CHINA'S NEXT STRATEGIC ADVANTAGE

CHINA'S NEXT STRATEGIC ADVANTAGE

From Imitation to Innovation

George S. Yip and Bruce McKern

The MIT Press
Cambridge, Massachusetts
London, England

Sset in Sabon and Helvetica Condensed by Toppan Best-set Premedia Limited. Printed and bound in the United States of America.

Library of Congress Cataloging-in-Publication Data

Names: Yip, George S., author. | McKern, Bruce, author.
Title: China's next strategic advantage : from imitation to innovation / George S. Yip and Bruce McKern.
Description: Cambridge, MA : The MIT Press, 2016. | Includes bibliographical references and index.
Identifiers: LCCN 2015039956 | ISBN 9780262034586 (hardcover : alk. paper)
Subjects: LCSH: Technological innovations--Economic aspects--China. | International business enterprises--Technological innovations--China. | Leadership–China.
Classification: LCC HC430.T4 Y57 2016 | DDC 338/.0640951--dc23 LC record available at http://lccn.loc.gov/2015039956

10 9 8 7 6 5 4 3 2

for Ng Chun (in memory) and for absent friends

CONTENTS

ACKNOWLEDGMENTS

There are many people we need to thank. The first are all those who were involved in setting up the Centre on China Innovation (CCI) at the China Europe International Business School (CEIBS), which has been the basis for all of our research on the topic of this book. Annette Nijs, CEIBS Executive Director–Global Initiative, made the major effort, with the help of CEIBS President Pedro Nueno, to recruit the first four sponsors to fund the start-up of the CCI in 2011: Akzo Nobel, DSM, Philips, and Shell. Each company provided a member of the CCI Advisory Board, which provided invaluable guidance for our research program. Of the board members, the originator of the idea for CCI was Dr. Frans Greidanus, Chief Technical Officer, Philips Asia. Upon his retirement, Frans was replaced by Klaas Vegter, Senior VP, Head of Philips R&D China. Kathy Zhang, Director of Business Development sometimes represented Philips on the Advisory Board. For Akzo Nobel: Chaodong Xiao, Research Development & Innovation Director, Akzo Nobel (China) was their first Advisory Board member, later replaced by Chen Ling, RD&I Director, China & North Asia, Decorative Paints. For DSM, Jaco Fok, Vice President Business Incubator and Director DSM China Innovation Centre, was the first Advisory Board member, later replaced by Jan-Anne Schelling, VP Human Resources. For Shell, X. D. Jing, External Research and Innovation Director, Shell (China) Projects and Technology was the first Advisory Board member, later joined by Jaco Fok, General Manager of Open Innovation (worldwide). The Bosch Group joined as a sponsor in our second year, its Advisory Board member being Martin Brett, VP, Bosch Engineering System, China, helped by Zhang Di, Senior Manager, Innovation Management, Bosch China.

At the global corporate level of the sponsor companies, supporters of CCI included at Akzo Nobel Graeme Armstrong, Executive Committee–Research, Development and Innovation, and Marjan Oudeman, former Executive Committee member responsible for China; at DSM, Feike Sijbesma, CEO, Stefan Doboczky, former Member of the Managing Board, Rob van Leen, Chief Innovation Officer, and Marcel Wubbolts, Chief Technology Officer; at Philips, Gottfried Dutinné and Hayko Kroese, former Members of the Group Board of Management; and at Shell, Gerald Schotman, Chief Technology Officer, and Thijs Jurgens, Vice President–Innovation. At the China country levels of the sponsor companies, supporters of CCI included at Bosch Peter Loeffler, Executive VP, CFO, Member of the Board, Bosch China, and Henri Catenos, Executive VP, Finance and Administration, Bosch China.

At CEIBS, Dean John Quelch appointed the two of us to co-direct CCI and provided encouragement and support, as did his successors, Dean Hellmut Schütte and Dean Ding Yuan. Co-Dean Zhang Weijiong and his staff provided operational support for CCI. After Bruce McKern retired from CEIBS, Jian Han helped to keep CCI afloat by taking over his role as Co-Director. We have had had great support from the CCI team. Our center managers have been Jess X. Zhang, Ivdis Tao (Tao Xiangyi), and now Wang Wingying, who all also contributed research to this book. A key research assistant was Eleonore Yang (Yang Yi). We have also had research help from two CEIBS MBA students, Gary Liu (Lü Hui) and Lizzie Zhang (Zhang Wei), as well as from teams of CEIBS MBA students. Kathy Xu has provided administrative help to the center and the book preparation.

We are very grateful to those who joined us in co-authoring some of the chapters: Yi Ta Chng, Dominique Jolly, Maja Schmitt, Lin Xu, and Yongqin Zeng. Others who have contributed to our research and thinking include Weiru Chen and Klaus Meyer of CEIBS, Max von Zedtwitz of GLORAD and Moscow School of Management Skolkovo, Mark Greeven of Zhejiang University, and

Wim Vanhaverbake and Nadine Roijakkers of Hasselt University. Our ideas were also shaped by collaborations with the seasoned China experts Steven Veldhoen, Director of Strategy& (formerly Booz and Company), and David Michael, Senior Partner and Managing Director, Greater China, for The Boston Consulting Group. We also thank the hundreds of executives who have given access to their dozens of companies, both Chinese and non-Chinese, and their valuable time for our interviews, or have joined our research forum discussions, as well as academic colleagues who provided comment and criticism of our ideas in their early stages. All of these people helped make this book possible; we alone take responsibility for its shortcomings.

We thank John Covell, Senior Acquisitions Editor for Economics, Finance, and Business at the MIT Press, for signing the book, and for his insights and encouragement. We also thank the anonymous reviewers. We thank the manuscript editor, Paul Bethge, for his meticulous work.

Bruce McKern thanks colleagues at SKEMA, INSEAD, and Oxford's Technology and Management Centre for Development for their hospitality during his stays. He thanks Stanford University's Hoover Institution for its generous support over several years and particularly David Brady, Deputy Director, for his wise counsel and unfailing kindness.

Last, but not least, we are very grateful to our wives, Moira and Cathryn, who have tolerated our frequent, long absences in China.

George Yip and Bruce McKern
August 2015

1

CHINA'S DRIVE FOR INNOVATION

In the eleventh century, the most advanced application of new technology in the world could be found in a Chinese city called Kaifeng, a capital of China during the Northern Song dynasty. It was a clock, standing 13 meters high, that displayed not only the time but also a variety of astronomical measures. Designed by Su Song, a talented scholar, statesman, scientist, and polymath, it was powered by water and employed a chain drive and a sophisticated escapement mechanism well in advance of any instrument then known in Europe.

Su Song's clock is but one example of China's early inventiveness: its discoveries of cast iron and steel technology predated the arrival of those technologies in Europe by more than a thousand years. Other Chinese innovations before the fourteenth century included agricultural technologies such as hydraulic engineering, iron ploughs, fertilizers, wheelbarrows, horse collars, and veterinary medicine. The Chinese also introduced paper, explosives, lacquers, pharmaceuticals, moveable type, and maritime innovations such as the compass and ships equipped with buoyancy chambers, rudders, and maneuverable sails.[1]

For reasons not fully understood, China's innovative ability languished after the fourteenth century. Today, however, China is determined not only to catch up with the West, but to re-establish itself at the forefront of technological innovation. Two forces are driving the surge of Chinese innovation described in this book. One is based on need—China's pressing need to solve the myriad domestic problems that rapid economic development has created.

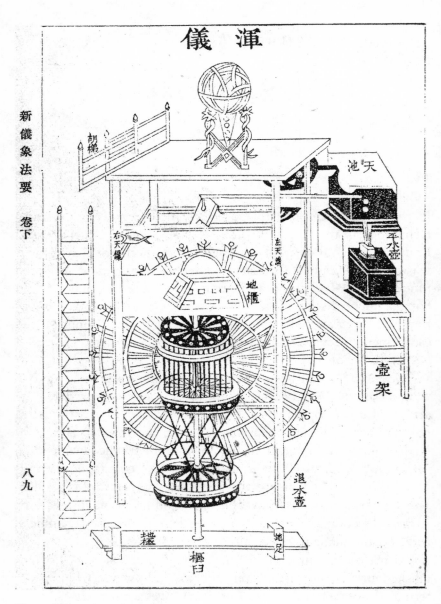

Figure 1.1

Su Song's astronomical clock of 1094 AD.

Source: J. Needham, *Science and Civilization in China*, volume 4 (Taipei: Caves Books Ltd., 1986). Image courtesy of the East Asian History of Science Library, Needham Research Institute, University of Cambridge.

The other is based on a new strategic direction for Chinese corporations: to enter high-value, high-margin sectors that are internationally competitive and where they will be matching global corporations, innovation for innovation. Much of this recent drive is through mergers with and acquisitions of successful Western firms that were made to gain brands, technology, and markets.

WHAT THIS BOOK IS ABOUT

Today every senior executive of a Western corporation needs to understand the tidal wave of innovation flowing from China that is about to engulf Western markets. Executives in Chinese corporations also need to understand the role of innovation in the rise of their firms. We believe this challenge is unprecedented in the global economy and more substantial and longer lasting than the Japanese challenge of the 1970s. We argue further that the only way to counter this challenge is to become embedded in the Chinese ecosystem. Firms not already in China also need to understand this new phenomenon, as it will affect home markets hitherto thought to be sanctuaries. We provide detailed evidence of the rapid evolution of China's innovation capacity and propose strategies that CEOs should develop to counter the challenge by creating carefully planned innovations in China, both for China and for the rest of the world.

What is innovation? A workable definition is provided in the *Oslo Manual*, subtitled *Guidelines for Collecting and Interpreting Innovation Data* (OECD/European Communities 2005): "the implementation of a new or significantly improved product (good or service), or process, a new marketing method, or a new organisational method in business practices, workplace organisation or external relations." In this book we adopt an equally broad definition of innovation. We define innovation as new ideas that are implemented in the form of products, processes, services, or business models that have commercial value. Whereas innovation is sometimes thought to be concerned only with the commercialization of ideas that are new to the world, our view of innovation includes (as does the definition in the *Oslo Manual*) ideas that may be not be

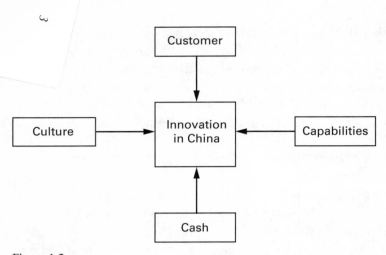

Figure 1.2
The four factors driving innovation in China.

new to the world but are new to a country or a company. This defi-nition includes improvements to existing products, processes, or services; it also includes their provision to new groups of users or customers. In fact, in our research with corporations in China we identified eight different modes of innovation, which we describe in detail in chapter 2.

In this book we discuss in detail the growth of China's innova-tive capacity and that of its innovative companies in terms of four factors, which for simplicity we call the Four Cs. These four factors are in two groups: *customers* and *culture* (which explain the devel-opment of China's innovative ecosystem at the macro level and the development of the first two phases of Chinese companies' growth, described below) and *capabilities* and *cash* (which explain the competitiveness of Chinese firms entering global markets in the third and most recent phase of their evolution). The Four Cs framework will be elaborated in the chapters that follow; here we will provide a brief introduction, summarized schematically in figure 1.2.

Customers refers to the deep understanding of customers that Chinese companies have acquired in responding to the large and dynamic China market. This powerful force underlies the rapid growth and the competitive intensity of Chinese enterprises, which we explain in chapters 2 and 3.

Culture embraces not only the entrepreneurial drive and vision of China's business leaders, but also the clear ambition of the Chinese government to make China technologically independent, realized through its sustained investment in the creation of a national innovation system. The grand strategy of the Chinese government in creating the indigenous innovation ecosystem, along with other strategies of support, has greatly assisted Chinese firms to satisfy customers' needs through innovation. We detail this strategy and its impact in this chapter; we return to it in chapter 6 in the context of open innovation.

These two factors (*customers* and *culture*) explain the first two phases in the development of Chinese companies, which we describe below. But Chinese companies have now entered into a third phase of growth, in which they will make a transition from seeking new resources to seeking new knowledge. This phase appears to fly in the face of the experience of established multinational companies (MNCs), which have competitive advantages derived from experience that they can deploy to enter new markets. What advantages do late-moving Chinese companies have that they can use in the face of entrenched MNC competitors in markets outside China?

In chapter 2 we discuss the innovation *capabilities* developed by Chinese companies and provide case examples of particularly successful firms. In chapter 3, we explain the sources of these managerial and innovative capabilities, detailing ten ways in which they differ from those of Western companies. Their profitability in domestic markets provides the funding—the *cash*—along with government assistance, to support their expansion into foreign markets against traditional multinational corporations.

How powerful are the Four Cs? Can multinational corporations learn from what Chinese companies have been doing in their home market? Can they counter them in their backyards? We believe that they can and, moreover, that to do so they will have to participate in the Chinese innovation ecology. In chapter 4 we discuss in detail the phases in the evolution of the innovation activities of multinationals already operating in China, from cost-driven R&D to market-driven and knowledge-driven R&D. We argue that today foreign companies must regard China as the lead market, in which they must be present. They need to be in China, not only to make and sell goods and services to China's increasingly sophisticated consumers, but also to take advantage of the remarkable growth in local knowledge and technology. By participating in this ecosystem, and by becoming embedded in the creation of new knowledge in China, they will be able to take advantage of new opportunities both for China and for world markets. But they will have to organize effectively in order to do so. In chapter 5 we address this important question and describe how multinationals can organize innovation activities in China to strengthen their global competitiveness.

In chapter 6 we look at a phenomenon that has become commonplace among Chinese firms and increasingly commonplace among multinationals operating in China: open innovation, which came naturally to Chinese companies in the early stages, but for which many Chinese companies are now setting up comprehensive platforms. Open innovation provides a critically important avenue for both Chinese companies and multinationals to gain access to the ideas and technologies bubbling up in myriad places throughout the country. For multinationals, however, their closeness to the local innovation ecosystem raises critical issues of protecting intellectual property rights. We will take on this topic directly in chapter 7, where we propose a number of strategies firms can use to protect their intellectual property in China. Both multinational corporations and Chinese companies can learn a great deal about leading innovation initiatives to deal with the very different customers and markets in China. In chapter 8 we provide advice on those leadership lessons, focusing on how foreign companies can improve not only their innovation processes from what they learn in China, but also many other aspects of management.

Our main argument in this book is that companies' experience of the mindset of "good enough for China," whether they be Chinese or foreign, has created innovative capabilities that are appropriate for them to extend to other developing country markets.

Those capabilities quickly become suitable for market segments in advanced countries and will eventually enable China to become the home of world-class multinational corporations. No company can afford to neglect the dynamic learning opportunities in China, which will be essential for global competitiveness.

One topic we have chosen not to address is how to manage government relations in China. There are many other works on that topic.[2] Because China's economy is significantly controlled by the Communist Party of China, politics is clearly important, and intervention by the Chinese government is often seen as a barrier or disincentive to innovation for foreign companies. But this doesn't mean that companies can't innovate in China, nor that they should ignore government relations. Quite the contrary: as in Western countries, companies must have a non-market strategy—a strategy for dealing with stakeholders other than customers. We provide many instances of how important these relationships are and what companies should do to establish and maintain them. In fact, in our extensive interviews with executives of foreign companies, we did not hear of government interference as a barrier to innovation. The one salient issue is that of protecting intellectual property, in which the Chinese government plays a role that is evolving. We address that issue in chapter 7, which also reports improving conditions in the role of the Chinese government in protecting IP. Similarly, it is not our objective in this book to criticize the Chinese system of government or its effect on innovation.[3] We take the Chinese political system as a fact of life and offer advice to help managers, in both foreign and Chinese companies, to innovate successfully within that system.

Our focus is deliberately concentrated on the immediate challenges and opportunities facing all large companies: China's rapidly developing innovative capacity. For those readers who would like to understand better the political and economic environment in which MNCs and Chinese companies operate, we suggest a number of other sources. One excellent book for managers is *Dragons at Your Door*, by Ming Zeng and Peter J. Williamson, the first book to address cost innovation as an aspect of innovation in China.[4] Some books take a macroeconomic or government policy ᴧrspective, including the role of the education system as a barrier to innovation in China.[5] Other books provide excellent research perspectives for academic readers. Notable among these is the comprehensive study by Fu Xiaolan.[6] In *How to Get China and India Right,* Anil Gupta and Haiyan Wang argue that multinationals need to have a strategy for both China and India.[7] A few books are addressed to managerial readers, but these do not take a strategic perspective.[8] Another excellent book for managers, Vijay Govindarajan and Chris Trimble's *Reverse Innovation,* focuses on emerging markets in general, not just on China.[9]

We believe that this book occupies a unique space, as in it we take a comprehensive approach, based on a strategic and international business perspective, intended for a managerial reader rather than an academic one. In summary, our book takes the perspective of the business leader, providing detailed understanding of business innovation in China based on our own in-depth research, in order to provide CEOs with a comprehensive guide to the innovation challenge from China and how to manage it.

Our research methodology for this book was to interview hundreds of R&D and innovation-related executives, and some CEOs and C-Suite executives, of dozens of Chinese and foreign firms, mostly in China but some in their European home countries. We also prepared several in-depth case studies of selected firms that are frontier practitioners of innovation in China. These firms do not represent a statistical average. Managers want to learn from the best practitioners, not from average ones. Lastly, we conducted an extensive review of the relevant existing literature of the past twenty years and closely monitored reports on innovation that appeared in the media in the years 2010–2014. In chapters 3–6 we report in more detail on the companies we studied in our field research.

INNOVATION: CHINA'S PATH TO GLOBAL COMPETITIVENESS

The need for innovation in China is all too apparent. China is faced with an array of problems arising from its phenomenal post-1978 growth, problems that cry out for solutions. Air quality, water, energy, food safety, health, and retirement insurance are among the most prominent. China's leadership has recognized that innovation will be a necessary part of the solutions to these problems in the next phase of economic growth.

But the choices made by Chinese corporations seeking world-class competitive strength have demonstrated their growing reliance on innovation. Recent surveys of Chinese executives show that they often have a greater awareness of the necessity for innovation than Western executives operating in China. This is constantly brought home to them as they expand abroad and face established competitors with deep reservoirs of technology and experience. And the leaders of the best Chinese companies are remarkably open to new ways of managing and organizing that maximize their potential for innovation.

Consider the household goods manufacturer Haier, which is experimenting with a new "individual-goal" organization in support of its growth strategy. By its own account Haier has already created 2,000 self-managed business units, designed to "let each employee become his or her own CEO" to facilitate innovation and entrepreneurship. Haier's visionary leadership has already helped make it the world's largest manufacturer of white goods (large household appliances). Whether this new organization will be right for the next phase of Haier's development is not clear. What is important is that the company's leadership has decided to make a major organizational innovation in order to foster an entrepreneurial and innovative environment to deal with global competition.

The Chinese economy's growth in size and sophistication since 1978 has been extraordinary, especially in view of China's very low degree of industrialization before World War II. There is no reason to assume that China's innovative capacity will not continue to expand. At some point the economy's growth will slow, as indeed it has already begun to do. But in a few years China will be the world's largest economy, and its companies will have become strong contenders in innovation, if not the global leaders.

This brings us back to Su Song's clock. Although China has not yet devised a modern-day equivalent of such a revolutionary ion as the steam engine, electricity, or penicillin, it has rapidly become very successful in coming up with innovations that are adaptive, incremental, and appropriate to its stage of development. China's own domestic critics point to the lack of a consumer innovation comparable to the iPhone as proof of China's inability to innovate. But such radical innovations tend to arise in countries with high disposable incomes. China's low level of income is at present a constraint, but it is a constraint that China will eventually throw off. And Chinese companies have already seized the opportunity to create incremental innovations that are right for China's present needs—a necessary precursor to more radical innovations.

Already China has put a man in space, built the most extensive high-speed rail network in the world, and created numerous successful companies in fields from heavy industry to the Internet. Just as the United States did for many years, China is placing heavy emphasis on funding innovation in research institutions and public universities. Many of the radical innovations the West takes for granted stem from path-breaking research funded by government agencies, and the Chinese are determined to reproduce that pattern.

The clock of Su Song, the iPhone of the eleventh century, demonstrates that China has, in the past, led the world in innovation. Today's flood of incremental innovations from Chinese companies is a harbinger of future radical and disruptive competition. And that future is not far off. The coming wave of competition from China will focus not on the Chinese market, but on the traditional high-value markets of established global businesses. The Chinese will bring the fight to their competitors' backyards. The following examples of China's established success reinforce this point.

CHINESE INNOVATION SUCCESSES

The challenge from China's innovating companies is already seen in their many innovation successes, such as the following:

- Huawei's Single RAN (radio access network), which allows a single base station to handle 1G, 2G, and 3G telephony

- TCL's TV set that can simultaneously show two different programs full screen
- innovative startups, such as Suzhou Nano-Micro Bio-Tech's world-beating nano-particles for purification of bio-pharmaceuticals, medical diagnosis, and flat panel displays
- Tencent's live chat application WeChat (Weixin), highly popular in China and now expanding to other countries
- Xiaomi's mobile phone business model, which makes clever use of an Android platform and rapid adaptations based on feedback from customers
- Alibaba, which has become the world's largest business-to-business Internet portal[10]
- innovations in solar-energy and wind-energy technologies[11]
- the Commercial Aircraft Corporation of China's C919 narrow-body jet, designed to compete with the Boeing 737 and the Airbus equivalent, which at the time of writing was expected to be test flown for the first time in late 2015

Evolving features of China's environment promise even more dynamic innovation in the future. Not only local companies but also MNCs can benefit from the opportunities and resources of this environment. For example:

- China's government has made innovation the lead plank in its two most recent Five-Year Plans.
- Chinese scientists trained in the best Western universities and companies are being lured back to China with tax incentives and other privileges by the "1,000 talents" program, recently supplemented with a "10,000 talents" program.[12]
- Huawei, TCL, and some other major Chinese companies are devoting 10 percent or more of their revenues to R&D. ZTE and Huawei are in the top three global companies in international patent applications.
- The large size and rapid growth of China's market and the country's rapidly increasing disposable income are creating both opportunity and demand for ever-more-sophisticated products, such as high-speed trains and multifunctional mobile devices.

A number of far-sighted multinationals have already tapped this potential, setting up more than 1,500 foreign R&D centers in China.[13] These continue to increase in number and scope, and many are turning their focus from cost-driven or market-driven to knowledge-driven innovations.

THE THREE PHASES OF CHINESE INNOVATION

In less than 40 years, Chinese companies have moved from outright imitation to pure business innovation, in parallel with and contributing to China's extraordinary economic growth. The three phases of this shift, though not strictly in chronological sequence, provide a narrative of relentless refinement of China's innovative capacity.

We call the first phase "from copying to fit for purpose." Adaptation to the Chinese market was evident even in China's earliest attempts at competing with the world's global manufacturers—simplification and cost reduction were present from the start. As Chinese companies refined the concept in a market that rapidly grew more discriminating, "fit for purpose" became a formidable competitive strategy. The second phase we call "from followers to world standard." Chinese companies have shown little inhibition about reproducing what successful companies elsewhere do. Where they are unusual is in the speed with which they have developed the ability to apply research and development and deep customer understanding to redefine products and business models, and capture leadership in their chosen markets. The third phase has taken Chinese companies "from new resources to new knowledge." The received wisdom is that Chinese corporate investment abroad is all about acquiring primary resources in emerging economies. We believe the reality is rather different; quietly, and often behind the scenes, Chinese companies are buying the market access, the brands, the technology, and the human expertise that will allow them to mount a formidable innovation challenge to the incumbent companies of the developed countries. We describe these three phases in more detail in the following subsections.

From copying to "fit for purpose"

Companies have to learn to innovate. The multinational corporations of the developed countries have vast troves of technology and know-how, the fruits of investment and learning over scores of years. Most Chinese companies had to start from scratch after markets were permitted after 1979, with no experience of modern management or technology, so they began by copying and then by making small improvements to an existing product or process—often foreign. Companies called *shanzhai,* meaning "mountain stronghold (of bandits)," copied brand-name products ranging from fashion accessories to telephones. The products were cheap and the quality was low, but customers didn't much care so long as they were affordable.

But the Chinese market changes very fast. As customers became more discriminating, entrepreneurs learned to move from imitation to incremental innovation, improving their products and their processes. Incremental innovation is a big step beyond imitation—it marks the recognition that innovation is at the heart of long-term competition. Chinese companies based in the Pearl River Delta, in Beijing, and in Shanghai began by making components for global supply chains in the information, computing, and telecommunications industries. Because they were under intense pressure to meet the cost and performance requirements demanded by their multinational customers, their technical capabilities had to be close to the state of the art. As they grew, they used the skills acquired in the hard school of cost reduction to explore opportunities in adjacent markets and with other customers, adapting and improving their existing technological base through incremental innovation. The capabilities developed through incremental innovation made them essential players in supply chains for products sold in the developed countries.[14] Early imitators of consumer products were often greatly aided by an open market for standardized components, such as Intel microprocessors and other components for personal computers, MediaTek wireless chipsets for mobile phones, and later Google's Android mobile operating system. These technologies provided them with a base to develop products for the burgeoning domestic market.

The special demand characteristics of the Chinese marketplace meant that in this first phase of innovation Chinese companies became adept at producing products or services designed with just the product attributes Chinese customers were willing to pay for, and no more. This "good enough" strategy worked both in markets that serve lower-income consumers and in industrial markets, such as food processing, mobile phones, household appliances, and electrical machinery. Companies learned to eliminate unwanted features, to economize on materials (and sometimes on durability), to reduce waste, and to streamline processes. Their products and services are not inferior, but rather "fit for purpose." They suit what customers need, whereas Western-designed alternatives may have costly features for which customers aren't prepared to pay. "Fit for purpose" is a strategy that has moved these companies well beyond copying and low-cost production; it also focuses on identifying emerging needs and, as segments mature, responding with higher-quality products and services. Taobao, Baidu, Tencent, and many other companies began by copying products, services, or business models from abroad. Taobao, for example, was created by Alibaba in response to eBay's entry into China. Its agility, its understanding of China's market and institutions, and its willingness to forgo medium-term profitability enabled it to drive eBay out of China. Baidu copied Google's search model, but moved more quickly to include paid search advertising. Tencent began with imitative online games and messaging services but then added its own successful WeChat live chat application, now being extended to other countries.

Academic studies confirm that Chinese companies learned to upgrade their own capabilities by competing with foreign entrants into China.[15] This adaptive copying strategy enabled Chinese companies to grow rapidly, to achieve economies of scale, to learn what customers want, and to move into other segments as customers' needs changed. Some call this process "secondary innovation." Initially based on foreign technology, it goes beyond imitation and adaptation to create something unique for China.[16] Many multinational corporations operating in China have adopted a similar strategy in order to penetrate markets that are very different from their home markets. But they have had to overcome internal concerns about quality and brand reputation and, at the same time, to catch up with local competitors' deep understanding of the specific characteristics of Chinese markets. Their Chinese competitors have no such inhibitions and have much deeper knowledge of their customers. We assert that this capability is also preparing Chinese firms to compete in foreign markets where they are already challenging Western multinationals.

From followers to world standard

The "fit for purpose" phase represents innovation driven by market necessity. But many Chinese companies have chosen a more ambitious route of innovation by choice: innovation that drives the market, rather than being driven by the market.

There are many examples of Chinese companies that began by supplying the fast-growing Chinese market with products that depended primarily on low-cost labor, but that now supply markets that depend primarily on innovation. These companies include Sany and Zoomlion (which make construction equipment), the online travel companies Ctrip and TongCheng (also known as 17u. com), TCL in consumer electronics and mobile phones, and Tencent in online games, instant messaging, and e-commerce. Some of these companies invested heavily in technical talent from the start; others have turned to innovation as a strategy for future competitiveness. Several are now active in global markets, competing against the very multinationals that served as their models. One of the most visible of these companies is the appliance manufacturer Haier. In 1984 Haier was a state-owned enterprise and was on the verge of bankruptcy. Today it is the largest producer of white goods in the world. Along the way Haier acquired refrigerator technology from German company Liebherr and Western management ideas wherever it could find them. By 2014 Haier's annual revenue had reached $31 billion (here and elsewhere we give the US dollar equivalent of Chinese renminbi), and it had 10 percent of the global market.[17] Haier moved from supplying underserved niche markets, such as those for bar refrigerators and wine coolers, to offering a full range of high-quality appliances.

Haier understood the need for innovation from the start. It spends 4 percent of annual revenue on R&D, and it has filed more than 4,000 domestic invention patents, including 541 in 2012 alone. But Haier understands that invention is not innovation. Its technical capability is accompanied by a deep understanding of its customers, an extensive distribution and service network, efficient logistics, and a willingness to serve segments that have been neglected. A legendary example of its readiness to innovate for the customer was its washing machine adapted for washing potatoes as well as clothes.

Like Haier, many Chinese companies developed strong innovation capabilities out of evolutionary necessity. Mindray (in medical devices), Neusoft (in software engineering, IT services, and medical information), Huawei (in telecommunications), Goodbaby (in strollers and juvenile products), and Yuwell (in self-monitoring medical devices) are all examples of companies that have created effective R&D departments and strong capabilities for innovation—incremental up to the present, but now ready to disrupt global markets.

A remarkable feature of the industrial landscape in China is the myriad of startups, seemingly in every field, many of which have developed world-class capacities to develop new products. One example is Han's Laser Technology Industry Group Co., which overcame a multitude of hurdles as a tiny startup to capture the majority market share in China in the field of laser printing, marking, cutting, and welding. Its dominant position is due in large part to its stream of incrementally innovative and patented products.

Other companies have created novel business models. For example, Xiaomi developed an Android-based smartphone that succeeded not only because of its high quality, but also because the company has developed an ecosystem of applications and customer relationships that is unique to China. The Four Dimension Johnson Industries Group in Beijing, which makes specialized cash-in-transit vehicles, uses a "mass customization" business model that exploits comparative advantage by combining body-panel manufacture in China with flat-pack shipments to Europe and final assembly close to European markets. That isn't radical innovation, but it is an innovative business model based on relative capabilities.

Established global companies operating in China are often astonished at the speed with which local companies introduce new products to the market. They follow the precept of "fail fast and learn" (one of the principles of the design thinking of companies such as IDEO). The product many not be perfect, but it doesn't have to be; on the basis of customers' reactions, it can quickly be succeeded by an improved model, and then a more improved model. And because the market is so large, a market launch in one location may not affect a company's overall reputation. Such an approach is very difficult to countenance for a large corporation with worldwide customers, but it is one that Chinese companies are entirely comfortable with.

From seeking new resources to seeking new knowledge

Since 2005, Chinese companies, and especially state-owned enterprises (SOEs), have been pushed to enter foreign markets by the government's "go global" policy. As of the time of writing, the official plan is to balance the stock of inward foreign direct investment with the stock of outward foreign direct investment (OFDI) by 2015, and to encourage overseas expansion by private-sector companies. This includes the creation of R&D centers overseas. China's government is fully committed to helping Chinese companies to become insiders in foreign markets. Although the FDI target for outward FDI stock was not reached in 2015 and will not be reached for many years, the outward *flow* of Chinese direct investment in 2014, at $103 billion, was not far below the inward flow of $120 billion. By May 2015, OFDI had reached 94 percent of inward FDI ($9.2 billion versus $9.8 billion in that month).

With foreign exchange reserves close to 4 trillion US dollars, China can buy the foreign industrial capacity it thinks it needs. Yet until recently, outward investment was overwhelmingly in the minerals and energy sectors of emerging economies where primary commodities are found. Although China's OFDI stock more than doubled between 2008 and 2012, only a small portion went into developed markets. The Heritage Foundation estimates that 71 percent of outward investment between 2005 and 2012 was invested in energy and metals, and our own detailed analysis of announced investments shows that during 2012 and 2013 (the most recent two years on record as of this writing) 66 percent of investment was still concentrated in energy and metals.[18] The limited diversification that has occurred has been in finance, real estate, transportation, and agriculture. Manufacturing remains a relatively small component.

So is China's foreign investment still fully fixated on the world's natural resources, at the expense of building up the kind of offshore manufacturing and services capacity that will give China an innovation platform abroad? We think not: behind the headlines, something very interesting is taking place.

The fact is that, in contrast to China's engagement with the rest of the world, much of recent Chinese investment in Europe is in manufacturing and services, and is driven by companies looking for new markets outside China. Their successes in the home market have given them surplus funds (*cash* in our Four Cs framework), manufacturing skills, and experience with consumer marketing. While Western competitors have been suffering from lackluster home markets (and in some cases losing money by entering China only to leave when profits failed to match expectations), Chinese companies have taken a longer view and have bought European manufacturing assets—especially assets that provide immediate market access and a strong brand name.

Recent acquisitions support the view that a marked shift is under way. For example, Lenovo recently bought Motorola Mobility, Dongfeng Motors (number 31 among global automobile firms in R&D expenditures) bought a 14 percent stake in Peugeot-Citroën, and Volvo was bought from Ford by Zhejiang Geely, an auto company with enormous ambitions but lacking a strong brand and short on design expertise. In stark contrast to the previous focus on acquiring physical assets, in 2014 two thirds of China's offshore investments were in services, about which Chinese firms still have much to learn.

Although Chinese companies have developed good manufacturing skills, they lack understanding of sophisticated markets—and they know this. They also know that they often lack the full range of scientific and engineering expertise needed for more demanding customers. This has led to a new phenomenon: the creation, through direct investment and acquisition, of Chinese corporate R&D centers in the United States and in Europe. A Chinese company creates such a center in order to embed itself in the innovation ecosystem of a developed country so as to acquire and develop technologies, brands, and marketing know-how.

Chinese companies, fully conscious of the need not only to tap into the local expertise but also to assimilate new knowledge into their global network, are internationalizing their innovation activities. They are challenging established MNCs in China, which are now finding their strongest competitors are not their traditional MNC peers but local companies.[19] They have established organizational processes for sharing newly developed knowledge among their R&D centers in China and other parts of the world. An example of that is Goodbaby, the world's largest producer of strollers and baby carriages (although its products are not yet branded with its name outside China). Goodbaby has established design and technical centers in China, Europe, the United States, and Japan, where local knowledge and expertise enable its branches to satisfy the idiosyncrasies of each market while sharing this consumer and product knowledge among its centers. And in 2014 the company made its first foreign acquisitions: of CYBEX (a leading child safety brand established in Germany) and Evenflo (a US company). These acquisitions broaden its product line while providing brand reputation and complementary expertise in areas such as child safety seats, as well as distribution in Europe and the United States.

The proportion of private companies (rather than SOEs) investing abroad is also growing, having increased from 4 percent in 2010 to 9.5 percent in 2012. Private firms tend to be more aware than their state-owned counterparts of the need to develop their capabilities, and they are usually able to act faster. They know they need to acquire brands, technologies, and markets as platforms for innovation in developed countries. In many cases they have already learned how to innovate at home, and they are battle-hardened from furious competition in the Chinese market.

n't the first time China has brought its resources and es to developed Western markets. Chinese labor was it in building the California end of the Transcontinental Railroad in the nineteenth century. Ironically, it may be Chinese technical know-how that will build California's high-speed railway (if it ever takes off) in the twenty-first.

INNOVATIVE CAPABILITIES OF CHINA'S COMPANIES

It is often said that China is a nation of copiers and that little genuine innovation takes place there. Does this mean that China's indigenous innovation goal is unrealistic? Our field research leaves us in no doubt about this important question. But to add support to our findings, we will summarize data from published sources. (Readers already convinced on this score may prefer to skip this section.) The innovation investments and outputs of Chinese companies are our starting point.

Several indices attempt to rank corporations in terms of innovation success. One of these, the 2014 EU Industrial R&D Investment Scoreboard, ranks 2,500 global companies by the sizes of their investments in R&D. Among the top 2,500 companies in R&D spending during 2013 were 804 US companies, 633 EU companies, 387 Japanese companies, and 676 others.[20]

Among the "others" were 199 Chinese companies with average R&D intensity of 1.5 percent, of which 62 were in the top 1,000.[21] In 2013, therefore, Chinese companies made up less than 8 percent of the world's top spenders on R&D, with an average R&D intensity well below the 3.2 percent average of the top 2,500. Among the top 100 in the EU list, there were only two Chinese companies: Huawei and PetroChina. However, the R&D investments of those two are comparable with those of multinational corporations based in developed countries. Huawei ranked 26 on the EU list in 2013 and spent $3.6 billion on R&D—not far behind Cisco Systems (ranked 18th), which spent $4.6 billion. Huawei is also an exception to the pattern of Chinese patenting: It has filed a considerable number of applications for PCT patents, the output of a large force of scientists and engineers. In fact, Huawei filed 3,442

PCT patent applications[22] in 2014 (ranked first among the top PCT filers).[23] PetroChina (64th) spent $1.7 billion on R&D in 2013, more than any other oil and gas company.[24] Furthermore, Chinese companies showed the highest growth rate of R&D spending over the year.

R&D spending is, however, not directly correlated with output of patents or, more important, innovative products.[25] Other indices attempt to measure specific indicators of innovative output at the company level, rather than focusing on countries. One such index, the Thomson Reuters Top 100 Global Innovators list, focuses on four criteria, all of which measure patenting output. No Chinese companies have yet entered that list.[26]

There are weaknesses with approaches based on R&D investment and patent output, as these are not of themselves direct measures of success in launching new products. Booz & Company's Global Innovation 1000 list tries to overcome this by soliciting the opinions of international executives. Executives who encounter competitors on the ground every day make judgments about innovativeness, which may not correlate well with the quantitative data cited earlier but may be more realistic. In 2014 the Booz ranking included 114 Chinese companies, an increase of 39 from the previous year.[27]

Yet another ranking, the 2014 Forbes 100 list of the World's Most Innovative Companies,[28] ranks companies according to the *premium in shareholder value* estimated to be attributable to innovation.[29] The 2014 list included six Chinese companies,[30] none of which was in the top 100 on the EU list.

These data show that, although very few Chinese firms are among the world's leaders in innovation yet, Chinese firms are steadily increasing their investments in R&D and some have translated that effort into a stream of patents. While a few outstanding companies (among them Haier, ZTE, and Huawei) have become not only prolific filers of patent applications but also successful global competitors, most have a considerable distance to go before they become world leaders on the basis of innovation alone. This is good news for MNCs; there is time to respond to the growing competitive challenge. Nevertheless, the trajectory is clear. More and more Chinese companies are seeking to compete outside China; they know they must innovate to succeed, and they are making substantial investments.

Critics, while recognizing that R&D investments and patenting are on the rise, question whether they will provide a basis for Chinese firms to engage in radical and disruptive innovation.[31] Our response to this important question is that *incremental innovation*, in which Chinese companies have been very successful, creates the capabilities for radical innovation in the future, as it did in the West. We address this question in more depth in chapter 2, where we provide detailed evidence of the development of these capabilities during three major phases of evolution.

CHINA'S ENABLERS OF INNOVATION

The market-opening reforms promulgated by Deng Xiaoping in 1978 radically transformed the economy and induced profound changes on both the supply side and the demand side in the remarkably brief period of 35 years.[32] These changes, in turn, stimulated the business strategies of Chinese firms and the development of their innovation capabilities.

China has several specific advantages for innovation, even relative to developed countries, on both the supply side and the demand side. These enablers of innovation provide incentives for both local companies and MNCs to innovate there. Here we will outline the main enablers; in later chapters we will focus in detail on the specific innovation strategies of local firms and multinationals in China.[33]

Supply enablers

One of the most obvious enablers of innovation in China has been its very large number of relatively low-cost engineers and scientists, although the cost advantage is diminishing quite rapidly, particularly in the coastal regions.[34] China graduates nearly as many PhDs in science and engineering (S&E) per year as the United States (31,410 in 2010, versus 32,649 in the US[35]), to which we should add the 5,000 PhDs in S&E awarded each year to Chinese nationals by US universities. Both Chinese and foreign companies are using this skilled labor force to develop innovations that would be too expensive to develop in advanced market economies. And Chinese companies can afford to allocate significantly more skilled people to innovation projects than their multinational competitors, enabling faster results. One major Chinese company boasts that one of the reasons for its success is the rich human resources in China. The company can hire any number of employees at a reasonable cost, such as 300,000 renminbi ($50,000) a year for an engineer; in Europe it would have to pay a secretary that much.

More valuable than China's home-grown PhDs (many of whom are not yet up to global standards) have been the increasing number of Chinese scientists returning to China after receiving training at prestigious Western universities, especially universities in the United States.[36] These *haigui* (literally "sea turtles," a pun on the homophones *hǎi* "ocean" and *guī* "to return") have the benefit of education at the best universities and experience in globally leading companies, and often have a patriotic zeal to help build China. They are able to work independently as researchers, and willing to take on a great deal of responsibility, in return for high salaries or entrepreneurial equity. Although many now command global level salaries and thus are no longer a cost advantage, they are valuable leaders for local R&D teams.

Government support is China's second enabler of innovation—an important part of the *culture* element of our Four Cs model. As we outlined above, China's investments in the National Innovation System have provided many initiatives and much support for innovation in order to catch up with the developed countries. Less well known is the fact that in China's quasi-federal economic system, many provincial and city governments—which account for some 85 percent of total government expenditures in the country—compete with one another to attract investment in ways analogous to the economic competition among states in the United States. This national and provincial government support is not just in infrastructure, education, and science parks, but also through direct grants for research and investment channeled into the many wholly or partially state-owned enterprises, as well as private firms.

Multinationals are able to benefit from government support in the form of land, buildings, and infrastructure. They have been less able to benefit from the central government-funded scientific initiatives, but in chapter 6 we show how they can participate in this ecosystem.

A third supply enabler (the other half of the *culture* factor) is the famed entrepreneurial spirit of Chinese business people, well demonstrated for many decades outside mainland China.[37] One of the co-authors of this book made a lecture tour of China in 1982 and was greatly impressed by the sense of latent entrepreneurship and business interest, waiting for an opportunity to be burst forth, despite the superficial conformity. The post-1978 reforms unleashed this previously suppressed entrepreneurship, whose manifestations can be seen from the English-speaking sidewalk sellers of pirated DVDs to the skyscrapers of the new financial and business Lujiazui district of Shanghai and the many innovative companies we discuss in the next chapter. Furthermore, the post-reforms generation is showing a strong desire for independence through entrepreneurship.

A fourth supply enabler is the rapidly and creatively evolving local Internet-related industry, which has been extensively funded by the Chinese government. Most prominently, Alibaba Group has rapidly become the world's largest e-commerce business. Its Taobao, Tmall, and Juhuasuan platforms generated merchandise revenue of $397 billion (with $12.4 billion in corporate revenue) in the year to March 31 2015 from 350 million active buyers and 10 million active sellers.[38] Likewise, Tencent has established a strong position in online multi-player games, complemented by its voice-messaging service WeChat. Many other internet companies have been established, such as Baidu (Web TV, search, maps, encyclopedia), Netease and Sohu (Web portal and online gaming), C-Trip (in travel) and Sina (Web search, microblogging). These businesses are almost exclusively the preserve of Chinese companies.

Demand enablers

The first demand enabler is the very rapid growth of China's vast market. Rapid growth makes it easy to introduce new products and services without having to displace incumbents. In addition, rapid growth is a much more forgiving environment for innovation failures, so companies can take more risks and try out new ideas. Companies can quickly experiment and find a market for their innovations. Customers' reactions in one part of the country may not transfer to another part, so loss of reputation is not a big concern. Chinese consumers are also relatively forgiving, so experimentation is less risky.

Second, because of the discontinuity created by the early years of the Communist system, China has many empty market spaces and little heritage in terms of customers' habits. That provides opportunities both for Chinese firms and for MNCs. For example, Philips has been highly successful in launching a garment steamer developed by its local R&D center, partly because the product takes up less space than a conventional ironing board. But the other reason is that Chinese consumers simply don't have a heritage of traditional ironing, and so are quite open to treating their garments with a hand-held steamer. Similarly, IBM's China Development Labs in Shanghai seek to take the global lead for many industrial needs, because in China there is a great diversity of applications across newly developing industries. China is a green field with no legacy, where IBM can undertake experiments and it can exploit its latecomer advantage to create leapfrog innovations.

The third demand enabler is China's need for simpler, cheaper products than those offered by companies from developed countries. Chinese companies' superior understanding of the niches in Chinese markets enables them to address this "good enough for China" market successfully through a range of products and services. Although developed-country companies have the same opportunity, they are often hampered by the organizational pressure to protect an existing global portfolio and global standards of quality[39] and often by their sheer ignorance of the diversity of customer segments and special needs. (We provide recent examples of this diversity in chapter 8.) Although both Chinese and foreign companies create such products,[40] foreign companies have been considerably less successful at it.

A fourth demand enabler is fast-moving large-scale government projects, made possible by the *culture* factor. Despite the increasing rise of a market economy, China's government remains very active in many sectors and able to undertake large-scale projects that in other countries might take years to implement. This means that the national government, and sometimes provincial governments, can rapidly implement large-scale projects, such as high-speed rail or new airports, that in turn create many opportunities for innovation.

These enablers have stimulated a rapid evolution of the Chinese marketplace and a rapid increase in the capabilities of companies to find and fulfill new opportunities. As we have already described, this evolution has taken place in three major phases.

CHINA'S NATIONAL INNOVATION SYSTEM AND ITS PERFORMANCE

Most innovation activities in a country derive from its National Innovation System (NIS), comprising its universities, research institutes, government policies, innovation personnel such as scientists and researchers, and the ecosystem of innovative companies, both domestic and foreign. This is particularly true for China, both because innovation there is at an emerging stage, and because of the large role of government in most aspects of business. Understanding the National Innovation System is critically important for any MNC serious about learning from China. In this section we outline the major features of China's National Innovation System and how it performs.

A developing national innovation system
The Chinese government is strongly fostering "indigenous innovation" through the development of a National Innovation System.[41, 42] The features of this system include sustained and growing investment in innovation, strengthening major research institutions and the top 100 universities, funding for commercial research that fits with national priorities, a push for transfer of foreign technology, and gradual reforms to the intellectual property regime. Its goal is

clearly to strengthen local companies to succeed against foreign competitors both in China and in overseas markets.

The Chinese NIS has been deeply transformed since 2005.[43] Selected universities are generously supported by the government to develop research capabilities. A number of public research institutes and centers are also funded by government. This investment is paying off. Reliable sources show a significant increase in the number of Chinese scientific publications in reputable journals, particularly in chemistry, physics, and computer science.[44] Consequently, the leading universities and public research institutes are increasingly a source of ideas that can be translated into innovative products and processes. Another impressive impetus from the central government led to the opening of more than 100 science and technology parks. (See figure 1.3.) Some of the parks, including

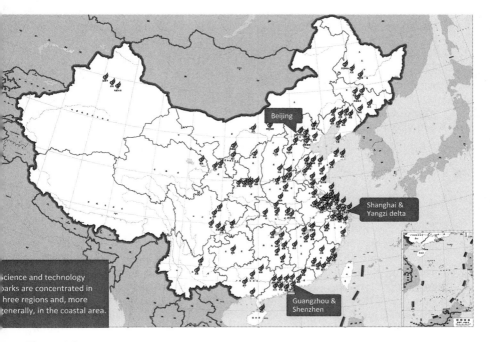

Figure 1.3

Locations of China's science and technology parks.

Source: http://www.gaoxinqu20.com

Zhangjiang in Shanghai and Zhonguancun in Beijing, have attracted major multinational companies and start-up ventures, so that
they have become important means of tapping into the innovation
ecosystem. Chinese technological intensity (R&D expenditure di-
vided by GDP) has now reached 2.1 percent (the level of Europe),
and is approaching the level of the United States (2.9 percent).[45]
And the number of patent applications in the country has surpassed 600,000 a year, exceeding the number filed in the United
States. Furthermore, courts and regulators increasingly recognize
and defend intellectual property rights in China.[46]

A frank preface to the National Medium-and Long-Term Program for Science and Technology Development contained this
passage:

In our effort to build a well-to-do society, we are faced with both rare historic
opportunities and grave challenges. The nation's economic growth shows an excessive dependence on the consumption of energy and resources, with high associated environmental costs; the economic structure is irrational, characterized by a
frail agricultural base and lagging high-tech industry and modern service industry; and firms lack core competitiveness and their economic returns are yet to be
improved as a result of weak indigenous innovation capability. There are a whole
range of problems concerning employment, distribution, health care, and national
security that need prompt solution. Internationally, the nation will be for a long
period of time under enormous pressures from developed nations who possess
economic and S&T superiority.[47]

While recognizing China's achievements in nuclear weaponry, sat-
ellite technology, manned space flight, high-performance computers, and other fields, the document also pointed out the gap between China's innovative capacity and that of other countries:

However, compared with the developed nations, China's overall S&T level still
has a fairly big gap to close. ... This is mainly reflected in the following areas: we
have a low rate of sufficiency in key technology supply and a limited number of
invention patents; the technological level remains low in some regions, particularly in the rural areas of the central and western regions; the quality of scientific
research still needs significant improvement due to a shortage of top notch S&T
talents; and investments in science and technology are still insufficient; and there
are numerous loopholes in the existing S&T system. Despite the size of economy,
our country is not yet an economic power primarily because of our weak innovative capacity.[48]

In proposing the development of a comprehensive innovation system, the Program stated the following guiding principles:

The guiding principles for our S&T undertakings over the next 15 years are: "indigenous innovation, leapfrogging in priority fields, enabling development, and leading the future." Indigenous innovation refers to enhancing original innovation, integrated innovation, and re-innovation based on assimilation and absorption of imported technology, in order improve our national innovation capability. Leapfrogging in priority fields is to select and concentrate efforts in those key areas of relative strength and advantage linked to the national economy and people's livelihood as well as national security, to strive for breakthroughs and realize leaping developments. Enabling development is an attempt to strive for breakthroughs in key, enabling technologies that are urgently needed for the sustainable and coordinated economic and social development. Leading the future reflects a vision in deploying for frontier technologies and basic research, which will, in turn, create new market demands and new industries expected to lead the future economic growth and social development.[49]

This ambitious document specified eleven broad sectors relevant to national needs, eight "frontier" technologies, and four programs of major scientific research. The program has as its goal the creation of an "innovation ecosystem" including scientific research, education, venture capital, and "market-driven entrepreneurship." As we will explain in chapter 6, this ecosystem is vitally important for open innovation, which has been a powerful force for growth in Chinese companies.

No Western government has spelled out such a critical assessment of its current situation or such a visionary and long-term plan to create the technological basis for its future. Although it may be easy to find fault with these ambitions, government support for fundamental research has been a common prerequisite of entrepreneurial success in the United States and other Western countries.[50] In China, funding from the central government has flowed to national research institutes, research universities, state-owned enterprises, and private companies operating in the sectors given high priority in the National Medium-and Long-Term Program for Science and Technology Development. At the same time, the government has been improving the overall quality of the research institutions and the universities, helping local companies to patent their discoveries, and strengthening the intellectual property protection regime. The "ecosystem" now includes 54 national-level Science and Technology Industrial Parks (STIPs),[51] which have been magnets for both local firms and multinational corporations,

and many provincial, municipal, and city-level high-tech development zones. The STIPs have become important contributors to
output and employment in the provinces and municipalities in
which they are located; on average, a STIP accounts for about 30
percent of the industrial output in the local area.[52] Multinational
corporations have established about1,500 R&D centers in the
larger STIPs, mainly those located in coastal regions: in Beijing, in
the Yangtze Delta (Shanghai and Suzhou), in Shenzhen, and in
Guangzhou. General Electric, for example, has three major centers
and three regional ones; Oracle has four. Most of the multinationals' R&D centers were initially established to support local operations, but increasingly they are seeking to tap China's National
Innovation System—something that we believe is necessary for future success, as we discuss in chapter 5.

It is possible for a multinational corporation to participate in
government-funded research programs if it is willing to form a
partnership with a Chinese company and a Chinese research center. Enlightened multinationals have recognized that the dynamic
Chinese market is not only an opportunity for revenue growth but
also a hotbed of stimuli for innovation. We return to this issue too
in chapter 5.

Political context[53]

The strong politicization of nearly all business activities in China,
including innovation, must be recognized. What most distinguishes
business in China from business in other parts of the world (ex-
cepting North Korea, Vietnam, and Cuba) is the tight linkage of
the government, the Communist Party, the private sector, and the
many wholly and partially state-owned state enterprises. The Party,
with a membership of 88 million as of 2015 (6.5 percent of the
total population and about 8 percent of the adult population), is a
dominant presence at the national level, at the provincial level, and
at the municipal level. Every company of more than fifty people
has a Party Secretary. This political presence not only shapes investment and product priorities and disadvantages multinational
corporations but also creates opportunities for corruption. The

present national government has taken bold steps to fight corruption, but its efforts will take a long time to work.

The political environment is changing. China is a more complicated place to do business today than it was in 2010. Government policy has become more nationalistic and "anti-corruption" mechanisms are everywhere. In universities, classrooms are being monitored to ensure that only politically correct statements are made. It is not hard to imagine that this might have some effect on innovation.

Despite these concerns, there is no doubt that the innovative activities of Chinese companies have developed with remarkable speed. As we will discuss in detail below, the Chinese government has shown great determination in creating a national innovation system, of which many entrepreneurial companies are the beneficiaries.

China's R&D investment: catching up with the West

China's thinking about developing its capacity for innovation was influenced by the policies of the United States, European countries, and Japan, which have for many years seen government investment in research and development as an important foundation for a national system of innovation. Fundamental and applied research on national projects is important for defense reasons, but the Chinese government also expects that publicly funded R&D will generate spill-overs into the commercial sector, as in other countries, and it has supported the indigenous innovation program with growing investment. Government funding for R&D by government research institutions and universities has averaged around 0.45 percent of GDP since 2005, keeping pace with the rapid growth of GDP ($8.23 trillion in 2012)[54] and reaching $43 billion in 2013.[55]

R&D investment by state-owned enterprises and corporations has also risen rapidly, to $146 billion,[56] bringing China's total investment to 1.18 trillion renminbi ($191 billion)[57] in 2013, and its R&D intensity (ratio of R&D to GDP) to 2.08 percent of GDP. OECD estimated that China's R&D intensity in 2012 was in fact slightly higher than that of the European Union.[58]

China is also catching up with the United States in R&D intensity. In 2012, spending on R&D by the US government (including
a component of defense R&D spending[59]) totaled $74 billion, or
0.45 percent of GDP (which was $1,624 billion in 2012[60]). State
governments, universities, and non-profit organizations invested a
further $31 billion. Thus, total US non-business R&D investment
was $104 billion in 2012. US *business* R&D spending is more than
twice China's reported total, amounting to $280 billion in 2012.
Adding these three components together gives a total gross expenditure on R&D (GERD) for the United States of $384 billion (2.36
percent of GDP). On this basis, China's total investment of $163
billion was 42 percent of the US total—comparable to the relative
size of its economy, which was 50 percent as large as the US economy in 2012. Moreover, it is increasing quickly.

Public funding is directing research at universities and research
institutions towards projects that will become important initiators
of home-based innovative successes, and there is increasing emphasis on the management of the system. For example, it is claimed
that the adoption of incentives and assessment for researchers
based on the quality of their publications in international journals
has led to an increase in the output of scientific papers[61] and to
changes in the rankings of universities within China.[62]

The Chinese government's support for research and development was influenced by the US experience of stimulus from government agencies such as the National Institutes of Health, the Department of Defense, the Department of Agriculture, and the
Department of Energy. The US government has been a major sup-
porter of high-risk R&D over the years, and many commercial innovations in many fields—particularly computing, communications, and pharmaceuticals—owe their success to government
investment in R&D.[63] The US approach works because government funding of high-risk research is only one component, though
an important one, of a broad ecosystem in which there are many
other actors, including startups, venture capitalists, universities'
commercialization offices, and large corporations. These participants in the ecosystem have strong incentives to commercialize
innovations—an area in which more needs to be done in China. In

the United States, research institutions compete for public funding, which is allocated to the best researchers on the basis of peer review. In 2013, for example, 32 percent of the R&D funded by the federal government was performed by universities.[64] Also, a remarkable feature of the US system is that public funds support fundamental research projects: 75 percent of research undertaken in US universities (much of it funded by government) is classified as basic or fundamental.[65] Fundamental research provides a basis for many business innovations, as the Bayh-Dole Act gives universities attractive incentives to look for opportunities to commercialize their R&D.

When China's program was being formulated, there was plenty of disagreement about the appropriate role for government in promoting innovation—particularly in view of the weak innovation record of state-owned enterprises, which today still account for more than 30 percent of China's GDP. Much of the Chinese funding is for large-scale projects aligned with national priorities. Critics argue that this, in combination with state control and excessive centralization in universities and SOEs, inhibits inventiveness.[66] Some critics argue that that the Chinese environment is not sufficiently free and that China's system of education doesn't encourage creativity.[67]

Another criticism of the Chinese approach is that it forces foreign companies to share technology with Chinese companies and research institutions. Limited evidence[68, 69] indicates that foreign companies are not transferring new technologies to Chinese counterparts to the extent that might be expected from the extensive presence of their local R&D centers.[70] Foreign sources provide only 1.3 percent of the total funding for R&D[71] and account for 18 percent of local patent applications (although there may be investment by JVs and foreign subsidiaries not captured in the data).

In efforts to improve the system, the Chinese government has introduced incentives for researchers and evaluation of their performance; it is also improving the system of intellectual property protection. In March 2014, Premier Li Keqiang proposed further actions on innovation intended to achieve the government's avowed goal of transforming the economy to a market-based system. These actions include allowing universities to commercialize innovations and introducing incentives linking remuneration for researchers to the market value of their research.[72] Premier Li also said the government would "let market competition determine which businesses survive," would "abolish preferential policies," and would "level the playing field for domestic and foreign enterprises to compete on fair terms."

This shift to a competitive and open system will require substantial changes in government organizations and in state-owned enterprises, and will take persistence and time to bear fruit. It may not succeed, although the government of Xi Jinping appears to be serious about its intent. A more nearly level playing field for multinational corporations, including changes in how they can participate in the National Innovation System, would be of benefit to China as well as to foreign corporations. It is clear, however, that Chinese business, in tandem with government, has increased its spending on R&D every year, and the investment is now being reflected in outputs of scientific publications, patents, and commercial innovations by Chinese companies. The corporate capabilities being developed in this process are the building blocks for new products, processes, and business models that are being launched in the domestic market and, increasingly, beyond that market. They will provide a basis for radical innovation and for competition in global markets. A look at the innovation outputs of China's research centers and companies provides evidence supporting this view.

China's growing innovation outputs

For comparisons of China's innovation output, we turn to five indicators, which tell a mixed story. No single one of these indicators is a sufficient measure of innovativeness, of course. R&D turns cash into ideas, whereas innovation turns ideas into cash. But R&D outputs are important precursors of success, particularly for radical innovation. Our output indicators include scientific scholarship (as measured by publications and international patenting), China's share of global high-technology manufacturing, China's share of global high-technology exports, and China's ranking on indices of innovativeness.

Scientific scholarship

China's share of articles published in leading international scientific journals has been growing in recent years, from 2.6 percent in 1999 to 11 percent in 2011[73] and to 14 percent in 2012.[74] Over the same period, the European Union's share of publications decreased to 31 percent, the United States' share to 19 percent, and Japan's share to 4 percent.[75] Although China's relative position is still behind those of the US and the EU, it is the one country whose overall share has been growing fast.[76]

In chemistry and in computer science, China's share of publications has been growing faster than other countries' shares. China was number one in the world in these fields in 2012, ahead of the United States. In mathematics, in physics, and in astronomy, China ranked second to the US. But China ranked well below the US and EU in publications in biochemistry, in molecular biology, in medicine, and in pharmaceuticals, no doubt because of the government's previous funding priorities.

In *citations* of scientific publications in other scientific publications (an indicator of research importance), the United States still leads by a wide margin. Although China's citation share has grown considerably, it has grown most strongly among Korean and Taiwanese researchers, for whom the Chinese language is of less an obstacle than it is for Westerners. Also, China's record has been tarnished by recent exposures of fake articles and payment for publications in bogus journals.[77] In 2011, Gupta and Wang argued that "China's research culture also suffers heavily from a focus on quantity over quality and the use of local rather than international standards to assess and reward research productivity."[78] As was noted above, China is taking measures to deal with the incentives for high-quality research and publications,. and the number of articles in respected journals is rising quickly.

Patent applications

Chinese companies and state-owned enterprises are very active in applying for patents: 648,219 "invention patent" applications were filed in China in 2012 through the State Intellectual Property Office (SIPO),[79] overtaking the number of applications to the US

Patent Office for utility patents (571,612).[80] (China's SIPO uses the term *invention patent* for original innovations; the US Patent Office uses the term *utility patent*.) Eighty-two percent of the Chinese invention applications were from domestic firms.

In addition to the applications for invention patents, the SIPO registered 692,845 applications for "utility model" patents, and 412,467 applications for industrial design patents.[81, 82] "Utility model" patents require little evidence of originality and are not subjected to a detailed examination process. Sometimes such a patent is used by a Chinese patent holder to pre-empt the legitimate owner of a foreign patent from exercising it locally. The United States doesn't have such a registration category, but does register design patents, for which it had 36,034 applications in 2013, again greatly outpaced by the vast increase in such applications in China.

Chinese companies overwhelmingly prefer to file patent applications in their own country. In 2013 they filed only 30,000 applications in other countries' patent offices—less than 4 percent of the world's total foreign filings.[83] This may reflect lower standards of acceptance by the SIPO or a generally lower quality of patent applications that the inventors fear might not succeed in patent offices outside China. To examine this international comparison further, it is useful to look at two other indicators of the international quality of patents: triadic patent families (that is, sets of patent applications filed in the patent offices of the United States, the European Union, and Japan) and applications for patents through the PCT[84] process. Triadic and PCT patent applications and patents issued are better indicators of valuable intellectual property for companies expanding globally.

In 2011, patent applications originating in Japan accounted for 31.4 percent of the total lodged in the three patent offices, applications originating in Europe for 27.5 percent, and applications originating in the United States for 29.0 percent. China accounted for only 2.2 percent of triadic filings.[85] But these data understate the speed at which China's triadic filings are growing, as filing in three jurisdictions takes some time. Chinese firms are in fact rapidly increasing their applications to the US Patent Office. The number of applications to the US Patent and Trademark Office (USPTO) from China grew from only 422 in 2000 to 8,619 in 2011, an average growth rate of 31 percent per annum.[86]

It is also interesting that China's success rate, measured by the ratio of issued patents to patent applications, is now at 79 percent, comparable to those of Korea and Japan. The USPTO speculates that the growth and higher success rate may be partially explained by more applications coming from Chinese inventors working for MNCs, which are more experienced in applying for patents in the United States.[87] Though it is not clear whether that is correct, it is certainly the case that patent applications to the USPTO originating in China are increasing very rapidly, as was true in the 1980s of applications originating in Korea.

The PCT process, used by inventors seeking eventually to obtain patents in multiple countries, is a more rigorous process than applying in only one country.[88] In 2013 the United States accounted for more than 24.1 percent of PCT patent applications, Europe for 28.2 percent, and China for 10.5 percent[89] (approximately equal to Germany's share). Thus, despite the fact that Chinese entities are filing great numbers of patent applications at home, few of them (although significantly more than are obtaining triadic family patents) are going through the PCT process. Also, China's share of PCT patent applications is growing fast, while the shares of the United States, Japan, and the European Union are declining. In fact, two companies—ZTE Corporation and Huawei Technologies—ranked first and fourth respectively among corporate PCT applicants in 2011 and 2012.[90] A new Chinese company entered the top 50 list in 2013: Shenzhen China Star Optoelectronics Technology Co., Ltd, ranking seventeenth.

Chinese research institutions are also becoming more prominent in applying for patents Among the PCT applications filed by the world's government research institutions in 2013, two Chinese government institutes were close to the top: the China Academy of Telecommunications Technology was third and the Institute of Microelectronics of the Chinese Academy of Sciences was fifth.[91]

The Chinese government must be concerned about the relatively low patenting activity by multinational corporations in China to

date. Despite the government's objective of urging foreign participation in the creation of intellectual capital, in 2011 only 8 percent
of the filings by Chinese firms included a foreign inventor.[92] One
reason for this is that China has very few immigrant inventors.
(The United States has more than 50 percent of the global total of
immigrant inventors,[93] and 40 percent of the *Fortune* 500 companies were founded by immigrants or their children.[94] Immigration-
related diversity appears to pay dividends in entrepreneurship.)
But another reason could well be a lack of sufficient incentives and
intellectual property protection. The China-based units of five of
the ten US-based companies that were awarded the most USPTO
patents between 2006 and 2010 did not receive any patents from
the USPTO during that period. By contrast, nine of those ten companies received patents for India-based innovations.[95] It is encouraging that the Chinese government appears to be taking these matters seriously and has been discussing making the playing field
more nearly level for multinationals.

High-technology manufacturing and exports
A third indicator of a country's success in innovative product development is its share of global high-technology manufacturing.
China's share of global high-tech manufacturing output[96] is growing. It reached 18.8 percent in 2010, close to the European Union's
share of 19.5 percent and closing on the United States' share of
27.6 percent.[97]

China's share of the world's high-technology exports reached
22 percent in 2010, surpassing the United States' 15.7 percent
and the European Union's 15.2 percent. China is a particularly
strong exporter in sectors related to mechanical and electrical
engineering. In 2012 it had 38.5 percent of the world's exports
of telecommunications equipment and 45.4 percent of the exports
of computers.[98] It should be noted, however, that about 60 percent
of the manufactured goods exported by China are made by
multinational corporations and that about 50 percent of those
exports are "processing" exports, in which the value added in
China is lower than for other exports (the iPhone being a classic
example).[99]

In those areas of manufacturing in which China's own companies are active, they are supported by specialization in China's patenting focus, which is strongest in digital communications, computer technology, electrical machinery, and energy.[100] China is active, but not dominant, in the manufacture of scientific instruments and semiconductors. It is much less significant in pharmaceuticals and aerospace. But it has very clear ambitions in commercial aviation: As of the time of writing, Commercial Aircraft Corporation of China plans the first flight of its C919 narrowbody jet in 2016, and China AVIC Avionics has a joint venture with GE to develop the needed avionics systems.

CONCLUSION

The data presented in this chapter show that Chinese companies are rapidly improving their global rankings for innovativeness relative to companies based in the developed countries. The numbers of Chinese companies that are highly ranked in innovativeness is increasing every year, and their capabilities are supported by the Chinese government's huge investment in the National Innovation System. This is clearly bearing fruit in the outputs of high-quality scientific publications and patent applications, which underpin the technological development of Chinese businesses. China's National Innovation System has aided its companies to gain capabilities and valuable experience in innovation. We have cited examples of successful Chinese innovative companies and explained how they have progressed through three phases of innovation to become challengers for dominance in the home markets of Western multinational corporations. A study published in late 2015 by the McKinsey Global Institute concludes that Chinese companies are currently using innovation to succeed globally in two types of industry sectors (efficiency-driven and customer-focused ones) but have yet to make much of a global impact in two other types of sectors (engineering-based and science-based ones).[101] We agree with this conclusion but expect rapid gains in all four types of sectors. *The Economist* argues forcefully that it is the private sector in China that is producing commercial innovations, a view that is reinforced by the findings we present in this book.[102] *The Econo-mist* also observes that state-owned enterprises have not been successful at innovation, despite their access to government support, because there is too much government interference in their decision making. According to a World Bank study the article quotes, the productivity of SOEs has increased at only one third of the rate for private companies. That study goes on to argue for greater freedom in universities and research institutes to pursue research, to let the play of market forces more effectively turn inventions into innovations. We don't disagree with this viewpoint, but we demonstrate in this book that Chinese companies are much more successful in innovation than previously thought and that foreign MNCs need to be active in China to understand what is happening and to become players in the innovation ecosystem.

China's growing capacity can't be dismissed as a Japan-like phenomenon that will fade in a few years. The four factors we detail in the rest of the book are, in our judgment, powerful and enduring. In support of these four factors, the size of China's population, the scale of its successful enterprises, the diversity of its markets and customer segments, the drive of its entrepreneurs and the determination of its government, as well as the emergence of sophisticated and demanding new clients, constitute a huge force pushing companies to higher levels of customer understanding, management systems, and innovative capacity.

Multinational corporations already operating in China have had the benefit of experiencing this vast laboratory of innovation. Companies not yet active in China need to reconsider their strategy to take advantage of what is becoming the lead market of the world. Not to be present in and actively innovating in China is to miss the opportunity of the century. In the rest of this book we explore this challenge in greater depth, explaining the major elements of the Four Cs framework,[103] how Chinese and foreign companies innovate in China and what both Chinese and foreign companies can learn from this unprecedented conjunction of forces.

2

HOW CHINESE COMPANIES INNOVATE

In chapter 1 we argued that Chinese companies are much more innovative than many think. They have responded to the enormous stimulus of the large, diverse, and rapidly expanding Chinese market—the first of our Four Cs, *customers*. In chapter 3 we will explore in depth the ten components of that factor. In this chapter, to provide a background for the discussion in the next and to develop the framework of our four factors further, we look at specific companies. We describe the innovations they are developing, the numerous modes they employ, and how the four factors have contributed to their success.

Chinese companies understand the value and the power of innovation. They are aware of where they stand in the hierarchy of global companies, and of the path they have to follow to rise in that hierarchy. At the Qingdao headquarters of the Haier Group, now the world's largest producer of "white goods," there is a display case containing a sledgehammer. It commemorates the day, many years ago, when the CEO of Haier, Zhang Ruimin, pulled 76 refrigerators off the production line. There was nothing much wrong with them, apart from minor defects such as scratches. But the message that Zhang Ruimin wanted to send to his employees was that minor defects are defects, and that Haier had ambitions to match the quality of any competitor in the world. So he and his managers took sledgehammers and smashed all the defective products. This story resonates throughout the Chinese corporate world. Any business-literate person in China knows it, and one of the sledgehammers is now in the National Museum of China in Beijing.

MANY MODES OF INNOVATION

The conventional wisdom is that most innovations by Chinese companies are about process or cost rather than product or technology, and furthermore that they tend to be incremental rather than disruptive or radical. This is only partly true; it is a simplification of complex and diverse phenomena. Chinese companies are evolving through three broad phases of innovation, as we described in the previous chapter, and these phases are underlaid by eight specific *modes* of innovation, which have changed in emphasis as China's market, infrastructure, and ecosystem have evolved. This evolution will become clearer as we look at examples in detail. The eight modes of innovation are, as we would expect, also visible in the expansion of these companies outside China; here we highlight how they are being used by Chinese companies in the Chinese context. And, as we show, a single innovation outcome might combine different modes of innovation; for example, some product innovations include technology innovation but others do not. Furthermore, we see the mode of innovation (whether in products, in processes, or elsewhere) and the degree of innovativeness (ranging from incremental to radical) as separate dimensions.[1]

Cost innovation—China's first advantage

Cost innovation occurs when changes in product design, production process, delivery process, technology, or materials result in reductions in the costs of production or delivery. Substitution of lower-cost labor for higher-cost labor is not particularly innovative in itself, but low-cost labor can be applied to all the dimensions of innovation.

As is well known, the extensive use of low-cost unskilled or semi-skilled labor in China makes many Chinese products cheaper than comparable products made in developed countries. This has been well documented by Ming Zeng and Peter Williamson.[2] Yet many Chinese companies are also now deploying highly skilled labor in R&D and engineering to reduce costs throughout the value chain, using capable people at lower cost than their competitors in more affluent countries. Chinese companies also often substitute low-cost labor for high-cost capital and machinery. Chint, a maker of electrical equipment such as transformers and power-supply units, flexibly substitutes labor for automation to reduce costs and to better align automatic production lines with manual lines.[3] The China Ocean Shipping Company (COSCO) used locally generated research on clean energy to reduce the fuel consumption of its container ships. According to calculations based on the energy-consumption index issued by China's Ministry of Transport, the fuel consumption of COSCO's container ships was 6 percent lower in 2010 than in 2009.

Process innovation—from Henry Ford to Guangzhou Crane

Process innovation occurs when a company creates a new process or technique for producing or delivering an existing product or service; it often goes hand in hand with innovation in a product or a service. The most famous example is Henry Ford's introduction of the assembly line. Mass customization was a later process innovation that provided flexibility yet also provided scale economies and also often made possible new product variants that hadn't been possible with the old process. In China, much process innovation seeks to reduce the cost of production. For example, the Guangzhou Crane Corporation has pioneered single rather than double welding of crane sections as a way to reduce costs while maintaining performance.[4] It is a simple innovation that makes it possible to provide better-tailored solutions to customers, enabling companies to transform the business models of their industries.

Through both product innovation and process innovation, BROAD Group has become the world's largest manufacturer of non-electric air conditioning systems. Its process innovation included reducing the installation cycle for customers from 100 days to just 14 days.[5] BROAD Group has also diversified into manufacturing sustainable buildings. Using factory-made modules, it can erect a six-story building in a day. Its sustainable buildings are five times as energy efficient as many other buildings, are free from "sick building syndrome," and have 1 percent construction waste.

Rapoo Technology was founded in Shenzhen in 2002. It originally designed computer mouses and other peripheral products.

Within ten years, Rapoo had progressed from ODM (original design manufacturing) to OBM (original brand manufacturing) and had entered international markets. Now it is one of the world's top three wireless peripheral companies and the industry leader in 2.4 wireless connection, intelligent connectors, and blue light tracing. Its leading technologies, stylish industrial design, and highly efficient production management enable it to outperform competitors in the wireless mouse market. Its wireless products have won multiple iF Design Awards.

Like many other computing, communication, and consumer (3C) companies, Rapoo faced a worsening labor shortage as the year 2000 approached. Its workers' salaries had been increasing at an average rate of 15–20 percent per year, which had slowed the growth of corporate profits. Moreover, high turnover had affected production and delivery. In response, Rapoo started a large-scale automation program in 2008, purchasing a large number of robots to improve production efficiency. By 2011, Rapoo had installed more than 70 robots on its production line to replace more than 300 workers working under repetitive conditions. Rapoo has become the first 3C company in China's domestic industry to have realized full automation on assembly lines.

Application innovation—the low-hanging fruit

Application innovation occurs when existing products, services, or technologies are combined in a new way to produce a new product. The sandwich and the credit card are two classic examples. Chinese companies, with their pragmatism and their focus on customers, eagerly embrace application innovation. The Antas Chemical Company has reformulated and repackaged butane-based sealants for easy use in the construction industry; BROAD Group uses waste heat or natural gas to generate cool air directly for skyscrapers, airport terminals, and other large buildings.

Supply-chain innovation—an opportunity in China

Supply-chain innovation occurs when one or more elements that are new to the world or to a country are introduced into a supply chain, or when existing elements of a supply chain are combined in a new way.[6] Examples include Amazon, other Internet retailers, and global purchasing networks. Paradoxically, while China has become critical in the global supply chains of foreign companies, supply chains inside China still have much room for improvement, not least because China's infrastructure has yet to catch up with the country's rapid growth. But increasingly there are examples of supply-chain innovation by Chinese companies. For example, the China Vanke Company was the first Chinese real-estate company to make extensive use of prefabrication in the construction of residential buildings. Previous methods of construction in China were primarily in-situ forms of construction involving the use of scaffolding. Vanke pioneered off-site mass production, reducing its reliance on the traditional supply chain for construction raw materials and on just-in-time delivery.

Likewise, the Haier Group is known for its well-developed supply chain. Because of its early insistence on quality in manufacture as well as in product delivery, Haier created a supply chain to eliminate bottlenecks and ensure quality in component supply, plus its own logistics network to deliver finished products and service to its customers safely and in timely fashion. It implemented electronic management of global order bidding, order placement, and stock control. It set up 42 logistics centers throughout China, built up a fleet of 16,000 vehicles, and began to track deliveries electronically. Haier claims to have reduced purchase and logistics costs considerably, to have reduced warehouse storage space by 90 percent, and to have shortened the holding period for raw materials by 77 percent with these reforms.[7]

Product innovation—from incremental to radical

Product innovation occurs when a final product or service has features of value to customers that are new to the world or to a country.[8] Radical innovations that change the way people live and work, such as the introduction of the personal computer, are unusual. China has produced relatively few product innovations that are truly new to the world. But its rapid development has spurred incremental innovation in many fields. For example, the construction in China of great bridges, highways, urban transit systems, high-speed trains, and towering skyscrapers has helped to foster much incremental innovation in the equipment industry.

But some Chinese companies are moving from incremental innovations toward radical ones. Huawei Technologies Co. Ltd. is an example: at the Long Term Evolution (LTE) World Summit 2010, the telecommunications industry's annual conference devoted to 4G technology, the company won several awards, including one for "best contribution to research and development for LTE." It was noted that Huawei had 2,500 engineers working in this field for more than six years in six R&D centers and had filed 181 patents,[9] and in the same year the company demonstrated a mobile technology breakthrough that achieved a downlink speed of up to 1.2 gigabytes per second. Then, in 2015, Huawei was given the award for "biggest contribution to 5G development" at the 5G World Summit. Huawei is working close to the boundary between incremental and radical innovation.

BROAD Group created its non-electric air conditioning products with direct-fired absorption technology to apply energy from fuel to air cooling directly, and to enhance energy efficiency by recycling the wasted heat. Its air conditioning has been sold in more than 80 countries, is used at a US Air Force base and at a US Navy base, and now can be found in airports in many countries. In another product category, BROAD Group now makes air-quality-detection machines the size of a small mobile phone that can detect particulate matter as small as 2.5 microns and other hazardous substances within 30 seconds.

Technological innovation—China's next phase
Technological innovation occurs when a product or a service itself or its production or delivery makes use of technologies that are new to the world, to a country, or to an industry category.[10] The first television sets and the first mobile phones were examples of radical technological and product innovation. China has yet to produce high-impact technology innovations with global significance, but Chinese companies have already shown the ability to use world-class technology to create innovations. SVG Optronics is a startup company that uses nanotechnology to create very thin

films that create holographic patterns that can be printed onto identity cards and are very difficult to copy. As a result, a Chinese identity card is now more secure than a European or an American driver's license. SVG Optronics developed this technology using its own engineers and scientists, with help from Chinese universities and institutes. Suzhou Nano-Micro BioTech is also active in nano-technology, producing very small particles of uniform size and shape and tailored to the customer's specific needs. Precisely sized and shaped particles are important for certain sophisticated applications—such as the separation and extraction of bio-pharmaceuticals, as spacers between the film layers used in liquid crystal displays, and to provide surface areas for LED lighting that improve emission and light diffusion efficiency by as much as 40 percent. This technological innovation grew out of the application of local research to needs identified by Chinese entrepreneurs.

DJI Innovation is a Chinese company developing and manufac-turing high-performance small unmanned aerial systems. Its core technology is the autopilot technology and gimbal stabilization system that enables the camera on a remote-controlled helicopter to film and deliver images of quality comparable to those shot by manned helicopters, but at a lower price. DJI also developed and expanded its technology into a fully integrated system including a cloud platform, a camera, and image-transfer devices. Its products have been widely used in rescue and relief work and in the produc-tion of television shows. GoPro, a US company that makes high-definition camcorders often used in extreme-action video photography, even sought collaboration with DJI to design an inte-grated aerial photograph product for the GoPro brand. (That potential collaboration failed to work out because of a lack of agreement on price.)

Business-model innovation—often copied and adapted
Business-model innovation occurs when changing more than one major element of a business model (that is, the way in which a business is configured to deliver value and make money) results in a new way of doing business.[11] A classic example is Federal Express, which created a distribution system modeled on the

telephone switching network, with initially just a single hub in Memphis through which all parcels were routed. In China, most business-model innovation has started by taking a Western model, adapting it to China, then further innovating the adaptation.

Tencent, China's largest Internet portal, experimented with multiple business models in order to monetize its products. It now generates most of its revenues through Internet value-added services, developing an ecosystem of service offerings centered on its QQ instant messaging service. Like other Internet service companies, Tencent typically offers a basic product or service free and then charges for extras (the "freemium" model). For example, it monetizes its games by allowing users to sign up at no cost and then charging for virtual goods.

However, for its instant messenger service QQ, Tencent did not copy the unprofitable business model of the global leader, ICQ. Instead, it created a new business model that was the first to include advertising. That business model enables Tencent to monetize all the value-added services surrounding the free QQ instant messenger application. Tencent also collaborated with the telecommunications giants China Mobile and China Unicom to provide instant messaging between QQ and mobile phones, capitalizing on their value-added services. This has created one of the few Chinese brands capable of generating its own licensing revenues: Tencent has licensed its popular penguin logo and has opened up stores selling QQ merchandise.

Non-customer innovation—another huge opportunity

Non-customer innovation occurs when a business is able to serve a customer segment not previously served in a certain category in the world or in a particular country. An example is Apple's iPad, whose simplicity drew in many older users who had previously been unable to use more complex personal computers. China's modern market economy is so new that there are many potential customers in almost every category. For example, in banking many small enterprises still have no bank accounts. Minsheng Bank succeeded in capturing small companies' business as the first mover. In 2009 the bank launched Shang Dai Tong, a specialized product designed for small companies. By 2011, this product alone accounted for loans of 200 billion renminbi ($32.6 billion), 19 percent of Minsheng Bank's loans. The product serves more than 120,000 individual customers, with a non-performing loan rate of only 0.13 percent. In just over two years, Minsheng Bank became one of the world's largest providers of financial services to small businesses.

FOUR CHINESE INNOVATION LEADERS

Having given brief examples of eight modes of Chinese innovation, we will now discuss four Chinese innovation leaders in depth, basing our discussion both on our original research at these companies and on published materials.

Three Chinese companies are regularly rated as among the most innovative in China (including in our own surveys with Strategy& in 2013 and 2014[12]). Those companies are Haier, Huawei, and Alibaba. In this section we will profile them. We also will discuss Yuwell, a mid-size manufacturer of medical equipment whose innovation approach is attracting increasing attention. Each of these four companies exemplifies one or more of the different innovation modes used by Chinese companies.

Haier—step-by-step innovation

The Haier Group, now the world's largest producer of domestic appliances and perhaps the most international Chinese company, represents Chinese companies' classic path of step-by-step, incremental innovation. The company describes its evolution through five phases: domestic brand building (1984–1991); diversification (1991–1998), international expansion (1998–2005), global brand strategy (2005–2012), and networking strategy (2012 onward).[13]

Haier is famous for early idiosyncratic product adaptations for the Chinese market—simple additions and alterations that turned out to be welcomed by consumers. The most famous is the adaptation of washing machines so that rural farmers could wash potatoes and vegetables. But Haier also took this approach in entering international markets. For the US market it added table tops to small refrigerators sold to college students, and added a third compartment to some household refrigerator models to keep ice cream at a temperature higher than that in the freezer so that one need not wait for the ice cream to soften.

Incremental but customer-focused

Haier now develops more technically based product innovations, intended to improve performance for the user. For example, Haier integrated many technologies into a new generation of washing machines, such as two drenching systems that can rinse clothes and clean the washing machine simultaneously. In the traditional washing process, after the rinse cycle, some dirt might still be left on the wash drum. The new design avoids that.

Haier's incremental improvements are a response to the Chinese market's diversity and its lack of preconceptions about products. For instance, many users of washing machines demand a quick washing cycle—non-stop washing in 15 minutes. Although it is not a revolutionary improvement, this feature requires a very high-powered machine. The breakthrough was to increase the energy efficiency, something that Haier achieved in collaboration with Fisher & Paykel, a New Zealand company that Haier later acquired. This innovation path—collaboration followed by acquisition—is increasingly common for Chinese companies, which fully intend to use acquired knowledge and talent to evolve from incremental to radical innovation. Haier is already doing this: one potentially disruptive innovation that Haier is developing today in collaboration with external resources is a washing machine that can clean the water during the washing process. The washing machine will work like a filter, and the final "waste" water will be of drinkable quality. Haier has five R&D labs (in China, the United States, Japan, Europe, and Australia) and has been granted 3,299 patents in China and other countries. Its labs work on a range of improvements and also on ambitious innovation projects, which include low-water-consumption and noise-free washing machines, cordless TVs, and low-energy refrigeration and air conditioning. If successful, much of this work will have radical implications for the appliance industry. As will be discussed in detail in chapter 6, Haier is also a Chinese pioneer in seeking ideas globally through its open innovation platform, and it sees itself as a global company with a "three thirds" ambition: to make one third of its products in China for China, one third in China for world markets, and one third abroad for global markets.

After-sales service in China—not an oxymoron

Chinese companies are beginning to embrace service, and Haier is a pioneer. As early as 1990, Haier had set up a computerized service center to keep track of its customers, and had happily repaired 10-year-old machines—a level of service not previously heard of in China.[14] Haier now provides simultaneous delivery and installation, and is putting effort into better ways to deliver goods bought online. But in Haier's view delivery is not the end of its service; it is a new start. The true value of its products should lie in the daily use. Although such a philosophy has long been practiced by Western companies, it is new for China. It is a warning to multinational companies that they may soon begin to lose their competitive advantage in service.

Business-model innovation—a platform for competitors

In a business-model innovation, Haier has created a distribution platform that sells not only Haier's products but also its competitors' products, both internationally and within China. The platform is branded as Goodaymart in China. Haier has used it to work with companies such as Black & Decker, a US manufacturer of small appliances. The platform allows Black & Decker to strengthen its China business in food mixers and clothing irons, while Haier is helping Black & Decker with design, manufacturing, quality control, and logistics. The Chinese company says that it now sees itself less as a traditional manufacturer and more as a combination of virtual and physical networks—quite an evolution for a Chinese company, but in line with its belief in knowledge as the most important competitive capability.

The meaning of ZZJYT

The most unusual part of the Haier innovation process is its organization. The company has instituted a new management approach, using what it calls self-managed teams, and referred to as ZZJYT (*zhi zhu jing ying ti*), both in general operations and in innovation.

Throughout the company, each individual manager or staff member elects to join a number of self-managed teams. One manager explained: "When we were separate units, we may have had conflicting goals and sometimes had disputes. Now we work for one goal but take on different 'key performance indicators' (KPIs). That's the major difference. For instance, Mrs. X may have only concerned herself with customer satisfaction in the past, but now she is in charge of the simultaneous delivery and installation. Before, she received tasks from her line manager, while now she has to respond to customers directly. I am the team leader, but she doesn't need to make any promise to me." There are now 2,000 such self-managed responsibility centers within Haier. This management approach is reproduced in innovation, which is a bottom-up process. Staff members are encouraged to come up with ideas and rewarded for them, even if by only 10 yuan (less than two dollars). CEO Zhang reinforces this approach: "Every day in the morning when I get up, I refresh myself with three words, *bu man yi* ['I am not satisfied']. We have to challenge ourselves constantly in order to find better solutions."

Huawei: the innovation powerhouse

Back in 1987, long before most people in the West had heard of any Chinese companies, a man named Ren Zhengfei had a vision of a Chinese technology business that would compete primarily on innovation. His chosen field was telecommunications—he saw enormous opportunity in the fact that China then relied entirely on imported telecommunications equipment. His first product was a simple small PBX switching machine, for offices and hotels, that could support 48 users. But Ren had ambitions to go much further. He gathered together a team of young engineering graduates to start building the telecommunications products of the future. Some of these early efforts at innovation came to nothing. Ren's clever young engineers cared more about new technology than about customers' needs. The company produced plenty of new products but could not produce customers to buy them. Eventually Ren decided that innovation for innovation's sake was not the way forward. In 1997, to mark that decision, he held a ceremony to give unsold prototype products to the engineers who had created them. He said to each engineer "Take this back to your home as a memory of your effort." From then on, innovation for the customer would be first and foremost. Ren's company was called Huawei. By around 1993, Huawei had successfully developed and rolled out C&C08, a digital switching system that expanded the gate number (the maximum potential number of voice users) from 2,000 to 10,000.

Today Huawei is consistently rated in China as one of the country's most innovative companies. It provides a wide range of ICT (information and communications technology) solutions, covering enterprise networking, cloud computing and data centers, enterprise wireless, network energy and infrastructure services; and more recently consumer devices, especially mobile phones. In 2014 it had sales of $46.5 billion and 170,000 employees worldwide, overtaking the Swedish company Ericsson to become the world's largest vendor of telecom equipment.[15] Huawei's products and solutions now have been deployed in more than 170 countries, serving 3 billion users and 45 of the world's top 50 telecom operators. The company is privately held, with most shares owned by the founder and by more than 80,000 employees.[16]

According to Tom Standage, Digital Editor at *The Economist*, "Huawei is the firm that is overturning the widely held preconception that Chinese companies are merely imitators rather than innovators."[17] By the end of 2014, Huawei had filed 48,719 patent applications in China and 23,917 in other countries outside China, and had been granted 38,825 patents. It spends more than 14.2 percent of revenues on R&D and claims that 76,000 of its 170,000 employees are engaged in R&D.

Huawei's great advantage in international markets has been that, as a newcomer, it has shown willingness to listen to customers and to develop solutions without preconceptions. For example, in 2003 Huawei joined a large project in the Netherlands. The customer—KPN, the Dutch national telecom service provider—had just received a new license to build up its 3G network. But in crowded Amsterdam and other Dutch cities there was no room in customers' facilities to install the equipment. So Huawei simply split the traditional base station, which was the size of a refrigerator, into two parts. One could be placed on top of the building and then linked by fiber to a base station elsewhere. In one step Huawei reduced the footprint of the product by 70 percent. This was not a significant technology innovation; it was an application innovation. It led to savings of more than 50 percent of the customer's operating expense. Huawei now has one third of the world's market for 3G telecommunications equipment, and its base station has become an industry standard.

Huawei's innovation stream

We were invited to visit Huawei's corporate headquarters in Shenzhen and to interview some senior executives involved with innovation in what until recently had been one of the world's most secretive companies.[18]

Huawei has created many other innovative products. In base stations for mobile phones, Huawei started with GSM, then moved to 3G and then to 4G. The challenge for the network operator is that the base station for each generation of mobile technology required its own cabinet the size of a small wardrobe, plus another for the main battery and yet another for the backup battery. Huawei's innovation was simply to put all those units into one chassis, so that the customer could plug one card in for GSM, another for 3G, or another for 4G. This became a single access network (the so-called SingleRAN), leading to savings in both operating expenses and capital expenditure. For these base stations, Huawei learned that in traditional equipment rooms air conditioners were used to reduce the temperature of the entire room, which consumed a lot of electrical power. By installing cooling systems inside the main equipment, Huawei helped to reduce the temperature of the equipment and thus reduce power consumption by more than 30 percent. Innovations of this kind are based on customers' needs, observed in actual operating conditions—that is, on what customers want and are willing to pay for, rather than on what engineers can do.

Huawei set up its innovation activity by combining extensive use of Western consultants with its own particular approaches. In the 1990s, Huawei, like most Chinese companies, was not accustomed to formal management processes and had a very loose management style. But in 1999 the company implemented an Integrated Product Development (IPD) program designed to formalize the evaluation of product development from a business perspective rather than from a technology perspective. The IPD process was implemented in a large consulting effort by IBM. Hundreds of IBM staffers were brought in, with the specific aim of creating a "customer-centric" innovation structure.

At first the IBM process was difficult for Huawei's employees—they weren't accustomed to any process at all. Huawei's chairman, Ren Zhengfei, acknowledged that the IBM process was very uncomfortable for Huawei's employees, but he insisted that they persevere. Huawei implemented the IBM IPD process without changing its fundamental structure, but the Chinese company did customize the process to address Huawei-specific needs. For example, the original IBM system did not have a clear product-testing function, so Huawei introduced a product-testing step into the IPD sequence. IBM worked with Huawei for at least five years to build and adapt the system and has been working continuously with Huawei ever since, participating in implementation and the process of new product development.

A structure for innovation

When we asked our hosts at Huawei "Who is in charge of R&D?" we were surprised to be told that there is no one particular person in charge. Innovation is driven by the IPD process. Although a new team is being constructed to supervise all R&D activities, that team is primarily in charge of personnel. The same goes for funding: Decisions on how to spend the 10 percent of Huawei's revenues allocated to R&D are driven by the IPD process, which also sets up the teams that get the funding.

But although Huawei has no corporate head of R&D, each business unit does have a head of R&D. Huawei has twenty business units within three main business groups (carrier, enterprise, and consumer), with a leader of R&D for each group. Huawei's philosophy is that today a company should not depend on one person to direct the complexities of R&D. Each of Huawei's business units will propose how much R&D investment is needed and submit the proposal to the strategy decision committee, which is led by Eric Xu, the current rotating CEO. (The three vice-chairmen take six-month turns as CEO, reporting to Ren, Huawei's chairman and founder.)

Globalizing the innovation process

Since the mid-2000s, Huawei has been building up a global innovation system with R&D centers in Silicon Valley, San Diego, and Dallas as well as in Germany, Italy, the United Kingdom, France, Finland, India, Taiwan, Singapore, Ireland, Russia, and China. Huawei's seventy R&D centers implement projects for the company's strategic business units or for its "*2012* project" (discussed below). The R&D centers are numerous because they are designed to make use of local capability wherever it is to be found, rather than to be close to customers. For example, in the United States, Huawei has no carrier customers, but it has an R&D center seeking new technologies. Similarly, Huawei has a center in Italy for microwave technology because that country has the world's leading scientists and research capabilities in that field.

In addition to the seventy R&D centers, Huawei has set up 28 joint innovation centers (JICs) with fourteen leading telecommunications operators, and these centers are intended to work closely with customers. In the telecommunications business, for example, Huawei has JICs with Vodafone, BT, France Telecom, China Mobile, China Telecom, and China Unicom. Because information technology and communications technology continue to converge rapidly, creating both technological and competitive challenges, Huawei maintains at least one JIC with each major telecommunications customer. For example, SingleRAN was a disruptive innovation that Huawei implemented in collaboration with Vodafone in 2008, but as will be noted in chapter 6, it is now sold throughout the sector and has become the industry standard. At a recent conference, the CEO of Vodafone was asked what distinguished Vodafone from Deutsche Telecom. "We have the SingleRAN from Huawei," he replied.

Since 2011, Huawei has operated a laboratory that works on technologies that may be feasible five years in the future. Huawei originally named that lab after the 2009 disaster movie *2012*. It works on what the company calls "stupid ideas"—ideas that may one day seem much less stupid.

The future of innovation at Huawei

Huawei has become a world pioneer in several areas and owns many state-of-the-art technologies. But the senior management is adamant that it will not pursue technical innovation for its own sake just because Huawei is now a larger and more powerful company than it once was. Focusing on customers is still its first principle, and every employee is expected to understand that priority. Huawei also feels that, as an industry leader, it has the responsibility to shape the industry—for example, by working with its competitor Ericsson to define 5G standards.

Huawei also sees an advantage in not being a publicly listed company. It cites the example of Motorola, a company that once was a dominant player in mobile-phone technology, but which, when faced with share price pressure, reduced its R&D efforts in 3G and as a result later had no new products for customers, who then turned to Huawei.

We expect that Huawei will keep its humble approach to innovation—"humble" being a word we heard several times from Huawei executives. As one executive told us: "We do not give our solutions to customers but collaborate with them in joint development. The relationship can be very complicated because of vertical integration, and much depends on who the customers are. For Huawei collaboration is very important."

Like many other Chinese companies, Huawei also wants to change its company culture to tolerate failure—for Huawei a big change. As one Huawei R&D leader put it, those who fail should be considered heroes because they demonstrate what doesn't work.

Alibaba: a thousand and one innovations

Often rated as the most innovative company in China, Alibaba Group is now one of the world's largest e-commerce companies, with more than $397 billion in transactions by more than 350 million active users and more than 10 million sellers, and with company revenues of more than $5.5 billion, in fiscal 2014.[19] After its initial public offering on the New York Stock Exchange in September 2014, which put its market capitalization at $230 billion, Alibaba became one of the world's most valuable companies, more valuable than Amazon and eBay combined.[20] Alibaba Group (including affiliated entities) employs more than 24,000 people in about seventy cities in China, India, Japan, Korea, the United Kingdom, and the United States.

Founded in 1999 in the eastern Chinese city of Hangzhou, Alibaba Group facilitates online business through three marketplaces: www.alibaba.com(a global online wholesale marketplace), www.1688.com(an online wholesale marketplace for domestic trade in China), and www.aliexpress.com (a global transaction-based wholesale platform for smaller buyers seeking fast shipment of small quantities of goods). Alibaba's other platforms include Taobao (which facilitates consumer-to-consumer online shopping), Tmall (which specializes in business-to-consumer shopping with big-brand suppliers), Juhuasuan (China's most popular online group buying marketplace), Alitrip.com (China's leading online tourism booking platform, and www.aliyun.com (a cloud computing service).

Alibaba Group also provides payment and escrow services for its marketplaces through its contractual arrangements with the Ant Financial Services Group, which operates Alipay.

Through the Zhejiang Cainiao Supply Chain Management Company, a 48 percent-owned affiliate formerly known as China Smart Logistics, Alibaba Group operates a central logistics information system that connects a network of express delivery companies in China.

An innovative and maverick founder

Alibaba Group's founder, Jack Ma (Ma Yun), a former schoolteacher sometimes called the Steve Jobs of China, is a renowned maverick with a very clear strategy. In 2005 he said: "eBay may be a shark in the ocean, but I am a crocodile in the Yangtze River. If we fight in the ocean, we lose—but if we fight in the river, we win."[21]

Now executive chairman, having stepped down as CEO, Ma has played a very important role in the success of Alibaba—a success that embodies many of his personal characteristics and that is also illustrative of the visionary optimism of Chinese entrepreneurs. Ma is seen as optimistic, iron-willed, far-sighted, and innovative. His managerial philosophy includes being more international than domestic enterprises and being more domestic than international enterprises. He stresses Alibaba's need to be prepared to perform better than its competitors in terms of business operations, team management, financing capacity, technology, human resources, and global market development. And he believes that a leader can perform his or her leadership function with a professional team even if that leader is not an expert in the field—an idea that may seem obvious to Westerners but that didn't seem obvious to many Chinese when Ma asserted it.

Ma also recognized from the startup of Alibaba that he would have to deal with the high level of dishonest behavior in China—indeed, he recognized that by dealing with dishonest behavior Alibaba could profit from it by becoming a uniquely trusted brand. Ma insisted that customers use their real names, and from the very start any buyer or seller who cheated in any way was expelled from the company's platforms.

Alibaba's many innovations all depend on a deep understanding of Chinese customers. Although most of its service offerings are adaptations of existing services that originated in the United States, such as eBay and Amazon, Alibaba's ability to implement the many, often idiosyncratic adaptations needed for China has allowed it to defeat its Western rivals in China. Alibaba is the champion of "Sinaptation"—that is, adaptation of foreign products and services, such as Amazon and eBay, to China.

Many innovations, one platform

Alibaba's business-to-consumer platform Taobao ("treasure hunt") was developed specifically to counter eBay's entry into China. Its development involved at least three of the modes of innovation we discussed earlier in this chapter: combining existing technologies to facilitate electronic fund transfers (which overcame the idiosyncrasies then present in China's banking system), business-model innovation (which enabled sellers to create many innovations themselves), and non-customer innovation (which brought in many new users of e-commerce, whereas previously it had been very difficult to match demand and supply). Taobao decreases the distance between individual suppliers and individual buyers and increases the speed of information sharing, creating a business-to-customer business of unprecedented scale, with a daily transaction volume that has exceeded 5.2 billion renminbi ($870 million) and annual sales surpassing those of all traditional retailers in China. Alibaba has indeed been an "open sesame" for Chinese consumers; it has also helped establish a legion of entrepreneurial small-business sellers.

Alibaba's business model is to provide a marketplace that connects buyers and sellers and to earn income from facilitating the transactions. The company doesn't compete with its sellers or with the various service providers. Its growth strategy has three elements: to expand the number of customers and their spending, to increase the number of product categories, and to extend the penetration of mobile commerce (which now accounts for more than 20 percent of online purchases made via Alibaba). In 2014, active users of the company's mobile-device payment application Alipay Wallet (renamed Alipay 9.0 in 2015) exceeded 190 million and the daily volume of mobile payment transaction exceeded 45 million, accounting for more than half of Alipay transactions.

The centerpiece of Alibaba's business model is its group of online business platforms, supported by its cloud computing system, which enable transactions and support a wide variety of related functions for suppliers, customers, app developers, and related service providers. Sellers's activities are helped by Qianniu (an integrated platform for communication and productivity tools) and Weitao (a mobile social media platform that enables sellers to provide information to buyers). The platforms also provide many other functions to a wide range of participants.

From enabling transactions to enabling financing

In China, financing has long been difficult for Chinese small and medium-size enterprises (SMEs) because banks prefer to lend to big companies and particularly to reputable state-owned enterprises. Yet while SMEs create more than 75 percent of the country's jobs and are responsible for more than half of its GDP, they receive less than 5 percent of bank lending. In response, Alibaba.com (Alibaba Group's business-to-business platform) found a unique way to help SMEs gain access to financing. Alibaba.com has online trading records of all its numerous SME members, up to 80 percent of whom needed financing but did not have a good enough credit rating or reputation to borrow from banks. In order to help those entrepreneurs get loans, Alibaba.com provides banks with those small companies' transaction records (the company doesn't offer any guarantee but only provides trade credit records), effectively creating China's first small-business credit rating system.

Building on this knowledge of customer credit, Alibaba started its own SME loan business in 2010. It provides "micro loans" to sellers operating on its wholesale and retail marketplaces through lending vehicles licensed by various local governments. At the end of 2013, the SME loan business had more than 342,000 borrowers with a total net outstanding loan balance of 12.4 billion renminbi (equal to $2 billion). In January 2015, China's first credit agency, Sesame Credit, was set up by Ant Financial Services Group, the company that (as has already been noted) operates Alipay. Alibaba has a 37.5 percent stake in Ant.

Trusted payments in a low-trust economy

In 2004, having repeatedly challenged China's lagging state-owned banks, Alibaba developed its own online payment system, Alipay, to provide an easy, safe, and secure way for millions of individuals and business to make and receive payments on the Internet. By the end of 2013, Alipay had more than 300 million registered users and facilitated about 188 million transactions a day, 45 million of them via mobile phones. In the fiscal year that ended June 30, 2014, Alipay processed nearly $800 billion in transactions[22] ($2.2 billion per day). Furthermore, Alipay's partners include more than

180 banks and financial institutions, including 19 leading national banks and 142 regional banks across China, two foreign banks, MasterCard, and Visa.

The key to Alipay's success was trust. Although Alipay operates similarly to PayPal, it differs in that it uses an escrow payment service that enables buyers to verify whether they are happy with goods they have purchased before releasing the payment to the sellers. Jack Ma put it this way: "China will take 30 years to become one of the rich countries in the world, but it will take 50 years for China and the people to understand being rich; this culture is very difficult to build in reality. ... Trustworthiness is one element in this culture, but due to some historic reasons, it was not emphasized in the past."[23]

Alibaba's ecosystem

Alibaba Group's various marketplaces attract millions of buyers and sellers. Apart from them, there are third-party service providers that build their businesses in this ecosystem and boost the development of Alibaba's business. Alibaba has announced a "Small and Beautiful" Strategy to provide a platform, finance, and data services to develop a million merchants with annual revenues of more than a million renminbi each, and to help these "small and beautiful" merchants transform themselves from merchants into manufacturers.

Alibaba has built a vast and complex ecosystem of platforms, connections, and agreements for its own operating needs and for use by third-party service providers. Examples include the following:

- Alimama.com, through which more than 620,000 marketing affiliates provide advertising and marketing services to merchants.
- Proxy operators—third-party retail operational partners, with e-commerce expertise, that provide services (e.g., product planning, supply-chain management, inventory storage and fulfillment, marketing promotion, storefront management) to sellers on Alibaba's Internet marketplaces.

- The Tao Girls Platform. Taobao has one site where more than 40,000 young women called "Tao Girls" show off their beauty and outfits and post prices for Internet modeling or personal delivery services (via a logistics company partnering with Taobao). In 2013, this platform created revenue of more than 3 billion renminbi. Meanwhile, more than 100,000 design firms, photographers, and service outsourcing agents are providing online shop decoration and customer service outsource services. About 15,000 independent software vendors are providing software services on store management, marketing, data analysis, and customer relationship management.
- Courses in e-commerce. More than 300 colleges and universities in China have set up such courses. In 2014, nearly 5,000 people received training in e-commerce.
- Apsara, a cloud computing platform. Built with proprietary technology by Alibaba's 7,000 engineers, Apsara offers a suite of cloud services for the company, including elastic computing, database storage and services, and large-scale data processing. In addition, cloud computing services are provided to Alibaba's sellers and other third parties. More than 980,000 customers use Alibaba Cloud Computing services, either directly or through independent software vendors. The customers include developers of mobile apps, Internet gaming operators, and systems integrators. Apsara processed 254 million orders within 24 hours during the company's "Singles Day" promotion on November 11, 2013.
- The Taobao Ad Network and Exchange (TANX). This real-time online advertising exchange, hosted by Alibaba Cloud Computing, automates the buying and selling of billions of advertising impressions per day by third parties. Participants include publishers, merchants, demand-side platforms, and third-party data and technology companies.
- In 2013, Alibaba and eight other companies established the China Smart Logistic Network. In 2014 that network employed more than 950,000 delivery people across China and handled 5 billion packages.

An e-commerce exemplar

Alibaba illustrates how rapidly Chinese companies can grow through innovation in the fast-moving and evolving Internet sector. It is a powerful example of a company that sees opportunities for innovation in every aspect of its business, providing growth and business assistance to a wide range of related parties. China's enormous population and huge number of Internet users have made it a pioneering source of innovation for e-commerce, and any company involved with e-commerce needs to monitor closely how China's Internet companies are leading the way.

Yuwell: innovating in many modes

Yuwell Medical Equipment is a medium-size company with $1.5 billion in revenue that focuses on medical equipment for the elderly and for others who want to monitor their own health. Its products include rehabilitation nursing equipment and clinical oxygen products. Six products account for more than two thirds of its revenues: a molecular-sieve oxygen generator, an ultra-light oxygen valve, a nebulizer, a blood pressure meter, a stethoscope, and wheelchairs. But Yuwell innovates in many different ways other than in products.

Yuwell's founder and chairman, Guangming Wu, explains that the company is built on the premise of innovation and change. It was originally a so-called Township and Village Enterprise named Yuyue ("jumping fish"). The name echoes the old Chinese expression "carp leaping over the dragon's gate," which once referred to students succeeding in the civil service examination in ancient times. Today, the expression refers to how the company achieved success and created a new identity. Yuyue transformed itself into a public company in 2008 and then, in 2013, changed its name to Yuwell to signify its health-care mission and to be more easily understood outside China.[24]

Product and process innovations

Yuwell has excelled in the market for medical devices by introducing regular improvements in production operations, product marketing, and quality control. Yuwell calls this "The secret engine of our constant growth and progress." The company has filed almost 100 product patents to date, while its systematic innovations have re-engineered 273 complicated manufacturing processes to just 69 simplified processes, which facilitated the fastest production line in the world for making desktop sphygmomanometers (which are blood pressure meters). With a combination of manual labor and automation, Yuwell also developed the world's longest production line for live line-testing of oxygen generators, and it was also the first Chinese company to win a US Food & Drug Administration certificate for oxygen generators for export to the US market. The company owns design patents for each of its products and has maintained a record of launching a new product every month.

The electronic blood pressure meter is an example of Yuwell's innovation focus. Although this product was not based on a novel technology, it effectively enhances the accuracy of blood pressure measurement. Blood pressure measurement in an individual depends on several factors, including blood-vessel structure, age, and sex. More than 10 percent of people are not suitable for the traditional method of measuring blood pressure, which can't differentiate between these individual variations. Yuwell's R&D personnel studied pulse patterns in patients to understand these variations, and developed a self-adapting oscillograph system, which ensured a more accurate result. This product alone generated about 100 million renminbi ($17 million) within the first three years after launch.[25]

Engaging creatively with customers

Yuwell made a commercial breakthrough by understanding and influencing customers' preferences in such a way as to cultivate a new market for medical devices. Before Yuwell, there was no real market for medical devices to be used in patients' homes. For instance, wheelchairs were mainly meant for handicapped people, as were most of the other medical devices that the company manufactured. Yuwell fostered the idea that a wheelchair could be an excellent gift to an aging parent. Giving a parent a wheelchair was portrayed as a new way for the younger generation to express gratitude and consideration toward senior family members, a sentiment that is respected in China. The company designed gift packages of products never previously considered as potential gifts, such as a blood pressure monitor, a blood glucose meter, an ear thermometer, and a pedometer. Wheelchairs were promoted as useful for family outings, and oxygen concentrators as study aids for students. Yuwell's sales and marketing director, Xiu Hua Sui, once said: "Innovation does not necessarily mean a technology invention; sometimes it is about reinventing culture. We often invite fashion models to the exhibitions to express our mission statement 'to bring beauty to people's lives.' The external appearance accounts for about a quarter of our marketing strategy."

Yuwell products are also often equipped with special features not available in competitors' products. For instance, air purifiers were certified as a medical device but had more comprehensive functions and could also be used for air sterilization, creating an entirely new niche in domestic sterilization applications where air quality is a concern, giving Yuwell distinctive positioning in a crowded traditional market.

Mergers, acquisitions, and investment to enhance innovation

As is also true of other Chinese companies we studied, Yuwell doesn't innovate for innovation's sake, and its approach to mergers and acquisitions is designed to serve its strategy of "market demand first." Talent, technology, and unique products are the main targets in Yuwell's acquisitions. Its present R&D facilities were established through several rounds of mergers and acquisitions, which brought in a team of twenty engineers who directly contributed to the development of the electronic blood pressure meter. In 2011, Yuwell gained a niche advantage in traditional medicine by buying all the shares of Suzhou Huatuo Company, a major manufacturer of an ISO-standard acupuncture needle that excelled in traditional Chinese medicine products and that held patents on 22 registered medical devices.

Investments, sourced from both internal company funds and government finance, are equally important. Although Yuwell increased its own expenditures on R&D from 3 percent to 5.4 percent of sales revenues (71 million renminbi, equal to $12 million) between 2007 and 2012, government has also played an important role. As we noted in chapter 1, an important national agenda priority in China is to shift from "Made in China" to "Created in China," and government departments at various levels support local companies in innovation. For instance, Yuwell enjoyed a 14 percent refund of the value-added tax as a "double-soft corporation." "Double-soft" refers not only to capability and technology for software products but also to management system, company culture, and capabilities for sustainable development. In order for a firm to qualify, half of its employees are expected to work on software, and 50 percent of revenue should come from software sales. Specifically, two types of Yuwell software for x-ray machines received five years' funding from the government, and government support contributed about 72 percent of Yuwell's total non-operating income in 2012.

Yuwell's innovation process

Yuwell has developed an effective process for innovation. It encourages employees at all levels to think up innovative ideas, and about 30–40 percent of the bottom-up proposals are accepted by the top management after going through an approval system. Once approved, ideas are realized quickly—for example, Yuwell spent only three months on development of the electronic blood pressure meter.

"Open innovation" collaborations are also being used. Two examples can be cited here. The first is that, through collaborations with universities and the government, Yuwell has built up an Engineering Technology Centre for health-care diagnostics. The second is that, by collaborating with the Chinese Academy of Sciences, Yuwell helped to develop the infrastructure for a provincial laboratory focusing on fundamental research and offering internships for master's candidates, doctoral candidates, and postdocs.

Yuwell provides a model for many other small and medium-size Chinese companies as they try to move up the innovation ladder. Having started with a manufacturing advantage, it has steadily made incremental product innovations, technology innovations, and process innovations, shifting quickly from the copying phase to the "fit for purpose" phase and then to the world-standard phase. In each phase, the innovations have been infused with creative thinking about how to meet customers' needs.

There are many other examples of innovative Chinese private-sector companies in the medical field or in biotechnology. Venus Medtech produces aortic heart valves, and Nurotron is a producer of cochlear implants.[26] A number of these companies are world class, despite the early lack of focus on this sector noted in chapter 1. A prominent example in biotechnology is BGI, an offshoot of the Chinese Academy of Sciences that operates as a private entity in Shenzhen and operates half the world's capacity for genome sequencing. BGI was responsible for sequencing the SARS virus and provides pharmaceutical research advice for Chinese and foreign clients.[27]

The Innovativeness of Chinese Companies Compared with That of Foreign Companies

So far in this chapter we have provided many mini-examples and four case studies of Chinese companies and how they innovate. We will now provide large-sample evidence of how Chinese companies' innovation compares with that of foreign multinationals. For three years, 2012–2014, we collaborated with Strategy& (formerly Booz & Company and now part of PwC) in an annual survey of executives in leading multinational companies and Chinese enterprises regarding innovation in China. The surveys were conducted online and were then sent to contacts known to Strategy&, to our own CEIBS Centre on China Innovation, and to other survey partners.[28] Analyzing these surveys, we found that Chinese companies are rapidly matching the capabilities of Western companies for innovation in China. As figure 2.1 shows, an increasing percentage of executives in multinational companies perceive their Chinese competitors as either equally innovative or more innovative in China. More specifically, executives see Chinese companies as better innovators in supply chain, in service, and in business model, but less innovative in new product innovation (figure 2.2).

We suspect that executives of multinational companies in China may be exaggerating the innovative capabilities of Chinese

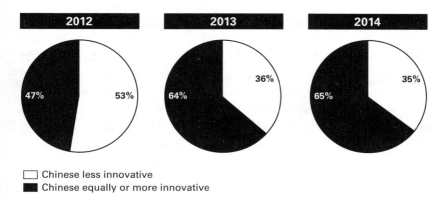

☐ Chinese less innovative
■ Chinese equally or more innovative

Figure 2.1

Evidence that Chinese companies have arrived as innovators (answers to "Please rate the work performed in your company's innovation performance in Mainland China").

Source: Strategy&, China's Innovations Going Global: 2014 China Innovation Survey.

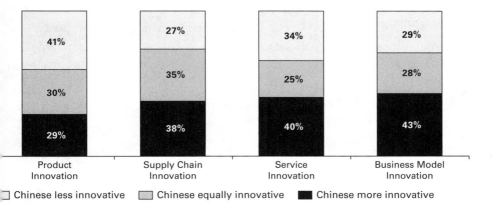

Figure 2.2

Comparison of Chinese firms and multinational corporations by type of innovation (answers to "Please rate the work performed in your company's innovation performance in Mainland China").

Source: Strategy&, China's Innovations Going Global: 2014 China Innovation Survey.

companies because they are living with the threat of their innovativeness every day. We found a weaker perception of innovation performance in a different study conducted by the CEIBS Centre on China Innovation, which was focused on 59 of the largest and most reputedly innovative companies in China. We found that none of the companies rated as highly in terms of innovativeness when the basis of comparison was "relative to global standards" as when the basis for comparison was "innovativeness relative to Chinese companies." In other words, these most innovative Chinese companies were all seen as behind world standards of innovativeness. This finding is consistent with the rankings reported in chapter 1, which find few examples of Chinese companies among the highly innovative companies (although the numbers are growing). But in a survey led by the consulting firm Strategy&, we did find that more than 80 percent of Chinese companies in each of the years 2012, 2013, and 2014 were conducting innovation efforts in China that also contributed to developing products and services for foreign markets (figure 2.3)—the third phase of evolution we described in chapter 1. The survey found that a higher proportion of Chinese firms than multinational corporations were using a

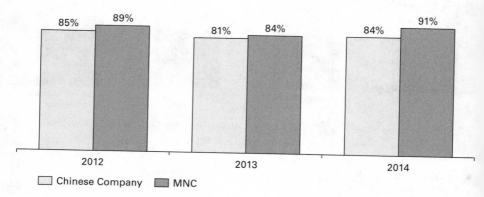

Figure 2.3

Innovation for foreign markets in China (answers to "Your company's innovation efforts in Mainland China contribute to developing products/services for foreign markets?")

Source: Strategy&, China's Innovations Going Global: 2014 China Innovation Survey.

"need seeker" strategy in China, which implied a greater focus on proactively engaging customers directly to generate new ideas.[29]

A possible conclusion is that Chinese companies have a competitive advantage over multinational companies in China. Their "need seeker" strategy demonstrates the centrality of their focus on *customers*—the first factor of our Four Cs framework. Not only are China's customers a powerful force for innovativeness, but Chinese firms see customer focus as essential to their strategy more often than do MNCs in China. In the next chapter we will discuss the reasons for these characteristics in more detail.

The 2014 survey also showed that Chinese companies use innovation as a tool in globalization to a surprising extent. Indeed, they prioritize innovation in globalization more than multinational corporations prioritize innovation in China. This strategic choice probably reflects the deep and well-trained reflexes of Chinese executives to innovate to succeed, regardless of the geography, and may also reflect multinational corporations' concerns about intellectual property protection in China (discussed further in chapter 7). It also shows that responsiveness to *customers* has become embedded in Chinese firms' *capabilities*—the third factor of our framework—and fundamental to their expansion.

As Chinese companies globalize, they will raise the innovation bar higher. We already see Chinese companies using innovation to address new customer segments, particularly in niche markets. They are eager to improve their global innovation capabilities, which many of them still perceive as lagging. Soon multinational corporations will face outside China the innovation intensity they now face from Chinese firms in China.

CHINESE COMPANIES GLOBALIZE INNOVATION DIFFERENTLY

Waves of globalization have originated in the United States, in Europe, in Japan, and (more recently) in Korea. Each wave has been accompanied by companies' globalizing their innovation capabilities, processes, and systems. Similarly, as China drives another wave of globalization, Chinese companies will globalize their innovation systems—indeed, they are already doing so. This globalization wave—more a tsunami of innovation—will be grounded in Chinese companies' Chinese roots, yet they will respond creatively to today's realities.

The 2014 survey mentioned above helps us to begin to define the specifically Chinese approach to globalizing innovation[30]:

- Chinese companies are more likely to globalize their innovation to gain access to talent and technologies. In other words, they seek capabilities rather than simple facts or knowledge. The top driver (68 percent) for a Chinese company setting up an innovation center is to acquire or monitor a leading technology; Chinese companies are planning for the long term. For multinational corporations, the leading driver (90 percent) is quite different: to capture customer trends and insights. We interpret these differences as demonstrating the superiority of Chinese companies in understanding their customers, coupled with an ability to invest in acquiring capabilities that they may lack. Success in domestic business provides the funding—our fourth factor, *cash*—that makes acquiring foreign capabilities possible.

- Chinese companies tend to rely less on in-house expansion than their multinational counterparts. They are more likely to partner with or even acquire other organizations insofar as that is consistent with their financial ability to acquire brands, market share, and missing technology.

- Chinese companies are more likely than multinational corporations to partner with organizations outside their regular value chains (such as universities and research institutes) as well as with organizations within their regular value chains (primarily suppliers but also competitors). For instance, 77 percent partner with universities, versus 45 percent of multinationals, and 68 percent partner with suppliers, versus 46 percent for multinationals. On the other hand, whereas 48 percent of multinationals partner with customers, only 27 percent of Chinese companies do so—perhaps because the Chinese companies already know a lot about their customers. Chinese companies are also hesitant to partner with companies in other industries because of the risk that those companies may cross industry lines and take market share. We provide more evidence on these characteristics in chapter 6, where we look at open innovation practices and see that such partnering is very common among Chinese firms and is strongly facilitated by the innovation ecosystem that has been systematically fostered by the government.

In sum, we are discovering a uniquely Chinese approach to globalizing innovation. Globalizing Chinese companies are open, seek collaboration, build capabilities, create networks, and are acquisitive when they lack needed capabilities. In contrast, previous waves of innovation were more focused on building in-house and self-standing assets.[31] And Chinese firms take this approach to foreign expansion because they have developed the internal capacity to seek out, understand, and absorb new knowledge.

CONCLUSION

In this chapter we have shown that Chinese companies make use of eight different modes in undertaking innovation, seeking sources of competitive advantage wherever it can be found. Some have overtaken foreign companies in China in innovation and some are reaching world-standard levels. We have also provided four examples of Chinese companies that have built up their capabilities for innovation. These cases shed more light on the variables underlying the Four Cs model.

The first factor—*customers*—clearly is the main preoccupation in the cases outlined above and in the survey results. First, Chinese companies employ every mode of innovation to satisfy the perceived needs of customers; and second, they are more focused on customers' needs than are multinational corporations operating in China. The cases show that Chinese companies' understanding of their customers has evolved, in tandem with their innovative capacity, from copying to "fit for purpose" and then to world standard.

The second factor, *culture*, includes leadership and entrepreneurial drive. This is evident from most cases of successful Chinese companies and in the case studies presented above, and it will be discussed in more depth in the next chapter. Our use of the term *culture* in the Four Cs framework is more extensive than the traditional description of national culture. It also includes the Chinese government's ambitions for the country's place and influence in the world, including its determination to create a world-class innovation environment. And, as we have seen, Chinese companies are more willing to partner with other organizations than are multinational corporations (though less so with customers or companies outside their industry domain) to make the leap to the next phase—that is, from new resources to new markets.

We have also seen, in this chapter and in the previous one, that the Chinese government, despite its commitments to the World Trade Organization, supports helping local companies to be successful in the local market so as to develop the capabilities and the *cash* to succeed in other markets. As the focus shifts from new resources to new markets, state-owned enterprises are less likely to have developed the management processes, the culture, or the internal capabilities they will need in order to enter more innovation-intensive markets. Private firms, as our joint surveys with Booz & Company (Strategy&) suggest, are more likely to have developed the needed capabilities, particularly the necessary understanding of customers. And where local firms lack capabilities, such as brands or technology, they have the cash to acquire them.

In chapter 1 we sketched the four factors that determine China's innovative capacity. In this chapter, we have pulled back the curtain to show how those four factors have influenced the growth of China's corporations. We have provided evidence from cases and surveys of the *customer* factor, the *culture* factor, and the *cash* factor, and we have sketched the outlines of the *capabilities* China's corporations have developed. Together, the four factors interact to explain the development of innovative capacity over the three phases of development. The four factors don't function independently, and we don't mean to suggest that it is easy, or even possible, to decompose the interactions between the underlying elements. Nevertheless, the four factors offer a simple way of viewing the drivers that have contributed to the remarkable surge of innovation in China.

3

WHAT IS DIFFERENT ABOUT CHINESE INNOVATION?

In this chapter we will broaden our explanation of the typical differences in innovation activities between Chinese and multinational companies. (Many Chinese companies are also multinational, but the common terminology in China uses "multinational" or "MNC" to refer to large companies from developed countries, particularly those from the United States, Western Europe, Japan, and Korea.)

This chapter is based on the many interviews we have conducted at Chinese companies, on comments by executives of Western companies about their Chinese competitors, on our study of the research literature and media reports, and on confirmations and critiques of our analysis in presentations to managerial and academic audiences.

We found ten major ways in which Chinese companies' innovation activities differ from those of multinational corporations:

- greater focus on local needs and customers
- acceptance of "good enough" standards
- incremental rather than radical innovation
- willingness to cater to special needs
- deploying large numbers of employees
- working employees harder
- faster, less formal processes
- fast trial and error
- more intervention by the boss
- closer ties to government

These are the underlying elements of the *capabilities* factor in our Four Cs model. They result from the companies' entrepreneurial drive, from learning through trial and error in the competitive domestic customer environment, and from the support and investment of the government in the innovation system.

GREATER FOCUS ON LOCAL NEEDS AND CUSTOMERS

All companies try to focus on customers' needs in their innovation activities, although Chinese firms do so more than others. For example, many Western technology-based companies can let technology capabilities dominate their innovation efforts, sometimes to the detriment of a focus on customers' needs. Lacking such technology advantages, in most cases, Chinese companies are forced to concentrate more on customers' needs. Conversely, the rapid and lower-cost execution capability of Chinese companies means that it is easier for them to respond to local needs with special variants of products.

In addition, there are specific characteristics of China that drive such a focus on the customer:

- Most Chinese customers have very different needs and tastes from customers in developed Western countries. It is much easier for Chinese companies to understand these needs. We have already cited Haier's adaptation to the needs of farmers to wash their vegetable crops. A Western company would probably have just added a warning label about not using the washing machine for that purpose.

- The rapid growth of China's economy means that customers' needs evolve more quickly than they do in the developed countries. Again, Chinese companies' fast and low-cost execution enable them to respond rapidly to these changing needs, whereas Western rivals would hesitate to react to each such change.

- The great diversity of China in geography, climate, and levels of development and urbanization engenders a great diversity of needs to satisfy. Sany, now one of the world's leading makers of construction equipment, explained that this diversity was why it had to develop many more versions of each machine than its foreign rivals. For example, Sany developed a special version of a machine used mostly in airport construction. Because the land in south China is soft, with lots of underground water, the machine has to be able to lay gravel under the earth and then tamp it down. Traditional machines could not do the tamping well.

- Because China has one of the world's most hierarchical cultures, customers' needs are always given high priority. This applies especially in business-to-business relationships, in which Chinese customers require exact satisfaction of their every demand.

Joyoung out-innovates Philips in blenders

For years, the Netherlands-based company Koninklijke Philips N.V. held the number 1 position in China for both juicer and blender products, categories in which it was also very strong in other countries. But after a Chinese company identified a particular preference among local customers, the situation changed. That company, Joyoung, knowing that Chinese consumers like to drink soybean milk, developed a "soybean milk cooker" that was actually a combination of a blender and a rice cooker. Joyoung quickly seized the market opportunity. By 2011 it had built a business worth 4.5 billion renminbi, ten times Philips' business, in the market for juicers and blenders—a market that Philips had been cultivating for more than ten years. Joyoung then moved aggressively into the blender and juicer market. As a result, Philips suffered a loss of 10 percent in revenue every year. As of 2012, Joyoung had 42 percent of the retail market for juicers in China, while Philips had only 20 percent.[1] Had Philips been the first mover to identify and cater to Chinese consumers' need for a soybean milk cooker, it would not have suffered such fierce competition. (This paragraph is based on our independent research, not on Philips' sources.)

The threat to multinational corporations

The story of Joyoung versus Philips illustrates how Chinese companies can use deeper understanding of local customers to overcome inherent advantages of multinational corporations.

Furthermore, if multinationals don't go deeper into understanding local Chinese needs and move faster to cater to those needs, they will allow Chinese rivals to build initial positions from which they will be able to threaten many more parts of the market. Chinese companies will use the experience and the financial resources they have earned in China to serve segments of foreign markets and will become strong competitors in those markets.

Another European giant (not named here) also sees Chinese closeness to customers as the biggest threat to itself in China— especially in mass markets, which are the markets with the lowest barriers to entry. That European company sees Chinese companies' approach to the mass market as very different from that of multinationals. These Chinese companies operate on a "brute force" approach, working closely with customers to satisfy their needs and making as much of an effort as was required. They learn from their customers and are quick to respond because they are so close to them. They add features that customers need. They can then move up the value ladder. One US multinational company commented that, whereas in the US market it faced a few large competitors, in China it faced hundreds of small ones, focused on parts of its product range. Most of these small companies in the mass market die— perhaps 95 percent—but those that survive are quite strong and innovative.

ACCEPTANCE OF "GOOD ENOUGH" STANDARDS

Because China is at a much lower level of economic development than most developed countries, and because most business and individual customers there are buying many products for the first time, low-cost fit-for-purpose ("good enough") products have great appeal. Companies from developed countries usually have to reduce the complexity of their better products to make them "good enough."[2] That is difficult for them. For example, an executive of the German firm Bosch, a global leader in automotive components, told us about a problem they face in China in regard to airbags. Bosch wants to ensure that the deployment time of its airbags is the same everywhere in the world. In the West, a car has six, eight, or even more airbags, but today a Chinese-built car has only two to four of them. From the engineering side, Bosch can't simply downgrade its global products. To maintain the deployment performance of its airbags, Bosch has to do new engineering for the airbag control system, or the production cost in China will be too high. But to do so in Europe would incur high engineering costs and would often encounter psychological barriers from Bosch's German engineers, who have been educated to design to the highest standards and who find it very difficult to "strip down" a product if asked to do so. So Bosch uses many local Chinese engineers for the redesign. They know what Chinese customers want; they also understand Bosch's standards, and can balance out apparently opposing needs. Nevertheless, meeting the "good enough" standard requires extra effort and money for Western companies. One rule of thumb is that companies coming from Europe or the United States should reduce the prices of their products by 30–60 percent for the Chinese market. Going the "good enough" route requires help from local personnel and a change of mindset by the parent firm. A multinational manufacturer of food-processing machinery that had found little success in China with its superbly engineered products found that the fastest solution was to acquire one of its local "good enough" competitors. It kept the acquired company's brand for local sales, and was surprised by two unexpected results: first, it found markets for the "good enough" product in India and also in developed markets for animal feed applications; second, over time, with growing concern about food quality in China, some of its Chinese customers moved up to the parent's higher-quality machines. Thus, China has acted as a lead market to stimulate "reverse innovation" by this firm.

In contrast to MNCs, most Chinese companies are starting from the bottom end of markets, so their initial challenge is building up, not down, to standards that are good enough for China. As a result of their success in satisfying local customers, Chinese companies have quickly captured the low end of most markets, denying space to Western companies, and are now moving up into the middle segment just as multinationals are moving downward from the top segment.[3]

The Chery QQ—the cute enough car

Chinese automakers, including Chery, Great Wall, and Geely, have
used cost innovation to develop vehicles that offer "good enough"
standards at very low prices. Take, for example, Chery's QQ.
The first unit of that subcompact model, designed to appeal to
young, white-collar buyers, rolled off the production line on
December 18, 2002, six months ahead of General Motors' new offering for the Chinese market, the Spark. By August 2003, 10,000
units had been sold.[4] The first Chery QQ had, indeed, all the "good
enough" features necessary for the Chinese market. Available with
either of two gasoline-powered engines (one displacing 0.8 liter,
the other 1.1 liters), it was fairly well equipped: air conditioning,
CD player, power windows, power steering). But it had many
faults. According to one review, "power windows jammed at
10,000 [kilometers], gearshift cable replaced at 38,000, alternator
blown out at 41,000, headlight bulb out at 42,000, power steering
oil pipe leaks at 44,000, reversing light switch does not work at
45,000."[5] Sources of customer-satisfaction data aren't as well developed in China as in the West, and perhaps customers were more
influenced by the low initial purchase price than by the lifetime
cost of ownership.

Nevertheless, despite its defects, the QQ outsold both GM's
Spark and Daewoo's Matiz (then the most successful subcompact
in the world) in China. In the 2000s, the QQ was often Chery's
best-selling model, and the company itself calls the car "a legend in
the Chinese history of the automobile … a mini model with the
highest cumulative sales in China."[6] Since 2010, owing in part
to Chinese consumers' rising aspirations and to the plethora of
user information now available on social networks, the QQ
has not been on the China Association of Automobile Manufacturers' list of the top ten sellers. Though no longer as popular as
it was, the QQ remained cheap—in 2012, one could be had for
about $4,000.

With such "good enough" products catering to both local and
international markets, Chery (which offered it first car in 1997) is
now the number-three auto company in China, behind the long-
established Shanghai GM and Shanghai Volkswagen.

Good enough for Western mass markets

Chinese companies can also take a high-end Western product and simplify it to reach a lower price point for mass customers. For example, Haier simplified the wine-cooler refrigerator, a classic high-end consumer good, into a much cheaper middle-market product, and secured more than 60 percent of the global market for such refrigerators.[7]

From good enough to world class

More and more Chinese companies are using the "good enough" segment as a base from which to move upwards in various markets, first within China and then in the rest of the world. For example, Huawei, initially established as a distributor of network equipment, has built and acquired the technical and managerial capabilities it needed to move up from the low end of the market.[8] A commitment to spending on R&D clearly has enabled Huawei's progress. As was discussed in chapter 2, Huawei is now a global leader in many products, and its R&D center in the United States now claims to be more advanced in some fields of communications technology than its US competitors.

INCREMENTAL RATHER THAN RADICAL INNOVATION

Incremental innovation improves a product's design, cost, operations process, or time-to-market, or caters to special needs of customers, without radical technological change. It entails maintaining the existing product, business model and manufacturing process and improving or adding to some of the elements. Because the technical capabilities of most Chinese companies lag behind those of their rivals in developed countries, most of them pursue incremental rather than radical innovation. And the nature of demand in the Chinese market has not yet required disruptive innovations. But because they are learning the basic skills that radical innovation requires, Chinese companies will soon develop the capability to be radical innovators when opportunities arise. As Clayton Christensen has demonstrated,[9] disruptive innovation often begins in a small niche of a large market, beneath the notice of the incumbents. In such niches, many Chinese companies are innovating incrementally in ways that will threaten Western incumbents in the near future. One such Chinese company is Gold Wind, now a leader in wind-turbine technology. Gold Wind gained its competitive advantage through incremental innovation. It developed a direct-drive wind turbine that eliminates the need for a gearbox, thereby reducing the number of moving parts and the likelihood of costly mechanical failure. That, together with the use of rare-earth metals found mostly in China in the turbine magnets, ensures a 98 percent operational success rate and secures Gold Wind's competitive edge.

Flooding the market with variants

Haier entered the US market for refrigerators by selling small models to college students. In addition to its lower cost, Haier innovated incrementally by adding a folding table top so that a refrigerator could double as a desk—very useful in crowded student accommodations. Chinese companies are also more capable than multinationals at incremental innovation, as they can better afford the engineering hours needed to create product variants. But Chinese companies don't just depend on innovating incrementally; often they also flood the market with huge numbers of product variants. Goodbaby, for example, offers more than 1,600 models of strollers, car seats, bassinets, and playpens—four times as many as its nearest competitor—all at prices tailored to a range of segments, from sophisticated to mass-market. Goodbaby is quick to respond to imitators, rapidly switching threatened new products into its mass-market line while introducing innovations in its high-end products. Similarly, Haier constantly improves each of its product lines and the specifications of its products. For example, Haier's freezers range in capacity from 62 to 535 liters. With that approach, Haier exploits economies of scope in production while blanketing every segment of the market.

TCL is now one of the world's largest consumer electronics companies. Its product portfolios serve as another example of the need to constantly improve each product line and the specifications of products. TCL's innovative TV products have features such as "Dual-display technology," "TV-Karaoke," and a "smart touch pen." "Dual-display technology" allows two people to watch different channels on one screen simultaneously, in high definition and even in 3D, by wearing special glasses. "TV-Karaoke" doesn't make use of any novel technology, but it does what many innovative products do: it combines existing technologies from different industries in a novel application. The content comes from the Internet rather than from a CD or a DVD, and users can easily access all kinds of songs—an incremental innovation that suits China's many karaoke fans. The "smart touch pen," however, is very innovative. It enables children to point at a specially designed cartoon book and cause the book's contents to be displayed on the TV screen—a potentially valuable tool for early education.

Preference for pragmatic innovation

Chinese companies seldom go for "moonshot" innovations—not for them "iPhone envy." They prefer pragmatic and predictable innovations. According to one Huawei manager, the company operates on a belief that "for any technology—if it's one year ahead of the market, you'll succeed; if it's too advanced, five years ahead of the market, you'll become a martyr. It's the university's and lab's responsibility to come up with the 'too-advanced' technology, not the company's."

Winning the incremental way

In China, companies often succeed by "presenting customers with an unmatched choice of products in what used to be considered standardized, mass-market segments."[10] This approach depends on many incremental innovations rather than on a single radical innovation. Certainly, this is the more practical choice for the short term, and it fits nicely with the Chinese preference for lower risks and short-term profits.

WILLINGNESS TO CATER TO SPECIAL NEEDS

Related to Chinese companies' preference for incremental innovation is the fact that they are more likely than multinational corporations to cater to special needs, something that often requires extra innovation. This willingness arises in part from their close focus on whatever customers want, in part from their ability to develop and build variants of products at low cost, and in part from their knowledge that the Chinese market for a product that satisifies a new need will be large.

Hisense, a leading TV manufacturer, has captured a large share of the market for TV sets in Sub-Saharan Africa. In Africa, the inhabitants of many villages can afford to buy only one communal TV set, so that set is used both indoors and outdoors, in the latter case for large audiences. The level of brightness has to be higher for outdoor viewing. Only Hisense was willing to expend extra innovation effort to create this brightness option and related operating technology.

Haier's Crystal series of washing machines illustrates that company's willingness to cater to special needs. By means of user surveys, Haier identified three special needs: American users want a machine that can wash heavy cloth materials such as towels and bedding, French users want a machine that can wash expensive and delicate fabrics, and Japanese users want a machine with drastically reduced operating noise. To cater to these special needs, Haier conducted 2,001 user surveys, 11,879 online surveys, and 628 discussions. In response, in 2012, Haier introduced its Crystal series, featuring functions to meet all the above needs, a maximum spin speed of 1,400 rpm, and low operating noise (40 decibels). Such innovations by Haier not only enable a new technology to be used for a broad model line but are also helping to build a new, positive image for "made in China."[11]

DEPLOYING LARGE NUMBERS OF EMPLOYEES

Chinese companies enjoy access to very large numbers of engineers and scientists, whose costs to employ are still well below those in developed countries. Of course, multinational corporations that have innovation operations in China can hire the same people, but generally not as many as Chinese firms are willing to hire. Having large numbers of engineers and scientists allows Chinese firms to take more of a "brute force" approach to innovation by putting large teams to work on many aspects of an innovation. For example, some Chinese pharmaceutical companies put many low-level scientists to work conducting tests on multiple compounds or formulations. The head of the China R&D center of a major Western pharmaceutical company told us that, whereas in the West a company's scientists might spend time deciding which of six tests to conduct, in China a company's scientists will conduct all six. This "parallel processing" approach is analogous to how IBM's Deep Blue machine defeated the world champion Garry Kasparov at chess in 1997.

By using large numbers of engineers and scientists, a Chinese firm can divide the innovation process into a number of small steps and then assign teams to work on each stage. The goal is an assembly-line system that accelerates the processes of innovation. WuXi AppTec (a pharmaceutical, biopharmaceutical, and medical company) has adopted this industrialized form of product development—each year, it hires thousands of graduates of trade colleges as R&D workers.[12]

An excellent example of this large-numbers approach is provided by the Four Dimension Johnson Industries Group, a Chinese conglomerate whose primary business is making cash-in-transit vehicles. FDJ has used China's low-cost engineers to change the production process in a way that is highly innovative, not just for China but for the entire industry. National regulation means that product specifications are different in each country, and in addition products are often customized for different banks and cash-in-transit companies. Sales volumes are also low (for example, only 500 vehicles per year in the United Kingdom). As a result, most of FDJ's competitors are local and use a labor-intensive batch production process. But FDJ found a way to turn this local operation into a global one, and to turn small-scale customization into mass customization. It employed 500 engineers in China over three years to determine the globally common needs for cash-in-transit vehicles. For example, it studied all the different types of vehicle exit windows, identified four globally common types, and asked customers to pick one of them for each order. It then developed a new business model that combined manufacture of body-panel modules in China with flat-pack shipment and final assembly in the UK, thereby combining customization with low-cost mass production. In two more examples of a Chinese company's acquiring needed technology, between 2004 and 2007 FDJ entrenched its foreign business by acquiring its UK partner Johnson, which supplied the specialized security technology for its CIT vehicles, and in 2010 it purchased KFB Extramobile GmbH, a German producer of ambulances. These were particularly valuable during China's SARS epidemic because of their sophisticated air-purification technology.

WORKING EMPLOYEES HARDER

Because Chinese culture puts a very high priority on work and achievement, work is emphasized much more than leisure. Within China this is more the case in Chinese companies than in China branches of multinational corporations, although in both cases Chinese employees work longer hours than their counterparts in the West.

Chinese entrepreneurs and business leaders tend to hold the view that Chinese companies should not follow in the footsteps of MNCs, but rather should pursue a more "Chinese" way.[13] Since China has the advantage of competing on labor cost and has a unique history, Chinese entrepreneurs, instead of emphasizing individual dignity and independence as the MNCs do, more often than not attempt to breed a spirit of hard work inside their companies, with reducing costs a primary concern.

The work ethic is further spurred by frequent use of individual incentives. Many pharmaceutical companies use "milestone-based" processes, which have an advantage over traditional scale-based processes in that with the milestone approach performance on a project can be reviewed individual by individual. This motivates R&D employees and encourages them to put in greater time and effort.[14]

Fosun Pharma's 24-hour R&D process

A former head of R&D at Fosun Pharma told us the following:

In our company, R&D staff need to work very hard. Our work day ends at 17:30, but usually R&D staff have to stay longer than that, because ongoing experiments need them, so they usually work till 20:00 or 22:00, or even later until experiments finish. R&D staff work follow the milestones, unlike task goals set for other employees. If R&D people work only eight hours a day, they can hardly reach the milestone within the stipulated time. So R&D staff typically have longer work hours, some have to give up the weekends, or even important holidays like the Chinese Spring Festival.

In addition to working employees harder to accelerate R&D, Fosun Pharma established "24-hour R&D," a novel way of using the company's global resources to increase the amount of time devoted to R&D activity. Fosun Pharma's micro-molecules team has successfully combined resources in San Francisco and in Chongqing. In San Francisco, Fosun has set up a small team to do the preliminary work, including drug design and early-stage experiments. Each day, when work in San Francisco is about to end, the experimental progress made that day is passed directly to the Chongqing team. The Chongqing team then conducts related experiments and reports the results back to the team in San Francisco. R&D activity is thus able to advance continuously, 24 hours a day.

The "wolf spirit" of Huawei

Ren Zhengfei, the founder and chairman of Huawei, has said: "Huawei people, especially the leaders, are destined to work hard for a lifetime and to devote more and suffer more than others."[15] This corporate culture, sometimes referred to as the "wolf spirit," was created by Ren from the start of the company. It emphasizes that individual aspirations are explicitly subordinated to the needs of the company. More specifically, Ren described it as a blend of three qualities: extreme resilience in the face of failure, a strong willingness to self-sacrifice, and sharp predator instincts: "In the battle with lions, wolves have terrifying abilities. With a strong desire to win and no fear of losing, they stick to the goal firmly, making the lions exhausted in every possible way."[16]

Huawei currently has more than 76,000 R&D employees—said to be more than 45 percent of Huawei's total employees worldwide. In the company's early days, R&D workers kept rolled-up mattresses under their desks. One could sleep during a lunch break or if one had worked late and couldn't or didn't want to go home.

At Huawei, managers face the same harsh policies as engineers and technicians. For example, one researcher found that promising managers who had been selected by the company to be sent overseas to explore new markets faced a very tough policy that the company had initiated in 1998: a manager who rejects overseas assignments will henceforth not be promoted.[17] The company now tells us that it is not a requirement that managers work overseas; however, it tends to give more rewards to employees who work overseas, especially in hardship regions. In addition to rewards, employees working overseas may have more career-development opportunities.

FASTER, LESS FORMAL PROCESSES

Chinese companies do everything faster than multinational corporations. We have heard this again and again from representatives of Chinese and Western companies. We have found that Chinese companies are motivated to innovate in a much faster way, while multinationals are constrained by elaborate, formal processes imposed by headquarters. Chinese companies speed up the innovation process by using simultaneous or concurrent activities, as we showed above. For example, Lenovo managed to cut its innovation cycle in half by applying concurrent engineering across the entire process. In every project, team members work on different elements in parallel, under the supervision of one leader.[18]

A senior innovation executive at a major German company summed up the speed issue this way: "It's not about the cost of the engineers themselves, but it's about their mindset and speed." Chinese innovators know that the market and the competitors don't wait for laggards.

In recent years the Internet industry has witnessed a shift in users' preferences from personal computers to mobile equipment.

That has caused changes in all segments of the Internet industry, including communications, social networking, online games, on-line media, and e-commerce. Mobile applications have become mainstream for most Internet service companies. Tencent, one of the Chinese giants in the industry, has a faster process for inno-vating and developing applications than any of its worldwide competitors.

One of Tencent's innovations, WeChat, first released in 2011, is a good illustration. A mobile text and voice messaging service, it was initially very similar to ICQ, a Western product first devel-oped in 1996 by an Israeli company and then sold to America Online. But in typical Chinese fashion, Tencent worked rapidly to adapt WeChat to the Chinese market. This fast innovation ap-proach has been a major reason for WeChat's phenomenal suc-cess. In 2015 WeChat had more than 800 million users in China and several million elsewhere. To quickly keep track of users' preferences, the company has a cohesive and feature-driven devel-opment process that emphasizes client-valued functionality. As in many other companies, the process has five stages: conception, design, development, testing, and release.[19] However, in order to innovate faster, Tencent applies less formal but more rapid pro-cesses at different stages. For instance, during the development and testing phase, outside users are usually picked from the user base, with priority given to subscription members.[20] Many prod-ucts and services go through a 'gray release' process—instead of testing with all the users, the company selects some of them to do the testing on the basis of their social background, gender, loca-tion and other characteristics, so as to introduce the products gradually and learn systematically from users' reactions. As Ten-cent has been successful in China since the early 2000s and has a very large user base, this process allows it to test its products very quickly. After conducting a million-user experiment, it might re-ceive 300,000 comments as feedback the next day. Generally, Ten-cent takes about three months to develop a basic product. After that, a product will be updated every week. New functions will be added, while the most valuable ones will be retained.

FAST TRIAL AND ERROR: FAIL FAST, BUT LEARN

Related to the penchant for speed in innovation, Chinese companies are also more willing to take risks in fast trial and error, and to
"fail faster, succeed sooner" (as David Kelly of the successful Western design firm IDEO put it). They do so because the fast-growing
Chinese markets are more forgiving than slow-growing markets in
developed countries. They have rapidly learned that in a fast-
growing market the bigger risk is *not* to try something for fear of
making a mistake and losing some money. This trial-and-error approach fits in well with the Chinese culture of pragmatism. Indeed,
China's first reforming Communist leader, Deng Xiaoping, liked to
talk about "crossing the river by feeling the stones." Kevin Wale,
formerly president and managing director of GM China, put it this
way: "What China does better than any place else in the world is
to innovate by commercialization, as opposed to constant research
and perfecting the theory, like the West."[21]

Warp speed for Internet businesses

In China, many Internet-based companies use fast trial and error to
test the market, learn from mistakes, and make adjustments, especially when starting a business. One example is provided by Mogu-
jie.com, a "social shopping" e-commerce website that provides
fashion-conscious young women, daunted by the myriad of op-
tions on the major websites, with selected products (clothes, shoes,
suitcases, cosmetics, and so on). Mogujie.com puts many products
onto its website, without any pre-testing. Relying on its excellent
execution capability and rapidly gathered customer data, it takes a
fast trial-and-error approach, investing resources to popularize
particular products only after it sees a relatively solid level of sales
after the trial.

A month after Mogujie.com launched, its CEO, Chen Qi, was
excited to see the photo gallery of Pinterest (a US website) and felt
that Mogujie.com, by presenting its products in a similar way,
could provide a balance between product demonstrations and users' experiences. A company team began to implement that idea
that same night and launched a "photo gallery" within three days.

This fast trial made the homepage of Mogujie.com rather messy in the beginning, but now, after rapid growth in its number of users the company is more cautious in its trials.

Xiaomi Mobile is well known for co-developing products with its users. The company sends out beta versions and then work with users to co-develop the products. Some of the products fail, but Xiaomi then quickly comes up with products that work.

Going too fast in electric vehicles

Having observed that China's auto industry doesn't spend much time investing in research, testing, and validation before trying to take products in the market, Kevin Wale of GM China pointed out the following:

> The Chinese system supports the idea that it's OK to fail if you fail in a government-sponsored direction. It's OK to make mistakes as long as you're moving forward. … There is no recrimination internally for doing that if that is the direction the country wants to move in. The electric vehicle is a good example. The Chinese view is that it's not going to be perfect, and they're not trying to make it perfect from day one. They've got a few more series of improvements to go, and they'll work on them in parallel with finding out what the customer really likes and adapting to that.[22]

Because of that attitude, the electric-vehicle industry in China has suffered many setbacks. For example, in recent years several accidents involving electric vehicles have been reported, including a self-ignition in Hangzhou and an explosion in Shenzhen. These accidents have put the safety of electric vehicles under the spotlight. Although no defects were found in the design and quality of the vehicles involved in the aforementioned accidents, customers' confidence was damaged.[23] But because the Chinese government favors electric vehicles officially, China's electric-vehicle industry continues to innovate and may become a global leader.

ICBC's fast trials by local subsidiaries

ICBC, the largest bank in China and in 2014 the most valuable in the world, encourages its local subsidiaries in various parts of China to conduct fast "field tests" of new products and collect feedback from customers. "In 2011," ICBC boasted, "we promoted our staff to brainstorm and collected *263 golden ideas* for innovation in banking services. Most suggestions came from the frontline, which are very practical and inspiring."[24] In 2011, ICBC launched a "Product Innovation Day & Product Experience Month Campaign." All bank branches in China took part in this national event. Branches in various regions adopted specific themes. For instance, branches in Zhejiang, Shandong, Jiangsu, and Henan promoted the innovative iPhone banking service to customers and conducted a survey to evaluate their experiences. With a deep understanding of the dynamic local setting, the Shenzhen subsidiary promoted to high-income customers the "Easy Loan credit card"— the first credit card in China for Chinese residents to pay for retail spending by installment.

A quick and dirty solution to a no-soap problem

The Chinese preference for fast trials can yield highly effective solutions. A partner of a leading Western consulting company told us that two of his clients in China bought production lines for soap from a major European packaged-goods firm, each of them paying about 20 million to 30 renminbi. Both of the Chinese companies encountered problems with the highly automated production lines. In particular, some boxes would go to supermarkets empty. The two Chinese companies took different approaches to the problem. One hired a Western-trained PhD, who then hired a team of fifteen people and was given a budget of 3 million renminbi. The team worked for three months and came up with a solution that entailed using automated robots to detect empty boxes and take them off the line. That solution cost another 2 million renminbi to implement. The other company took a classic Chinese approach. The head of the factory called in the line team leader and told him to solve the problem within a week or he would be fired. After trying many different practical solutions, the team leader installed a large fan in the ceiling, which blew off the production line any boxes that were empty.

MORE INTERVENTION BY THE BOSS

"Autocratic" and "intervening" are two adjectives often used to differentiate Chinese bosses from Western ones. There are two reasons for this. First, after thousands of years of a culture of benevolent paternalism and enforced hierarchy, Chinese employees expect top-down leadership. People in China like to follow a strong leader with passion and drive. So although Chinese executives recognize that they must give employees real decision-making power and push responsibility further down in the organization, they struggle against a long history.[25] The one-directional mode of instruction in the Chinese education system reinforces the culture of waiting for commands from the boss. Second, contrary to common belief, Chinese people are obedient to authority only when closely monitored. As one head of a Chinese company told us, you have to really watch your director of purchasing to make sure he isn't doing some business for himself on the side. This view is captured in the popular Chinese saying *shān gāo, huáng dī yuǎn* ("the mountain is high, and the Emperor is far away"). One observer put it this way: "You can't be a hands-off manager in China. You can—but you won't last long."[26]

Dong Mingzhu—the head of Gree, the largest manufacturer of household air conditioners in China—is a typical Chinese boss. A popular saying about her is "Where Sister Dong walks, no grass grows." Chinese executives like to cite Steve Jobs of Apple as a strong boss who produced brilliant innovations. But the norm in the West is a lesser role for the boss. As a Chinese Chief Technology Officer said to us: "In the West, it is 90 percent process and 10 percent boss. In China, it is 30 percent process and 70 percent boss." We have seen many successful boss-driven innovation programs in China—by Zhang Ruimin at Haier, Liu Chuanzhi at Lenovo, Ren Zhengfei at Huawei, and Zhang Yue at BROAD Group. Zhang Yue told us that he was responsible for 90 percent of the innovations at BROAD. But strong interventions by the boss have both positive and negative effects, in China as elsewhere. At Haier, in a search for the right balance, Zhang Ruimin has recently introduced a new organization structure with 2,000 responsibility centers in an effort to make every employee accountable for innovation and execution. No doubt the role of the boss will change as a younger generation with less respect for age and authority enters Chinese companies.

Bossing BYD[27]

BYD, a maker of batteries and electric vehicles, is often cited as one of the most innovative companies in China. It has come up with many product innovations in its range of batteries—technological innovations (such as its Fe battery and its lithium-ferrous-phosphate technology), cost innovations (such as its semi-automated production process and molding factory), and business-model innovations (such as self-research and development, self-production, and the self-owned brand).

Success in making batteries made Wang Chuanfu, the CEO of BYD, the richest man in mainland China in 2009,[28] and drew an investment of $230 million from the world's wisest investor, Warren Buffett. However, BYD fell into deep trouble just two years after that moment of glory, suffering a 45 percent loss of net profit in 2011. Too much intervention by the boss had nearly led to a disaster in the new electric-vehicle industry. Wang had been too ambitious. Under his direction, BYD had invested nearly 10 billion yuan in the electric-vehicle industry and intended to come up with novel applications for electric vehicles. "The boss's huge appetite should be blamed for the disaster" is a frequent comment from both BYD managers and observers.

Aside from his strategic bias, Wang Chuanfu sometimes micromanaged. He put strong emphasis on quality management and personally test-drove each of BYD's new cars. "Our CEO gave us over 100 suggestions for a single car during his half-year test," BYD's head of quality control said. "He just picked the problems but didn't mention our efforts and progress."

Horizontal flexibility with vertical hierarchy

Despite the top-down, boss-oriented hierarchy, there is also in Chinese companies a high degree of horizontal flexibility that allows for smooth and rapid flows of resources and knowledge between peers in various departments and functions. One study refers to this as a "huddle and act" mode of problem solving that is based more on personal relationships than on formal process.[29]

Don't contradict the boss

Perhaps a personal experience best sums up the Chinese boss. The Chinese father of one of us once said "You should never contradict me, especially when I am wrong."

Strong leaders of Chinese companies inspire their employees with their devotion to their company's success, often with colorful actions or phrases. Ma Yun (Jack Ma), Alibaba's founder, is renowned for his exhortations to his people to fight eBay as underdogs—"the ant's way." As we noted in chapter 2, Haier's CEO Zhang Ruimin, who became a national legend with his smashing of defective products, today says "Every day in the morning when I get up, I refresh myself with three words, *bu man yi* ("I am not satisfied"). And when Huawei's chairman Ren Zhengfei was experiencing difficulty in implementing the integrated product development process with IBM, he is said to have told members of his staff "Put your feet into the new shoes even if it hurts." These leaders' obsessions with cost, quality, and hard work are as essential to China's strategic advantage in innovation as is the Chinese government's long-term vision of technological independence.

CLOSER TIES TO GOVERNMENT

One-party rule and high levels of state ownership and intervention require Chinese companies, whether state-owned or private, to work more closely with government than most Western companies do. And, of course, Chinese companies can get much closer to Chinese government (national, provincial, or local) than foreign companies can. For example, many R&D grants, particularly those from the central government, are available only to Chinese companies. But, surprisingly, one European company told us that it has found a way to register some of its research entities as local Chinese entities so that they can qualify for government grants. However, for foreign companies, the major dilemma in innovation is the increasingly stronger pressure from the Chinese government to share technology with China. As one article puts it: "[The government's rules] reverse decades of granting foreign companies increasing access to Chinese markets and put CEOs in a terrible bind: they can either comply with the rules and share their technologies with Chinese competitors—or refuse and miss out on the world's fastest-growing market."[30]

For Chinese companies, national and local government can give much in the way of direct support for innovation. A Chinese company may not have MIT or Stanford up the street, but it may have a very supportive local mayor. There are also some ways for MNCs to take advantage of local support; we discuss them in chapter 6.

CRCC on the fast track

Government also exercises a powerful role in delivering advanced technologies to state-owned enterprises. Multinationals often have to subcontract the manufacturing of simple components to SOEs and transfer end-to-end systems to local players. In 2009 the Chinese central government began requiring foreign companies wanting to bid on high-speed railway projects to form joint ventures with the state-owned equipment producers CSR and CNR.[31] Bombardier, Kawasaki, Alstom, and Siemens won contracts in exchange for providing technology and know-how to assembly joint ventures with the government rail companies China North Car and China South Car, which merged in 2015 to form the China Railway Rolling Stock Corporation (CRRC).

Construction of the track and related infrastructure is the responsibility of China Railway Construction Corporation (CRCC). As a result of technology transfer, continuing heavy investment, and rapid advances by it and the local rolling stock builders, CRCC's high-speed rail network has become in just a few years the most extensive in the world, with more than 16,000 kilometers of track as of 2015 and with 25,000 kilometers planned by 2020.

As a major constructor of high-speed-railway tracks, CRCC aims to become a world leader in that sector and in other infrastructure sectors. By 2011, it was already ranked number 105 among the *Fortune*'s Global 500 Companies. Government incentives are major drivers for innovations at this huge SOE. In 2011, a government grant of 173.2 million renminbi constituted about 33 percent of CRCC's total non-operating income of 521.5 million renminbi.

In addition to railroads, China's twelfth five-year plan certainly favored SOEs in the seven "new strategic industries," which include energy saving and environmental protection, information technology, biotechnology, high-tech manufacturing, new energy, new materials, and clean-energy vehicles. According to one report, "the government aspires to increase the share of GDP these industries contribute from about 1 percent today to 8 percent by 2015 and to 15 percent by 2020."[32]

Thanks to huge investment by the government, CRCC made a breakthrough in establishing a national-level innovation platform. China Railway 12th Bureau Group Company, a subsidiary of CRCC, has set up a technology center as a certificated hub for technological innovation. With a fund of 8,470 million renminbi, three projects at CRCC were listed as major national research projects; 22 provincial and ministerial level research projects were added in 2011. CRCC filed 1,037 patents, 57 of which were certified as inventions. CRCC also initiated cutting-edge projects in construction. The Danyang–Kunshan Grand Bridge, which is part of the Shanghai-Beijing high-speed railway, is the world's longest (165 kilometers) and is designed for the highest operating speed (up to 350 kilometers per hour).

China's experience with high-speed rail is by far the most recent and extensive of any country's and is now the basis of a growing export sector. In 2010 alone, CRCC signed 156 new overseas contracts with a value of 25,912.5 million renminbi. A subsidiary of CRCC completed China's first overseas railway project, the Tanzam Railway between Tanzania and Zambia, in 1975 and is now completing the $8.3 billion Nigerian Railway Modernization Project, China's largest overseas project to date. And in July 2015 the first high-speed train to be exported to Europe rolled off the production line at Zhuzhou Electric Locomotive Co., Ltd., a subsidiary of CRRC.[33]

Riding the government wind

Alternative energy is a "sunrise" industry in which the Chinese government is investing lots of money. The Xinjiang Goldwind Science & Technology Company Ltd. (Goldwind), a manufacturer of wind turbines, headquartered in Urumqi in Xinjiang Province, is the second-largest such company in China and the third-largest in the world. Goldwind is the world's largest manufacturer of permanent-magnet direct-drive wind turbines, a more reliable and efficient technology that the company developed. It was named twice on the list of "The 50 Most Innovative Companies" by *MIT Technology Review*. The official website of Chinese National Energy Administration claims that "Goldwind is an outstanding player effectively penetrating the US as well."[34] In 2011, Goldwind made a breakthrough in the US market by building the 106.5-megawatt Shady Oaks wind farm in Illinois, the first large-scale wind project in the US to use Chinese turbines. The wind farm used Goldwind's 1.5-megawatt DDPM WTG (direct-drive permanent magnet wind turbine generators), which passed Intertek's ETL certification, fulfilling the safety standards of the United States and Canada. Goldwind was the first Chinese WTG maker to receive this certification.

The Chinese government promoted Goldwind's innovations primarily through funding and supportive policies. "Government subsidies for the R&D projects and upgrades of production facilities" are a major element of Goldwind's reported other income. In 2011, Goldwind's total other income was 770 million renminbi, a 15.7 percent increase from 666 million renminbi in 2010, due both to increased government subsidies and wind farm disposal gains. Under the approval of the central government, Goldwind built the National Wind Power Engineering Technology Research Centre in 2008 and collaborated with seventeen higher-education institutions on research projects and design engineering courses. In 2010, the China Development Bank signed a strategic agreement with Goldwind and offered a credit line of $6 billion for its international expansion.

The Chinese government has also aided Goldwind by erecting high barriers against MNCs, which found that they couldn't efficiently improve their supply chains in China with acceptable local purchasing. Foreign companies have not won a single central government-funded wind energy project in China since 2005.

Goldwind's top executives hold many government-related positions of influence. For instance, Wu Gang, the chairman and CEO, was once the deputy director of the Chinese Renewable Energy Industries Association and a member of the expert consultants' group for the government of Xinjiang. Wang Sanyou, an independent director of Goldwind, was the deputy vice chairman of the government of Xinjiang for 1991–1996, then was vice chairman of the Chinese People's Political Consultative Conference for five years. Three members of Goldwind's board receive special allowances granted by the State Council; and most of the firm's senior executives either have strong links to the government or good political reputations. When China's president Hu Jintao visited Goldwind for the second time in 2009, he recognized the company's performance and highlighted the government's strategy of "indigenous innovation."[35]

CONCLUSION AND RECOMMENDATIONS

The ten distinguishing characteristics discussed above have fostered a distinctive style of Chinese innovation. The traditional product-life theory[36] of the past argued that companies based in developing economies could only slowly gather the strengths to compete worldwide against multinational corporations from developed countries, which had the advantage of home-developed capabilities in technology, brand reputation, and management that supported their entry into worldwide markets. China's rapid rise fundamentally questions this concept. Government intervention, the complex nature of the Chinese market, and a large entrepreneurial class have combined to create an acceleration of the product life cycle in China that challenges established multinational innovation models.[37] China is moving much faster than had been expected toward being an innovative country, and its competitive vision is no longer "Made in China" but "Created in China." China is reclaiming its historic place as the "central country," and this has profound implications for companies in China and the rest of the world. Multinationals have much to learn from this great leap forward.

Our recommendation for Chinese companies is that they should continue to learn from their experience with these ten unique characteristics that are their main sources of competitive advantages. At the same time, they should adopt (and adapt) the more systematic methods of innovation used by Western companies. This is not to imply that they should abandon their speed and intensity, but it is to say that they should be more analytical and less intuitive in the less-understood markets of the West. The recently published government initiative for "Made in China 2025,"[38] which calls for a big shift in capabilities across the board and not only in innovation, urges local firms to put greater effort into understanding overseas cultures and markets and to develop stronger management of operational and financial risks.[39]

Western companies should learn from many, if not all, of these ten characteristics of Chinese innovators, and should apply those lessons to their business in China. In particular, they will benefit from stronger efforts to understand local customers and local decision makers, from greater delegation of decision making to their China units so that prototypes can be launched more quickly, from re-engineering of products to meet "fit for purpose" standards (with a local partner if necessary), and from looking for opportunities to take ideas from China into the rest of the world. MNCs have great resources of advanced technology, strong brands, and proven systematic innovation processes, which constitute a priceless advantage. Building on those capabilities by learning from the Chinese example will, as we argue in chapter 8, enable Western companies to develop innovations that will be of great value to their business in the rest of the world.

4

MULTINATIONAL CORPORATIONS' INNOVATION IN CHINA

(with Dominique Jolly)

In this chapter we turn from Chinese companies to foreign multinationals and what they are doing about innovation and R&D in China. (Although many Chinese companies are now themselves multinational, the term "multinationals" or the abbreviation MNCs is commonly used in China to refer only to foreign companies.) Because multinationals' innovation activities in China are diverse and are evolving quickly, a historical and evolutionary perspective is appropriate.[1]

China is now central to many multinational companies' plans for globalizing their R&D activities. In terms of our Four Cs framework, the Chinese are strengthening their innovation capabilities by making use of the maturing local technological capacity of their country. MNCs face the growing technological sophistication of local competitors, as well as the locals' superior knowledge of local customers and culture. Thus, it not surprising that, as an essential part of their innovative capacity, they deploy their one great asset—technology—in China. Because it is hard to observe all innovation efforts of companies, we use R&D centers as a close proxy for total innovation activity. There are now more than 1,500 foreign R&D centers in China, and each year more are being set up there than in any other country.[2] For example, since 2003 General Electric has established major R&D centers in Beijing, Shanghai, and Wuxi and also has established three regional innovation centers. In 2013 alone, Oracle opened its fourth R&D center in China, and R&D centers were also opened there by Daimler AG, Medtronic, Covidien, Boston Scientific, Continental AG, Toyota, Arkema, and other companies. In 2010 Johnson & Johnson set up in Suzhou's industrial park a new R&D center responsible for all medical diagnostics and devices product development in the Asia-Pacific region. In addition, many multinationals, including the Bosch Group, General Electric, IBM, Philips, and Shell, are continuing to upgrade and enlarge their R&D facilities in China. These investments contributed $5.5 billion to China's global lead in inward "greenfield" R&D investment over the period 2010–2014. In the same period the United States attracted less than half as much greenfield R&D investment.[3] We explain the reasons for the dramatic increase in greenfield R&D investment below.

In terms of our Four Cs, the expansion of MNCs into China has traditionally been motivated not by a desire to develop new capabilities, but rather by a desire to exploit capabilities already developed in their home country (or through previous international experience). The capabilities MNCs already possess have usually provided competitive advantages over local incumbents. But in China, *customers* and *culture* both act as substantial barriers. So, as we detail below, MNCs have traditionally begun in China with products or services for needs that are most like those at home— higher-income consumers, or technologically sophisticated industrial clients. They initially entered the Chinese market by exporting home-based products relying on their proprietary technologies, brands, or superior management skills, often with products later in their life cycles.[4] This was followed by local manufacturing or service operations; R&D centers were set up to support them, mainly for cost reasons. MNCs then adapted their products or processes to suit the Chinese market, setting up market-driven R&D centers and introducing new products designed for local requirements.

For a foreign newcomer, although surging market growth has been a positive enabler as it is for local firms, understanding customers and dealing with culture (and particularly the powerful role of government) has been the biggest challenge. Thus, it is not surprising that foreign newcomers did not initially focus on exploiting the local innovation ecosystem. China was not even considered as a knowledge source to be tapped by foreign subsidiaries during the 1990s.[5] A weak national system of innovation plus a lack of protection of intellectual property rights discouraged MNCs.[6] Then, in the 2000s, the rationale for international location decisions began to change. Studies of foreign R&D efforts show that foreign R&D centers in China are not only important vehicles for local market development but also, contrary to expectations, increasingly important sources of locally developed technology,[7] especially inside the many industrial clusters that were established by the national government's innovation initiatives.[8] Technological richness and diversity and the knowledge linkages of the subsidiary with other entities have been shown to drive innovation.[9]

Several MNCs have recognized the threat, as well as the opportunity, presented by the growth of Chinese firms' capabilities and are actively seeking access to the China knowledge base. They are attempting to benefit from the same sources of advantage that Chinese firms are tapping. In what follows in this chapter, we argue that more MNCs need to adopt a knowledge-based China strategy by becoming active participants in the innovation ecosystem. To fully explain what we mean by a firm's R&D process, figure 4.1 shows how the three major stages (fundamental research, applied research, and development) are associated with various external entities. At the first stage, that of fundamental research, a firm often associates with universities and research institutes; at the second, that of applied research, it often collaborates with startups; at

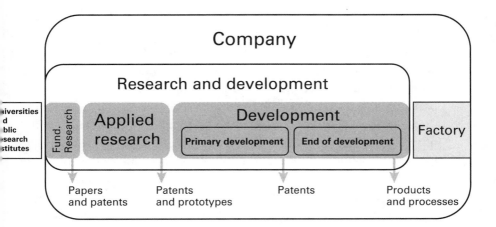

Figure 4.1
What constitutes R&D. *Source:* Dominique Jolly

the development stage, it is more likely to be associating with suppliers and (increasingly) with customers. When an innovation enters into production, the primary R&D activity in the early stages of an MNC's presence in China is to provide quality-control and testing services to the operations or factory end of the value chain. Over time, R&D activities evolve and the company's commitment to the Chinese customer deepens. Eventually, innovations created for China are offered to global customers.

THE EVOLUTION OF MULTINATIONAL R&D IN CHINA

Most of this chapter is based on in-depth interviews conducted at the China R&D centers of 52 MNCs from twelve countries (including the United States and some European and Asian countries). The chapter also draws on interviews conducted in China and at the home-country head offices of seven major European multinational companies. (For further details of our research method, see the appendix to the chapter.)

We found three major types of *motivations* for R&D: cost-driven, market-driven (plus a "government-driven" subset), and knowledge-driven. Each of these types of motivations is associated with one of the evolving stages in the company's R&D activities outlined above. Cost-driven R&D is more related to end-of-development activities done close to the factory. Market-driven R&D adds primary new product development. Knowledge-driven R&D extends from primary product development to applied research and to fundamental research. We also found that the three different motivations coincided with three phases in the evolution of a company's strategy for China. As firms evolved from simple adaptation (localization) of the parent company's products and services to innovating in China for the Chinese market, and then to innovating in China for global markets, their R&D activities evolved from cost-based to market-based to knowledge-based. We also found that the younger the industry of the R&D unit, generally the larger was the interest in doing knowledge-driven R&D, as the data in table 4.1. show. The relationships between motivation and type of R&D activity are illustrated in figure 4.2.

Table 4.1
Types of R&D in China: numbers of companies among the 52 we studied.

	Cost-driven	Market-driven	Knowledge-driven	Total
Automotive	3	6		9
Chemicals		11	2	13
Electrical, glass, food, consumer goods	2	9	3	14
IT, semiconductors, pharmaceuticals	4	3	9	16
Total	9	29	14	52

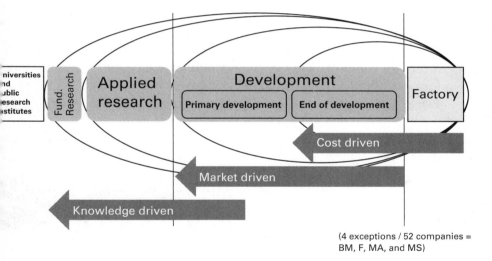

(4 exceptions / 52 companies = BM, F, MA, and MS)

Figure 4.2
Three motivations for R&D in China.
Source: Dominique Jolly

Cost-driven R&D

Historically, it has been a desire to reduce costs of local operations that has motivated foreign companies to conduct R&D in China.[10] Companies initially targeted repetitive operations, such as coding and testing a piece of software, with operations split between China and the home country. This cost-driven R&D was chosen by companies selling global products with few (or no) local features for the local market, or for export from China into the parent company's supply chain.[11] Their offshored R&D activities were concentrated in the development phase, and often at the end part of development, where new technology is less relevant and where budget control is most important. This phase usually requires more human resources, which may represent the largest share of the R&D costs. A multinational's R&D entity in China was typically set up in house, or perhaps a subcontractor was used for less advanced activities. Figure 4.3 illustrates the focus of cost-driven R&D in China at the operations end of the value chain. This form of R&D activity has limited spill-over impact on the MNC's worldwide operations, although there can be useful transfers of

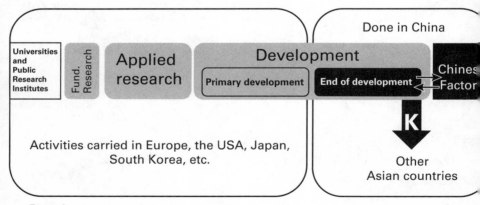

Examples
Contribution to a global project: Outsourcing of testing
Match with manufacturing: Small domestic appliances

Figure 4.3

Cost-driven R&D.

Source: Dominique Jolly

knowledge to similar (e.g., other Asian) markets, as indicated by the arrow labeled K in figure 4.3.

Because many firms have experienced this model, the corresponding factors for success in China are well known. R&D and production operations need to be well connected. Recruitment focuses on graduates with local bachelor's and master's degrees, rather than doctorates. And limited new knowledge is developed locally. Most of the knowledge comes from headquarters, so there is no need for the R&D activity be located inside a local system of innovation. Adaptations to manufacturing processes may be kept secret or may not be regarded as sufficiently consequential to be patented. But protection of intellectual property should be considered an important part of local R&D activities, including applying for patents in China for existing technologies developed abroad, as well as for new-to-the-world processes or products. (For more on protecting intellectual property in China, see chapter 7 below.)

The cost-driven model fits with the second (foreign production) stage of the product cycle, in which the MNC takes advantage of the foreign location's attributes—specifically low labor costs in China, including R&D costs. This was necessary to compete with local firms and also valuable for ensuring the quality of exports entering a global supply chain. However, wage increases in China have averaged some 10 percentage points above the rate of inflation since 2005, and local governments have been increasing minimum wages by 15–20 percent per year.[13] With fewer countries having a significant R&D salary gap relative to China, the cost-driven R&D model has become less relevant, except where it coincides with a shift of a company's production operations toward inland cities such as Chengdu and Chongqing, where labor costs are lower. Furthermore, the increasing sophistication of customers and the rise of local competitors necessitate localization and market responsiveness through market-driven R&D, the second stage in the evolution of MNC R&D.

Market-driven R&D

The second phase, market-driven R&D, occurs where localization is needed (as it is for culture-bound products such as food, flavors, and fragrances), or as in the case of automobiles, where local conditions, inputs, or regulation require it.[14] China's many differences from the rest of the world and numerous micro-segments spur the need for adaptation, as we demonstrated in chapter 3. Furthermore, increasing affluence and sophistication mean that Chinese customers are less and less willing to put up with Western "hand-me-downs." They want made-for-China products—i.e., products designed in China for China. Market-driven R&D means taking technologies developed outside China, importing them into China, and modifying those technologies locally to be in line with the Chinese market. Local competitors are superb at identifying and supplying market needs, and MNCs have had to deepen their knowledge of the Chinese market so as to match local demand. Products must be not just "good enough"[15]; they must also be "fit for purpose," meeting customers' expectations of functionality and price. (Figure 4.4 illustrates the focus and the drivers of market-driven R&D in China.)

To achieve "fitness for purpose," companies need to deepen their knowledge of the Chinese market so as to match it with local

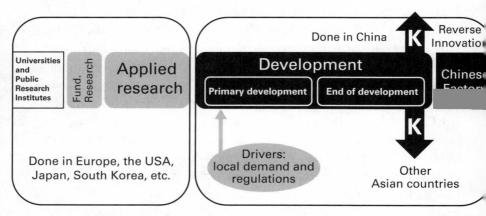

Figure 4.4

Market-driven R&D. Products and industries that need local adaptation include cosmetics, automobiles, electrical engineering, mechanical engineering, localized electronic products, and agriculture. Production processes that have to be adapted include construction materials, basic chemicals, and pharma clinical trials.

Source: Dominique Jolly

demand. This requires direct contact with customers and identifying the multiple segments that exist in each market; it also requires knowledge of the conditions of use, which can be very different from those in companies' home countries. Indeed, an engineer based in North America usually has little idea of Chinese customers' expectations. Sometimes, local adaptation in China is driven less by differences in customers' needs or tastes than by differences in local conditions (such as climate) or raw materials. For example, development could be about testing the combination of different raw materials sourced locally to find the right mix that satisfies Chinese customers' real needs or cost conditions. A striking example is the recent development by Chinese metals companies of nickel-iron as a substitute for nickel in response to the quadrupling in the price of pure nickel.

The need for local regulatory approval spurs some market-driven R&D in China. One example is provided by the pharmaceutical industry. Drug efficacy is not country-related; drugs are much the same all around the world, although some diseases are more prevalent in China than in the West (liver cancer, for example). Yet gaining Chinese approval for a drug already tested and approved by other agencies (e.g., the US Food and Drug Administration, the European Medicines Agency, or Japan's Pharmaceuticals and Medical Devices Agency) requires R&D in China—a form of market-driven R&D. Most of the major pharmaceutical companies do some so-called Phase 3 development in China to gain approval for sale in China. The China Food & Drug Administration, in fact, requires that drug tests be conducted on Chinese people to verify that the drug in question poses no particular problem for the Chinese physiology. Testing on as many as 5,000 patients may be required. The product is usually not modified, although the dose can be changed. Such testing on local populations has often been the historical start of R&D activities by foreign pharmaceutical companies in China. Novartis began such local testing in the 1990s.

Market adaptation in China can mean using, rather than fighting, traditional preferences. Johnson & Johnson pioneered a synthetic surgical suture, for which it has a very large market share in the developed countries. It is superior to silk sutures because it degrades rapidly and therefore patients don't have to be kept in hospital as long as they once did. In China, however, surgeons have long used silk sutures and have a strong preference for them. Johnson & Johnson's old approach would have been to attack the silk sutures directly with their superior product, but this would simply have created resistance by senior surgeons. But as a result of an innovation brainstorming session held at its new R&D unit in Suzhou, the company decided to embrace silk rather than fight it. Specifically, it created an artificial suture with silk-like characteristics, especially in texture, which has been well accepted.

Market adaptation in China can also mean adapting to the attitudes of a company's own sales force. The head of Johnson & Johnson's R&D unit got that company's China sales organization to adopt and promote a new low-cost electrocardiogram machine, developed for emerging markets, by offering a customized version for China that differed from the Indian version and which its sales people found easier to support. The only real differences were first, that the Chinese version eliminated two features that weren't used much in China and second, that the color of the device's face was changed from gray to brick.

Success in market-driven R&D in one country can result in an innovation that can be sold in other markets. Those markets are most likely to be adjacent to the source country in income or culture, but in some instances the market can be global. This is the phenomenon of "reverse innovation," most famously illustrated by the GE cardiac monitor.[16] Another example is a low-priced GE ultrasound machine, developed for China, that sold well in developed markets as a portable device or as a device for physician's surgeries. In chapter 3 we mentioned another example: the "good enough" food-processing equipment of one MNC's Chinese business, now sold for less demanding applications in developed as well as developing countries. Though such extensions to other markets have been more fortuitous than deliberate, we argue below, and throughout this book, that the third type of R&D in China, which is knowledge-driven, can be purposely used to drive new innovations for the world.

Government-driven R&D

A special case of market-driven R&D is government-driven R&D.[17] This type of R&D is undertaken in order to satisfy a wish of government, so as to gain access to contracts or big projects. It is alternatively labeled "PR&D" to stress the public relations dimension of this strategy. Such R&D usually starts with political agreements signed at the highest levels, often between countries. The impetus may be to satisfy the Chinese government's demand for more domestic technological innovation. This is common within business-to-government activities in concentrated businesses with very few global competitors. Such agreements are implemented by state-owned companies (under government control) on the Chinese side and, on the foreign side, by MNCs that are close to their home countries' governments. An important objective for the Chinese entity in such arrangements is joint technology development. High-speed rail, aerospace, and avionics are examples. For the Chinese entity the driving force is acquisition of technology, whereas for the MNC it is market access. Government intervention in this manner has compressed the evolution of the product cycle in China by accelerating inward technology transfer as well as indigenous innovation. The direct intervention of the Chinese government is stimulating the rise of local competitors, equipped with state-of-the-art technology, more rapidly than happened before in other industrialzing economies. For the MNCs, the price of participation in these big opportunities has been the creation of potential global competitors.

Knowledge-driven R&D

The third phase, knowledge-driven R&D, differs from cost-driven R&D and market-driven R&D in the number of steps in the innovation process undertaken in China. Whereas cost-driven R&D is focused on the end stage of development and operations, and market-driven R&D usually doesn't go beyond development, the activities of companies that perform knowledge-driven R&D encompass the full spectrum: fundamental research, applied research, and development. There are also important differences between the three types of R&D strategies in the direction of related knowledge

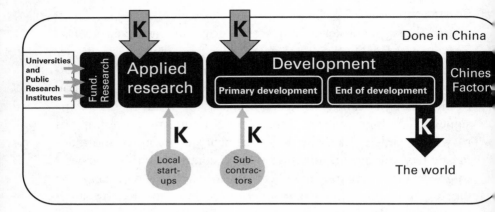

Figure 4.5

Knowledge-driven R&D in global businesses (same product all around the world, no need for local adaptation): software, energy, pharmaceutical companies for new drugs, specialized chemicals, global electronic products, semiconductor industry.

Source: Dominique Jolly

flows. Figure 4.5 illustrates the focus of knowledge-driven R&D in China.

The crucial question is whether to rely on imported knowledge or on knowledge created in China. When cost-driven R&D is the objective, knowledge comes from foreign R&D locations. Limited value is added to this knowledge in China, and there is little return flow to the home R&D location. With market-driven R&D, both the flows of imported knowledge and the value created in China are more significant. Foreign companies import into China complete technologies that were developed abroad. These technologies are then re-engineered and re-developed by the MNC's R&D center in China to fit with local requirements, creating more value in China. This new body of knowledge is created specifically for China and is not initially exported.

In contrast to the two previous modes, knowledge-driven R&D doesn't rely mainly on technology imports from abroad. Rather, it aims to take advantage of China's growing knowledge base. Value creation occurs in China thanks to technologies fully created in China—an example of how the birthplace of innovations changes as incomes and scientific capability become more uniform globally, a pattern seen historically across the globe.[18] Ideally, technologies developed in China will later be transferred to the rest of the world. This means that one prerequisite is that the MNC be willing to position its R&D activity in China from a global perspective (and not to centralize knowledge development at home). Connecting with the Chinese national innovation system (NIS) is also imperative, because in China more than in most developing countries that is where the innovative ideas are being created. Even companies in consumer mass markets, such as Philips and Unilever, have decided to locate some of their R&D labs that have global responsibilities in China. Some companies in business-to-business markets, including the Belgian chemical company Solvay, have adopted the same strategy.

Of the MNCs in our sample of R&D centers, 68 percent were operating in mature industries and only 32 percent in new industries. We believe there are two reasons for this: (1) MNCs are reluctant to undertake R&D on advanced technologies in China. (2) In the second phase of the product cycle (operations in the host country), MNCs have considered adaptation of the parent's technology sufficient, assuming that local firms weren't sufficiently innovative to be threatening. Although there are justifications for the first reason, the second is now challenged by the Chinese advances in indigenous innovation. Chinese firms are accelerating their development by developing technologies locally so that they can compete better domestically and expand abroad. This process is accelerated because of the increasing technological output of the NIS, stimulated by government encouragement and special treatment of domestic companies. These two forces accelerate the development of new technology and provide profits for local firms to invest in innovation, strengthening *capabilities* and generating *cash*. Not only are Chinese companies proficient at accelerating their internal innovation processes[19]; they also increasingly benefit from the acceleration of the product cycle, thanks to new knowledge generated by the NIS. This will undoubtedly lead to disruptive innovations.

Microsoft R&D in China

Microsoft provides a powerful example of how MNCs are conducting knowledge-driven R&D in China. With 3,300 people, including 300 in basic research, Microsoft's China R&D center is its largest outside the United States. Microsoft's R&D in China is based in three cities: Beijing, Shanghai, and Shenzhen, Beijing being its largest location. Microsoft obtained land in the Zhonguancun district of that city and built two tower blocks, placing it close to the top universities and academic research centers. The company started research activities in China in 1999, and development activities in 2006. This sequence is opposite to what most other foreign companies do. Microsoft's first reason to enter China was to gain access to talent and benefit from the quantity and quality of those people: China has many times as many engineers as does the United States and twice as many as India. Another advantage is that proportionately many more clever young people in China choose engineering and science as professions, in contrast to Americans and Europeans (a major concern to their governments). The size of the market is another factor: China has also the largest number of IT hardware manufacturers and the largest number of solution providers of any country. So R&D teams in China benefit from closeness to this huge pool of talented people and innovative companies. Earlier than most, Microsoft saw China as an emerging "lead market."

The goal for Microsoft's research operation in China is to be the leading lab for computer sciences in Asia. Members of the R&D staff are encouraged to publish and to register intellectual property that can later be transferred to product development. The performance of the members of the research group is measured, as in academic institutions, by the number of papers and patents produced.

Ninety percent of the workload of Microsoft's R&D employees in China serves the company's global needs. The remaining locally oriented 10 percent relates to "last mile innovation": localization, in which 300 people are employed. This includes minor adaptations such as for language, regulations, and for variations in the IT infrastructures among cities.

Linking to venture capital in China

The increasing availability of venture capital in China is spurring R&D-related startups. Half of the total current venture-capital funding of about $5 billion a year goes into the Information Technology field and the R&D head of Microsoft in China serves on the boards of several venture-capital firms. This experience convinced him to establish a "cloud integrator program." This is embodied in a floor dedicated to startups in one of Microsoft's buildings in the Zhonguancun district of Beijing, and includes a mentorship program with venture-capital firms. A total of 100 startups, selected by Microsoft, are lodged free for six months. Microsoft doesn't fund them or take equity, but assists them to use and create cloud-based applications, while the venture capitalists provide startup funding.

SHOULD A COMPANY MOVE TO KNOWLEDGE-DRIVEN R&D?

Knowledge-driven R&D in China is not right for all companies. Much depends on the industry. As in most countries, China's NIS is not equally strong in supporting all sectors. Multinational firms engage in knowledge-based R&D in China mainly in new and rapidly growing industries. They find less value from the Chinese knowledge base in mature industries, in which MNCs have years of experience and existing patents. In the sample of companies we studied, 9 of the 14 doing knowledge-driven R&D in China were operating in new industries, and 31 of the 38 undertaking cost-driven or market-driven R&D were operating in mature industries.

The first, easier approach is to conduct knowledge-driven R&D in sectors in which Chinese companies themselves are world leaders in R&D spending, primarily because of their size, dominance, and government R&D funding. These sectors include railways, telecommunications, oil, coal, and solar energy. The second and more difficult approach is to tap China's supply of scientists and engineers who can best support the MNC's innovation goals. The abundance (even dominance) of Chinese mathematicians and computer scientists (both home-grown and overseas-trained) enables frontier research in computer-related and telecom-related sectors. In addition to Microsoft, IBM and British Telecom have important knowledge-driven R&D labs in China. And despite China's relatively lower public investment in the medical sector, Chinese scientists in bioscience and medicine have attracted Astra Zeneca, GlaxoSmithKline, and Johnson & Johnson to set up fundamental research labs in China. The companies we interviewed reported that China's research in the domains of interest to them was growing rapidly in scale and quality, as evidenced by the growing volume of scientific publications and patents noted in chapter 1.

More broadly, China's emphasis on, and Chinese students' preference for, "STEM" subjects (science, technology, engineering, and mathematics) creates many opportunities for foreign companies to use the country's huge talent pool of qualified scientists and engineers. For example, besides PATAC (the Pan Asia Technical Automotive Center—the R&D joint venture for development that General Motors started in Shanghai with its local partner SAIC), GM started its own R&D unit a few years later—the ATC (Advanced Technical Center). That wholly owned entity, also based in Shanghai, was set up to gain access to local talent in magnesium metallurgy, advanced design, and battery development for global projects such as lightweight materials, vehicle entertainment, and battery systems.

In many fields, Chinese universities and research centers are publishing high-quality research at the international level (such as in the case of coal conversion into synthetic gas). In addition, an increasing number of Chinese startups provide opportunities for collaboration. There are, for example, hundreds of startups in chemistry. Having an R&D center in China allows a multinational to know quickly which Chinese startups could be of interest to partner with, or even to acquire. In some of these areas, venture capital is already active. As will be discussed more fully in chapter 7, MNCs that are practicing open innovation increasingly benefit from being close to the ecosystem. Those were important considerations for Microsoft in establishing knowledge-driven R&D in China.

WHERE IN CHINA SHOULD A COMPANY LOCATE KNOWLEDGE-DRIVEN R&D?

The question of where to locate a foreign R&D center raises two questions: Should a company settle on the coast or locate inland? Should a company establish its own science-and-technology park, or should it locate in an existing one?

When knowledge-driven R&D is chosen, the answer to those questions is straightforward. All fourteen of the companies we interviewed that had adopted a knowledge-driven R&D strategy in China chose a location close to a center where technology creation was taking place.

The best universities and the leading public research centers in China are located in the coastal provinces, never far from a leading science-and-technology park. Microsoft, Intel, AMD, Oracle, and Orange all have established their R&D centers in the Zhonguancun district of Beijing—the best science-and-technology park in China for information technology. Indeed, in several IT sectors, China is ahead of the rest of the world. Zhonguancun is a cluster of scientific and educational resources (including Peking University, Tsinghua University, and the Beijing University of Aeronautics and Astronautics), more than 200 scientific institutions (including the Chinese Academy of Social Sciences and the Chinese Academy of Engineering), state laboratories, and national engineering and technological research centers. Zhonguancun is the base for a number of leading Chinese IT companies, including Baidu, Sina, Youku, 360buy, and Lenovo.

MNCs that locate in top places for research can much more easily attract and retain the best scientists from those locations and can facilitate interconnections between their R&D center and the public research entities they want to work with. They will also be closer to the startups and venture capitalists that are creating innovate businesses and potential acquisitions. Although China doesn't yet have a direct equivalent to the innovation ecosystem of Silicon Valley, being part of the Chinese NIS is the closest alternative.

Another question is whether to have one or more locations. Having a single R&D center in China makes it easier to reach a critical mass of sufficient number of researchers, with benefits of shared equipment and support functions and closeness to local ideas. That is the case, for example, with Unilever in Shanghai. It has concentrated into a single location several entities that were previously scattered among different manufacturing sites across China. This location helped to tighten relationships with the local scientific milieu. Another argument is the agglomeration effect: the benefits of participation in an industry cluster. For example, 15 of the largest 18 companies in the world's chemical industry have established their R&D centers in Shanghai. Only one of these companies' R&D centers in China is elsewhere, in Tianjin.

The first rule for a newcomer is that a leading science-and-technology park should be the preferred option if the park's focus is in line with its business (for example, IT is concentrated in Zhonguancun in Beijing, and pharma in Zhangjiang in Shanghai). One shortcoming is that most of the science-and-technology parks are new, without much history, and it takes time for a multinational to develop deep roots in the networks. There is also less informal interaction among executives, venture capitalists, entrepreneurs, and supporting service professionals in China than in established clusters such as Silicon Valley. A second rule is that more than one location may be needed if the company is diversified and needs to cover multiple scientific domains.

CHALLENGES TO EXISTING AND NEW R&D CENTERS

The challenge to existing R&D centers is that multinationals already doing R&D in China may not be located in the right place, as the right location for knowledge-driven R&D is often not the same as the right location for market-driven R&D. The location criterion for a market-driven R&D center has been proximity to customers. Yet customers may not be located at the same place as the leading universities and public research centers, where a knowledge-driven R&D center needs to be. Thus, established

MNCs need to take a deliberate strategic decision whether or not to change location as they shift toward knowledge-driven R&D.

A multinational with an established R&D center may also find that the personnel it has recruited to do market-driven R&D may not have enough depth of expertise and experience for knowledge-driven R&D. A similar disadvantage may exist with the universities with which they have established connections. Existing MNCs need to undertake a thorough competency analysis of their staff and make adjustments, including the possibility of hiring new leaders.

The challenge for new "greenfield" R&D centers is different. They need to establish their company's reputation for R&D with the government, with research institutions, and with potential members of their research staff in China. A company may be known locally for manufacturing, but not for technology creation. The MNC can't assume that its home-country reputation for innovative R&D precedes it to China. An advance program of creating awareness must be planned and implemented carefully. In addition to visiting the leading universities and public research centers to identify and meet useful collaborators, this will include promoting the company's image within the Chinese NIS, including officials of the central ministries and municipal governments.

PARTNERS FOR KNOWLEDGE-DRIVEN R&D

The most important interactions with the Chinese NIS occur with knowledge-driven R&D centers rather than with cost-driven or market-driven ones. It is through the knowledge-driven R&D mode that collaborations, partnerships, and joint ventures are built with Chinese universities, public research centers, startups, incubators, and venture capitalists. There is, first, a need for a mapping exercise to identify who and where are the most reputed professors and research teams to partner with. Companies need to engage in thorough scouting to identify the best people and places in their field. Some of the companies we studied, including Air Liquide (a business-to-business industrial gases company from France), spent several years mapping the relevant research domains in the

Chinese NIS before investing in large R&D centers. The aim was to identify appropriate partners for collaboration. We also encountered companies that decided not to do this mapping alone and to get help from a consulting firm; one of them was Solvay. Solvay's partner examined scientific publications from different labs, identified the best-fitting places, and made road trips with Solvay executives to investigate them.

Not all partnerships exhibit the same level of involvement. Some companies choose a cautious strategy of establishing a small team for managing the externalization of basic research to Chinese universities. (Pfizer and Sanofi did this.) Other companies, more ambitious in their strategies, have built an in-house research center in China, either alone (Novartis, Unilever) or with partners (Solvay with Rhodia). A limited number of foreign MNCs, including Astra-Zeneca, have set up licensing agreements. In recent years, it has become more and more common for foreign companies to take over Chinese R&D entities, a practice that enables them to avoid starting from scratch. The ideal acquired firm is a Chinese company that already has an R&D center with a good track record (as the one bought by L'Oréal did). The various patterns of partnerships are explained in greater detail below.

Ad hoc sponsored research

Most MNCs begin by funding research projects carried out by a university, a research center, a hospital, or some other institution. Such ad hoc sponsored research is a low-risk way of entering the NIS and making connections. One-shot contracts allow testing of the Chinese partner. A major energy company, for example, began this way by establishing an R&D office in Beijing and commissioning research projects with many of the best university research departments. As a result, the company is now well known among the relevant Chinese technologists.

Repeated short-term collaborations

The next level of engagement with China's NIS is to set up repeated short-term collaborations with universities and other research entities.[20] The pharmaceutical industry illustrates this pattern. Bayer,

GSK, and some other companies have the same strategy. Each company manages a network of external partners for building connections with the scientific milieu (including biotech startups and contract research organizations), but without initially creating its own laboratories (although they did so later). Even if those companies dedicate only a limited number of local employees to discovery, their strategy allows them to gain access to hundreds of people in the entities with which they collaborate. One major US pharma company has three or four contracts with Chinese research organizations, four or five with universities and two or three with biotech research centers. The French construction company St. Gobain is another example; it has signed between fifteen and twenty contracts with various universities every year.

Long-term collaborations

Some foreign companies use long-term collaborations for R&D in China. Rather than set up a full R&D center, one major energy company's primary mode for research in China is to use long-term sponsored research. The company has relationships with Tsinghua University, with the Shanghai Advanced Research Institute of the Chinese Academy of Sciences, and with the Chinese University of Petroleum. To manage these external relationships and to head the China research entity, the aforementioned company assigned an ethnic Chinese professor from Imperial College London, one of the world's top science-based universities, who had also previously worked for the company in other countries. In contrast to that company's approach of corporate-level basic research, innovation that is more applied (and which will be implemented within two years) is located in operating businesses.

General Electric, in addition to its China Technical Center in Shanghai and its five other centers in China, has long-term relationships with several Chinese universities. These include the top ten engineering schools, including those in Shanghai, Beijing, Guangzhou, Nanjing, and Harbin. These relationships include hiring, collaborative research, and scholarships. GE has also tried to set up joint labs with some universities, but that effort has been less successful. GE's head of R&D in China is not sure that Chinese universities have enough capability to offer essential expertise to the company and finds it more effective to make small contracts (valued at about $50,000 each) for specific projects. GE makes about twenty or thirty such agreements each year.

Relationships have to be built step by step. For example, one leading European cosmetics company collaborates with the Shanghai Institute of Organic Chemistry (SIOC), which is under the Chinese Academy of Sciences. The relationship started a few years ago with fee-based contracts that helped the two organizations to become familiar with each other. They are now running a joint research program, with the objective of producing joint intellectual property. The development of trust between the two parties has generated closer involvement: ten people from the company are now permanently based at SIOC.

The joint research laboratory

A greater commitment is to set up a joint research laboratory with an entity of China's NIS. Until now, many of the joint research laboratories in China have been concentrated in the IT and bioscience sectors. A joint lab provides for close collaboration and the development of trust, but requires skillful management and dedicating specific research personnel to the venture. A joint lab may even be based inside a university or institute to develop a stronger symbiosis with the milieu.

In 2012 General Electric set up a joint lab with Shanghai Jiaotong University, with a research group focused on manufacturing and materials technologies and located at the university. GE has donated some equipment but has no employees there on a permanent basis. The agreement stipulates that students are cosupervised and that GE's employees go to the lab on demand for up to a week every month. Solvay/Rhodia, a major European chemical company, takes this approach for fundamental research. In 2011 it started a joint lab in Shanghai with the Centre Nationale de la Recherche Scientifique (France's national center for scientific research), the École Normale Supérieure de Lyon, and East China Normal University. A group of 130 scientists work on new economical and environmentally friendly processes for the production of plastics with raw materials from biomass. The performance of this lab is measured on criteria such as scientific publications and patent applications. This international partnership has recently been extended to Fudan University in China and Lille University in France.

"Licensing in" of new technologies from Chinese startups

Foreign companies can also engage with Chinese startups. The easier route is to license in new technologies from startups (often spinoffs from public institutions). The Chinese government encourages research institutes and universities to create their own spinoffs at the business end of their research. Astra Zeneca was the first foreign company to sign a licensing agreement with a Chinese biotech firm, a unit of the Hong Kong company Hutchison. This biotech operation is based in Shanghai's Zhangjiang district, with $20 million of capital funded from Hong Kong and a total of $100 million planned as it meets agreed milestones.

Joint ventures with Chinese companies

Very few of the companies we researched had formed a joint venture with a Chinese partner for the purpose of R&D, even if the MNC expected to facilitate recruitment of scientists by entrusting responsibility for that to the local partner. Most foreign companies now have many years of experience in China. They no longer need a local partner to guide them, and several have painful memories of joint management with a Chinese partner ("sleeping in the same bed but dreaming different dreams"—or, too often, nightmares). Control of recruitment, knowledge management, and property rights is much simpler in a wholly owned foreign enterprise (WOFE) than in a joint venture. Besides, a WOFE helps to reduce the risk of knowledge leaks, which were frequent in Sino-foreign joint ventures.

Acquisitions for knowledge access

The greatest commitment for engaging with China's NIS for knowledge access is to acquire a Chinese company or institute. Among the companies we studied, acquisition of a startup had most often been motivated by the desire to enter a business, in which acquiring expertise is one of the main motivations. R&D teams can help the business leaders in their scouting. For example, take-over has been one means for pharmaceutical companies to enter into traditional Chinese medicine. Several MNCs acquired local Chinese companies to gain a foothold in traditional formulas and to gain know-how for modern formulations.

Foreign MNCs are also eagerly scouting biotechnology companies, mostly founded by returnees with experience in drug discovery. At present, the field is competitive, as there are fewer than a hundred of these companies in China of a reasonable size (employing more than 200 people).

CONCLUSION AND RECOMMENDATIONS

Multinational corporations have evolved their R&D presence in China from cost-driven innovation to market-driven innovation, and some have begun to take advantage of knowledge developed in China. Figure 4.6 illustrates this change. As of 2015 most MNCs understand the customer and the culture much better than before,

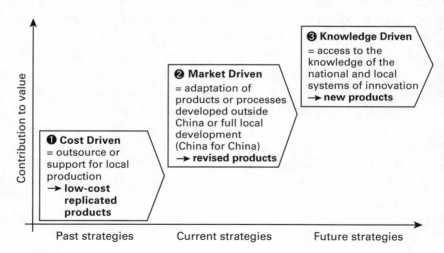

Figure 4.6

Changing drivers for R&D in China.

Source: Dominique Jolly

and have hard-earned experience of dealing with local competitors and government agencies.

But the opportunities are changing fast, domestic competitors are very agile, and the conditions for foreign participation are changing, particularly under the new government. Because China is becoming the global lead market and an important source of revenue growth and new ideas, MNCs can't afford to be absent from the world's new hub of innovation. By becoming part of the national innovation ecosystem, MNCs can build on the customer and culture factors of the Four Cs framework to develop capabilities that are complementary to those they already possess. This has become essential for firms in many sectors, which will face determined entries into their home markets by Chinese MNCs. They can't do this from afar; they need to be firmly present in China and embedded in China's national innovation system. Our advice to MNCs not yet tapping the China knowledge ecosystem is "Don't wait until it is too late."

To implement knowledge-driven R&D successfully in China, local managers of foreign MNCs need to plan a sequence of actions to gain the support of their most important stakeholders.

First, they have to convince headquarters in the home country. For most of the MNCs we researched, market-driven R&D was easy to sell to HQ. However, convincing HQ that the Chinese R&D center should be switched to a knowledge-driven R&D center is much harder and requires a strategic campaign. Such a campaign needs to deal with such important questions as protection of intellectual property and competition for resources within the corporation. These issues have been less difficult to manage when the top leadership of the MNC makes China a priority and establishes the China R&D center with a global mandate, or even moves the headquarters of a business unit to China. (We provide recommendations on how MNCs can protect intellectual property in chapter 7.)

Second, corporate leadership needs to be clear about the career path for R&D staffers of Chinese origin recruited from the United States or from Europe. Ideally they will be people who are happy to remain in China, but some may be looking for a global career within the company, and may see working in China as a useful development experience. Corporate policies need to be sensitive to such aspirations and ensure that there is a potential path to other assignments.

Third, MNCs need to have the good connections (*guanxi*) to enter and collaborate with the best universities and research centers. Because of the importance of hierarchy in China, the process has to start at the highest possible level—with the President of China, the Minister for Science & Technology, and the President of the Chinese Academy of Sciences. People of such importance in the hierarchy will expect to meet with no less than the top leadership of the company.

Fourth, the support of local authorities is another prerequisite. This means that the foreign company will do best if it is able to position itself in a domain that is targeted for growth by the Chinese government and local authorities. (In chapter 6 we provide examples of how MNCs have become insiders in the national innovation system.)

Fifth, companies will certainly benefit from experienced advisors—patent attorneys, consultants who can help to identify the good universities and public research centers, consultants who can help to identify startups, and experienced Chinese residents and foreign expatriates in China who can make introductions at the right level.

APPENDIX: RESEARCH METHOD

We researched 52 multinationals with R&D operations in China. We visited 21 of the 52 companies twice or more when complementary data were needed after the first visit to a site. We conducted 69 in-depth interviews, ranging in length from one hour to two and a half hours. The field of responsibility of most of the interviewees (44 of 69) refers explicitly to "research and development." A second group (18 of 69) had overlapping responsibilities, covering engineering, innovation, open innovation, or technology. A remaining group of interviewees (7) came with a different title (e.g., strategic business development). The level of responsibility of the interviewee was mostly that of a director or an associate director (38 of 69). We also interviewed a group (16 of 69) at the level of vice-president or senior vice-president. The remaining group (15) was at other levels, such as managers or site heads. (In addition, we conducted 50 interviews with embassy and consular officials and consultants.)

The industries covered included pharmaceuticals, chemicals, information technology, automotive, and electronics. (These are important sectors to MNCs in China: the pharmaceuticals sector received the most foreign investment between 2012 and 2014, followed by business equipment and consumer electronics.[21]) The research examined several facets of R&D operations in China, including the spectrum of R&D activities conducted in China, drivers of entry, location choice, interactions with the milieu, organizational choices, "people issues," knowledge management, and issues of intellectual property rights.

5

HOW MULTINATIONAL CORPORATIONS CAN ORGANIZE FOR INNOVATION IN CHINA

In the previous chapter we discussed the evolution of multinational corporations' R&D activities in China. In this chapter we examine how MNCs organize those activities. Our findings are based mostly on in-depth interviews conducted at the headquarters and at the China affiliates of several major European MNCs. We took this dual-focus approach because, in addition to the perspective of the Chinese executives, we wanted to understand how those in the MNCs' headquarters viewed the strategic role of China in their worldwide business and why the MNCs' China operations were organized as they were. We met with, typically, the head of the R&D unit in China and one or more senior executives at headquarters in Europe who supervised the R&D activities in China. In some cases these interviewees were the corporate chief innovation officers.[1] Some companies were willing to be identified here; others were not.

ORGANIZATIONAL MODES

We have found a pattern that multinationals typically follow as they evolve the scope of their China R&D units. The R&D strategy evolves as the corporation's depth of business in China changes. We identified the following strategies for R&D in China:

- The local server is a small R&D unit that is focused on localization and product adaptation; it is embedded in and serves the local China organization.

- The autonomous player has an R&D program, with significant numbers of scientists and engineers, that, while still serving the China business, has a life of its own.
- The global network member has strong connections to the MNC's headquarters and its global R&D network, with some sharing of projects and some exchange of employees.
- The global mandate holder is set up to conduct specific innovation activities for the MNC's global business as a knowledge-oriented and knowledge-seeking strategy.

These modes tend to be sequential, although some companies follow different paths and some skip modes.[2] In addition, some companies may use more than one mode at the same time. Also, the R&D/innovation organization tends to grow larger as companies progress through the stages. Finally, in companies with multiple business units, different business units may be at different stages in the evolutionary path. Each organizational stage also places emphasis on one of the three different types of R&D, as described in the previous chapter, although this is fluid, as many of the companies are in transition. As is illustrated in table 5.1, the local server mode emphasizes cost-driven R&D. The autonomous player mode emphasizes market-driven R&D, as does the global network member mode, which also includes steps toward serious efforts in knowledge-driven R&D. The global mandate holder very much emphasizes knowledge-driven R&D.

Table 5.1
Organizational modes and types of R&D.

	Cost-driven R&D	Market-driven R&D	Knowledge-driven R&D
Global mandate holder	*	* *	* * *
Global network member	*	* * *	* *
Autonomous player	* *	* * *	*
Local server	* * *	* *	

* * *major emphasis
* *moderate emphasis
*minor emphasis

Local server

The first innovation activities for multinationals in China are typically created to support an existing manufacturing or delivery presence. The focus is very much on localizing products or processes to China. In this stage, any product innovation is about adapting products developed in the home or other countries. Likewise, process innovations are directed toward satisfying local regulatory standards or adapting to environmental differences, as well as the specific nature of customers and suppliers. This strategy is very much related to the cost-driven innovation stage that we discussed in chapter 4.

A typical experience is that of Bosch China, which started very small, with R&D done in China only to support production and product localization. For that reason, Bosch's first engineers in China were based in the manufacturing plants. Only as the company moved from product localization to local product development, around 2002, did R&D by Bosch in China really begin. Bosch China hired its first patent attorney in 2008. That year Bosch filed only eight patents in China. But by 2012 the company had more than 200 invention reports, and almost 100 patent filings. Bosch China now has seven patent attorneys, 2,700 engineers across all divisions in China, and 13 technical centers (eight in automotive, three in industrial sectors, and two in consumer goods sectors). All of Bosch's divisions that are active in China now have technology centers.

Bosch faces typical challenges of localization in China. For example, in the automotive sector, the function or specification of products is generally higher in the West and in Japan than in China, so many of Bosch's products are overspecified for the local market and, hence, not competitive on cost.

German engineers are educated to achieve high standards. If they are asked to strip a product down or to lower its quality level, it is very difficult for them to do so. But the local Chinese engineers know what the local customer wants; they also understand Bosch's standards. Thus, the local engineers can balance the two. In contrast, engineers raised and based in Germany don't know the dynamics in China and don't feel the market pressures every day. As they are much farther away from China customers' needs, they don't see the cost concern so clearly. So for Bosch the motivation for hiring local Chinese people is not about reducing the cost of the engineers themselves, but about benefiting from their mindset and speed. "Local for local" is simply faster. As a Bosch executive put it: "Germans are not accustomed to working with the speed of Chinese customer demand, and they have no experience of how to handle Chinese customers." Also, companies need to be more responsive to China's ways of doing business. Germans would ask customers to give them the list of specifications, but in China the supplier has to provide the specifications. Thus, there is also a difference in business process.

BMW started doing R&D in China to undertake homologation to meet local standards for the vehicles it was importing. That initial activity evolved to include local sourcing of components, required by the state. For example, China requires a specific percentage of components of an engine to be made locally. Some units of BMW wanted to localize components such as the fuel tank, which is costly to ship from Germany. Batteries are also too expensive to ship by air. The switch to local sourcing required BMW to set up local R&D to qualify suppliers and test their products.

EuroEng (a pseudonym), a major global engineering and technology based company, set up R&D in China, motivated by its insight that each region has its own engineering and research mindset and also by the specific technology and application needs. For instance, products and systems for the Chinese market need to be much more SMART (Simple, Maintenance-friendly, Affordable, Robust, and Timely to market) than comparable products and systems for developed markets. EuroEng's aim was to set up local R&D units in its major markets, so as to capture and fuse local mindsets—to be global but local—and to be stronger than a purely German research emphasis would have been.

Philips' China R&D was initially set up for localization of supply in lighting products. Because of regulation by municipal and city authorities, high cost, and intense price pressure from competitors, platforms that had been developed in Europe would not be optimal for China. For that reason, Philips has pursued an ongoing process of adaptation. If a product is specifically intended for the local market, it is more likely to be developed in China. Products for which the market is considered to be global will more likely be designed in one of the global R&D units in Europe or the United States. At the same time, some innovations that have succeeded in the Chinese market have been able to expand globally. In its Consumer Lifestyle business, Philips has produced an innovative LED book light in China; it also has produced a garment steamer to suit Chinese consumers' preference for a non-traditional ironing system, a soy milk processor, and a tea-brewing appliance, all of which have found markets outside China. As a result, innovations for local and global markets are not sequential but rather parallel.

Globular (a pseudonym for a major global company) has taken a similar approach of using R&D in China to localize its production for local conditions. In its innovation work, the key success factor is local "pull"—what the local businesses need. Innovation is an enabler of the business activities and very much a result of them. For that reason, Globular takes the view that it is very difficult to innovate in a country without having both local R&D assets and also businesses. It needs pull from a local business unit that wants to apply the output of the innovation.

Autonomous player

Many multinationals enhance their China innovation operations to go beyond the local server stage. A multinational's operation becomes an autonomous player when it is doing more than simply serving local needs in production or adaptation, and when it has an R&D program with significant numbers of scientists and engineers. While still serving the China business, the R&D unit has a life of its own. The operation begins to look for promising areas for its work, even without prompting from business units. This mode is very much related to the market-driven innovation stage that we discussed in chapter 4, and to a lesser extent it is related to cost-driven innovation.

The development of the autonomous player is usually driven by the recognition that successful innovation in China needs to be conducted rather independently from HQ, with a local approach that differs from the standard corporate approach. Why should some R&D be done closer to the market? The board of a European company Matco (a pseudonym) has debated this question. In theory it could, perhaps, do all the R&D at the center. But to understand what is really going on overseas, it needs people located in the market. For example, Matco is one of the world's largest producers of a certain material, but it was not cost competitive in China. Its R&D people in China said "Do you realize that our cost of materials alone is already higher than the market price?" So Matco needed to reengineer the manufacturing process. It needed to get a proper understanding of Chinese customers' needs—to be in front of the customers in order to live their needs every day. Matco considered the emotional and experiential aspects critical to really understanding a local market.

Thus, Matco established a center of excellence in China with a completely different way of thinking. The company had perceived its products as premier in the market. The design and application of its products is controlled strictly in terms of temperatures and humidity in Europe, so the products perform very well there. However, Chinese customers viewed these Matco products as "delicate." For example, the local Chinese customer can't afford a climate-controlled factory. Therefore, Matco had to adjust its products to be tolerant of less nearly ideal conditions in China, but still to provide similar performance.

The second challenge faced by Matco was price pressure. Even though the performance of products may translate into real value, companies have to cut prices to meet the competition. Brand and reputation are also affected in this way. In many cases, the company has to either re-engineer the products or completely re-design them. However, for its high-value or premier products, the company can never cut the cost to a level that local customers accept. This is a completely new problem for Matco. It is sharply different from traditional European thinking, according to which a price reduction will only cheapen a high-performance product.

Philips provides an example of how an autonomous player can operate. Seeing a need for a portable light source for use in China's small, crowded homes and college dormitories, its China R&D

center invented an LED lighting device that can distribute light all over a plastic panel the size of a book page. Light is shed nowhere else and hence doesn't disturb other family members or roommates. In addition, being rechargeable, this portable light is useful in the many rural areas with irregular electricity supply. Philips' researchers in China created the product and proved that it could work. But because no business wanted to pick up the product, the R&D unit went further than usual and created a prototype. This reading light is now sold successfully not just in China but around the world.

EuroEng goes so far as to say that employees of its Corporate Technology unit in China have the same mission as their German counterparts: the development of leading-edge technologies in defined technology fields, either through their own research or through partnering with Chinese research partners. The company began to expand its R&D effort in 2004 in Beijing, and the number of employees there soon increased to nearly 400. The overriding objective is to come up with innovations driven by customers' needs. EuroEng has a vertical structure in China organized by technology fields, which gives the business operations access to the company's advanced technologies worldwide. Relative to its German peers, however, EuroEng tends to be closer to actual product development, if only to support the business units' R&D teams in China, which usually need more support and training than the more established BU R&D teams in Germany. But EuroEng has learned that China may need even better technology than does Germany. The company had initially thought that the world's best available technology was appropriate for China applications. In the case of urban rapid transit construction, the worldwide standard in 2005 was to run subway trains at three-minute intervals. But in the city of Guangzhou the government's requirement was for intervals of 90 seconds. This was necessitated by the very large population there. EuroEng developed innovations to address that requirement, and currently those innovations are applied in both local and global markets.

After starting with local server activities, BMW managers in China saw the large number of technical graduates from universities and the stream of published papers and patents. It became obvious to them that the world would soon see innovations developed in China, so BMW decided to increase R&D in China starting in mid 2010. Some of this activity was intended to adapt BMW's vehicles for the local market. Chinese customers buy BMWs because of their German engineering, but BMW needed to adapt their cars for China in certain ways—for example, Chinese customers want softer seats. Thus, the rear seats of BMW's China models have thicker upholstery than the German models, as do Chinese Mercedes and Audi models. Visually, BMW would not compromise for Chinese taste, but it does offer other modifications, such as tinted windows (through the aftermarket) and storage for two or three mobile phones. In 1998, when GM began selling its Buick Century in China, it made more than 600 modifications to the US design, not only for regulatory reasons but also to respond to Chinese customers' tastes. These included giving the passenger area more leg space and equipping it with controls for the radio, the heater, and sunroof for the benefit of executives accustomed to having a driver.

Global network member

The typical later stage of evolution for China R&D in a multinational is to add to its other roles that of a global network member. This mode has strong connections to the multinational's headquarters and to its global R&D network, with some sharing of projects and some exchange of employees. This mode is very much related to the market-driven innovation stage that we discussed in chapter 4, and is often the basis for moving to knowledge-driven innovation.

Nestlé R&D (China) Limited, henceforth referred to as Nestlé R&D China, typifies this type of network R&D organization. Globally, all of Nestlé's R&D centers report to its Global Head of R&D, based in Switzerland, as R&D resources are shared among markets. Obviously Nestlé R&D China has the purpose and the priority of supporting the company's business in that country. However, this doesn't exclude supporting other markets, especially in Asia Pacific. Nestlé R&D China has not only a local role but also a regional one. Its resources are located in four centers in China.

A good example of how Nestlé R&D works in a global network is the innovation from China of the on-the-go ready-to-drink coffee called SmoovLatte. This was the first coffee sold in a recyclable polyethylene terephthalate bottle. It was developed in China because Nestlé saw the opportunity for an innovative on-the-go coffee in the growing category of ready-to-drink. Many members of the global R&D network were involved in this project to ensure that a product with the right taste and the right packaging was created to delight Chinese consumers. The result is a smooth latte drink customized for Chinese consumers—one that appeals especially to young adults. Nestlé learned that younger consumers around the world want the same strong taste and good mouth feel of premium coffee. When tested in other markets the same recipe came out well as a winner. In another example, Nestlé R&D China developed culinary products with an innovative format that was successfully deployed to many markets in Asia. Through network and sharing within the global R&D network, the product in this novel format was introduced to many markets in other parts of the world.

A leading telecommunications company, one of the world's largest, had a network role in mind from the very start of its R&D operation in China in 2012. When the company opened its R&D lab there, it installed some elements of its cloud computing platform. The company chose cloud computing for China because this was a current topic of research in its home country and its global services business unit was interested in it, and because there were people with the necessary technological capabilities in China.

The US-based Dow Chemical Company has a strong commitment to China. Its R&D operation in China has a regional mandate and acts as a center for the whole Asia-Pacific region. It undertakes Asia-Pacific corporate R&D (funded by Dow's corporate headquarters), business R&D (shorter range in outlook), and technical service development (TSD) for Dow's business units. Of Dow's 400 scientists in China, 130 work on corporate R&D, focusing on a few major areas, including materials to support batteries for electric vehicles. The others work on business-oriented R&D and TSD.

In common with many of the other multinationals in China, Dow's R&D operation was initially set up as a local server to provide better TSD support for local Dow business, which was not properly served by the long chain between the customer and US TSD. Five years ago, Dow's main customers in China were multinationals, and the concept was to "leverage" R&D from the United States.

But there are now many more Chinese-based customers, and there is much more need to provide innovative solutions for local customers, which can't be done by simple adaptation of existing products. So Dow shifted the role of its R&D toward being an autonomous player in China. In addition, however, there was early recognition in Dow that China is well ahead of Western technology in some areas. Placing some fundamental R&D in China was seen as a good long-term strategy. Fields in which China is a world leader include video display technologies, a field in which leadership in technology has shifted from Japan to Korea and now to China as the locus of production has moved. Future developments in this industry will include organic LEDs, flexible display materials, and quantum dot technology and much of that will take place in the country that is the center of global production. As a consequence, Dow R&D China has become increasingly a global network member, working on projects of corporate interest, as well as contributing to development in China and the Asian region. The company reasons that because of the enormous growth in China and Asia more broadly, the technology will advance much faster there than in the West, where growth is more stagnant. Because Dow's customers in China will be innovating much faster than customers anywhere else in the world, Dow needs fundamental R&D in China to respond to their needs and keep ahead of its competitors elsewhere in the world. In fact, in at least one area, ESD Materials (Electrostatic Discharge Materials), Dow's China Centre has a global mandate.

There are still some tensions within the Dow organization about the R&D effort in China. Those tensions are due in part to the traditional commodity mindset. But this is undergoing substantial change under Andrew Liveris, the CEO who is leading the company's strategy toward high-value specialty chemicals and who sees China as an important part of this direction.

Philips' R&D operation in China is a major participant in global networks. Ideas that come from China are being used elsewhere in innovations, as mentioned earlier, sometimes combined with other applications and brought to markets in other countries. For example, Philips' health-care center in China is gaining deeper understanding of certain types of liver cancer and related physiological processes and is exporting that knowledge to other places in its research network, including India and the United States, so that other Philips units can use those insights in their research in that field.

Globular's new China R&D center is not intended to stand alone. It has the same function as Globular's R&D centers in Europe and the United States, where Globular has big business hubs and the R&D centers are closely involved with the businesses. Globular doesn't want fragmented R&D networks, preferring a small number of big centers. (Its Indian IT center is an exception, but that center has a specialized mission.)

Global mandate holder

The global (or regional) mandate holder is set up to conduct specific innovation activities for the entire world (or region), with a knowledge-oriented and knowledge-seeking strategy for R&D. A few companies started their China R&D in this mode; one of them was Microsoft, which we discussed in chapter 4. However, most other multinationals have evolved their China R&D operations to add a role as a global or regional mandate holder.

An example of establishing a regional mandate holder from scratch is the R&D unit that Johnson & Johnson set up in 2010 in the Suzhou Industrial Park. It has responsibility for all product development in the Asia-Pacific region for medical diagnostics and devices, one of the company's three business sectors. The head of the unit told us that he recognizes that he has to look beyond R&D to all of Johnson & Johnson's business functions. To succeed, J&J

believes, it must sell not only products but entire solutions, because a focus on products alone would open them up to imitation by lower-cost Chinese players. To help provide an end-to end-service to its customers in the medical field, J&J has established a simulated hospital environment in the Suzhou R&D center, where products are tested with medical practitioners. Understanding the conditions in the Chinese medical system and adapting to them is critical. The silk-like suture discussed in chapter 4 is an example of the value of gaining such understanding of the user's actual experience.

From the very beginning Philips set up the R&D center for its lighting products in China to operate with a global mandate, not just to serve China. This was because functionality and usage in this category are not too different around the world. The other driver was the intense cost pressure in the lighting industry: it is hard today for a European-based company to meet the costs of foreign competitors. So R&D has to be co-located with production, most of which now occurs in China. Philips has also given a global mandate to China for developing rice cookers.

IBM China Research Lab, established in Beijing in 1995, is one of IBM's nine research institutes around the world and has earned respect for the quality of its research. IBM China Development Labs, founded in 1999, has rapidly developed into a global behemoth, with its main campus in Shanghai. With 7,000 R&D personnel, it is today the largest software development center founded by a multinational corporation in China. Its employees operate under IBM's globally integrated enterprise organizational structure, with certain regional specializations. In IBM, each lab normally leads in certain competencies and Shanghai was designated by the company as its global headquarters for "Growth Markets." IBM China Development Labs has become IBM's main software development center engaged in the development of the company's core brand software (including WebSphere, Information Management, Tivoli, and Rational) and its industrial products and solutions (Lotus, Business Analytics, Industry Solutions). It leads in industry solutions because many different industries are starting up in China. So there is a green field, with no legacy, in which IBM can perform experiments. This is a latecomer advantage, as it allows IBM to use China to leapfrog competitors elsewhere.

Former CEO Sam Palmisano said that if a product fits a market and the market is growing, then one should move the company's competency base to that country. IBM's automotive industry competency was in Japan and Germany in the past, but now IBM is moving that to China. The executive who was IBM's auto-industry leader, formerly based in Germany, has now moved to Shanghai.

IMPLEMENTATION CHALLENGES

Implementing each of the above-mentioned organizational modes for successful R&D is challenging. The companies we studied identified a number of common issues:

- challenges in building up of local capabilities
- home-country engineers and scientists not valuing local capabilities
- difficulty in understanding needs in countries with higher standards
- desire to protect home-country employment
- unwillingness at headquarters to allocate resources to China
- fear of loss of intellectual property and core capabilities

A broader issue than organizing and expanding the role of R&D, but relevant to it, is that there are markets in China in which foreign companies are simply not allowed to compete. Portions of the information systems industry are a good example. The information systems industry is one of the eight core pillars of the Chinese government's industrial policy. At every step along the way, local companies have been strongly encouraged to grow in this area with government support. Unquestionably, Alibaba has been a great success. Some of its success, however, has been due to the government's having put strong constraints on the operations of Google and eBay, both of which eventually left China.

It is very difficult for a non-Chinese firm to do business in information systems in China. Foreign companies are tolerated as long as they bring value to China today by bringing new technologies into the country and improving services. Expansion of R&D activities plays a major part in delivering such benefits to China. But after local competition has been set up, foreign companies become much less desirable to the Chinese government (the "obsolescing bargain" observed by development economists).[3] Thus, an additional question when it comes to expanding the role of R&D in China is whether multinationals have a long-term future there. China's need for the technologies and skills of the MNC are sometimes at odds with its desire for independence. and some statements that the Chinese government made in 2014 and 2015 carried mixed messages. (We discuss this further in chapter 8.)

Challenges in building up local capabilities
A major difficulty in China for MNCs is the hiring of qualified R&D and innovation staffers. Despite the huge numbers of graduates each year, questions continue about the quality and creativity of China-trained researchers. A stereotype with much truth is that China's education system doesn't produce independent-minded researchers. One Western company's head of R&D in China said: "I could easily go to my team in China and argue that one plus one is three and they would not argue back. Those from Hong Kong are a bit more brave about speaking their mind. In our culture we don't care who comes up with the idea, but that is not Chinese culture, which is quite hierarchical. So there is a mismatch between behavior and our requirements." For this executive, the ideal is to recruit Chinese who have had exposure to Western thinking at some point, whether through work or through study, so that they are more confident and risk taking than other Chinese but still have all the Chinese virtues. But some companies see virtue in an entirely Chinese staff. One executive said: "You want to hire Chinese exactly because they are Chinese, because with that comes the Chinese attitude. If you open an R&D operation in China and staff it only with American-born Chinese, then you could run the whole show in America. I don't believe in relying too much on Chinese expats." Some companies find that local Chinese hires are satisfactory for R&D provided they are led by a Chinese with

overseas experience, or by an expatriate who is expected to groom a suitable local replacement.

A second problem is retention, because of China's exceptionally high turnover rates. Experienced R&D people in China can find jobs easily and move readily instead of staying long in one company. Third, inflexible human-resources policies that hinder a company's ability to adapt to the Chinese employment market can be a difficulty. Because of the well-publicized success of many Chinese companies, the employment advantages and prestige of working for a multinational enterprise are less attractive to local engineers and scientists than in the past. Multinationals' executives noted that local companies were sometimes more flexible than their own companies, offering attractive packages including housing loans and cars to persuade valuable employees to join them. Fourth, most multinationals' R&D centers in China depend a great deal on the use of Chinese scientists and engineers returning from overseas (the *haigui,* or "sea turtles," that we mentioned in chapter 1). Integrating returnees with local hires can be a serious challenge, as we noted above.

One European multinational, Europa (a pseudonym), finds it hard to hire senior people locally, so it is hiring large numbers of junior people. There are not many very senior people working in R&D in China, where R&D is still new, so by definition it is relatively difficult to find people with much local experience. Europa China also tries to attract returning Chinese scientists. Its US labs are a potential source, since 15–20 percent of Europa's employees in the United States are Chinese. Europa looks for people with both good ability and experience in applications development. It recognizes the importance of understanding the local market. Having R&D people with good abilities but little experience in China would be a disaster. And building competence usually takes about ten years.

Europa finds that Chinese researchers are very pragmatic and that they focus on getting results, the *what,* but sometimes lack the *how,* in terms of skils and competence. Today, many returning Chinese students are working in Europa's R&D centers in China, and they connect easily to experts around the world. Through the company's global network, the experts in different R&D centers can complement one another.

In contrast, Matco finds that the number of talented research people in China is growing rapidly. That is one of the reasons it has chosen to have one of its six global RD&I (R&D and Innovation) Centers in China. The company has learned that people need to be encouraged to show what they can do. People are eager to learn and amenable to adapting, and personal improvement and development are rapid. China's schools and universities also offer a lot of support for training of the workforce, and companies such as Matco can profit from that. Thus, in Matco's view, China has bright and well-educated R&D people, but the nature of the Chinese education system means that they are relatively limited in their knowledge and experience in their chosen fields. Further training and development in laboratory practices, safety, self-management, independent thinking, and teamwork are necessary, as is early exposure to international business.

The company we are calling EuroEng sees advantages in working with Chinese technical people and researchers: They are engaged, eager to learn, and highly capable of learning. The learning curve that EuroEng observes in China is much steeper than the learning curve it observes anywhere else, and Chinese technical people and researchers are much more pragmatic than those elsewhere—they are much more focused on getting a useful outcome out of a project. They are also focused on getting things done quickly—much more so than their foreign counterparts. The one thing that Chinese recruits have to acquire after joining EuroEng is the art of independent thinking. The Chinese way of learning, in their experience, is still very much influenced by Confucius and his value system: the teacher teaches, the student listens.

Not valuing local capabilities

Engineers and scientists from developed countries who have been assigned to China find it hard to accept that their Chinese counterparts can be highly capable. For that reason they are reluctant, at first, to approve of foreign adaptations to headquarters-generated products and processes. They are even more reluctant to accept that Chinese R&D employees have the capabilities necessary to develop products for the market in their company's headquarters country and for markets in other developed countries. This is a version of the Not Invented Here syndrome, sometimes arising from genuine concern that corporate standards of quality may be prejudiced.

A senior German R&D executive at a major German engineering-based company said that a critical consideration regarding whether China R&D centers will get global mandates is the mindset of headquarters scientists and executives. Chinese engineers are capable, but the incumbents in Germany will have to change their view of those capabilities. He also sees an advantage in the relative youth of Chinese engineers. In Germany the company's engineers are on average older and therefore are more experienced, but less acquainted with the thinking of the younger generation. To bring both advantages together is a challenge, but it seems likely to lead to successful results.

In a group discussion we had with twelve executives of multinational corporations in China, most of them professed aspirations for their Chinese R&D people to achieve senior corporate appointments. But when asked how many had promoted a Chinese executive to an executive position in their company's headquarters, none of them said they had yet done so. They cited many reasons for this, including the difficulty of attracting good scientists with managerial experience, the competition for talent throughout China, and their own relatively limited experience in doing R&D in China.

In contrast, Royal DSM (a Dutch global company active in health, nutrition, and materials) does a good job of building up the capabilities of and respect for Chinese engineers and scientists. DSM feels that this building up of trust is important, and it has limited the amount of expatriate managers in China to a much lower level. DSM continues to enhance the message that Chinese can innovate, can run the local business, and can reach senior positions in the company. It now has some Chinese scientists in corporate R&D at headquarters, and the CTO would like to increase that number, in part because of its aspirational impact.

Difficulty in understanding needs in countries with higher standards

Even if there are no attitudinal barriers, it can be genuinely hard for employees based in China to undertake work on products for more developed countries. It is always difficult for R&D and innovation personnel based in one country to understand the needs of another country, and it is harder to go "upstream" than to go "downstream." For example, Chinese employees accustomed to the typically lower or "good enough" standards in China find it difficult to understand the more exacting needs of customers in countries with higher incomes and higher standards, such as Germany.

Protecting domestic employment

Most senior managers at headquarters have some preference and pressure to protect domestic employment. This seems to be even more the case for employees in R&D and innovation. In comparison with employees in production operations, R&D employees have much more in common with the senior managers who make location decisions: they often work in the same locations and eat in the same cafeterias, and they may have attended the same universities. Another strong reason for caution about increasing the emphasis on China is the difficulty of moving an entire R&D operation to that country. It is not simply a question of individuals; it is a matter of their connections to the whole innovation ecosystem. People who have worked in the headquarters location for years have built up not only scientific knowledge but also knowledge of processes and routines inside the company; they also have built up connections with scientific and engineering leaders in their home country and in other developed countries.

This desire to protect domestic employment is particularly strong in most European companies, suffering from slow growth in their home markets. For this reason, there is psychological resistance to strengthening capabilities in emerging markets. One company whose corporate executives we interviewed is careful about the message it sends. It is building activities in China, but not reducing its R&D staff in the headquarters country. The CTO tries to make sure that he is not damaging domestic capabilities while building up new capabilities in different regions. He reserves a special budget for China. Another European company claims to be reducing some R&D activities at the corporate headquarters and, at the same time, offering employees the opportunity to move. In the past that was easy because the opportunities for expatriates were attractive, but those opportunities are much less attractive today.

But it is possible to move R&D to China. In 2012 one division of a British consumer-packaged-goods company had two Chinese people based in China and a team of seven in the UK. The company disbanded the R&D team in the UK and moved its members to other areas of the business, with the exception that one manager stayed in the UK in order to train people from China. One of the Chinese employees moved back to China, and the company then recruited more Chinese staff members in China. Was there resistance to the disbanding of the unit in the UK? Not really. There was more resistance from the rest of the company's R&D staff, who asked "Is this the first step in shutting down R&D in the UK?" Now part of the delivery team has also moved to China. One manager moved there from the UK, and five Chinese chemists have been recruited to work on formulation projects and project management.

It is easier for a growing business to move innovation activities to China than for a more stable business, as there is no need to reduce the head count at headquarters. When home country employment is not growing, it becomes very hard to motivate head office personnel to transfer to China or to help develop competencies in China. But, as we argue throughout this book, innovation involves not only scientific and technical capabilities but also deep connections with the local market and with the ecosystem of innovative ideas. Because China is a large and diverse market, multinationals must be present there to be exposed to all of the stimuli for innovation we have detailed in previous chapters.

Unwillingness to allocate resources to China

Some multinational parent companies have not yet found a way to put enough investment into their R&D activities in China. This is due in part to the economic problems Europe and the United States have faced since 2008, in part to insufficient strategic emphasis on the Chinese market, and in part to concerns about protection of brands and of intellectual property rights.

Fear of loss of intellectual property and core capabilities

In most companies, R&D and innovation are seen as more central than other activities to the company's special capabilities. Because of China's reputation for rapid imitation and outright theft of intellectual property, there is fear of losing intellectual property and core capabilities if R&D and innovation activities are set up in China, or if China-based R&D centers are fully integrated into global networks. This fear can be amplified by home-country government policies to protect intellectual property rights in particular industries, such as those considered strategic by home countries— for example, aerospace and defense. We will discuss this matter in more depth in chapter 7.

ENABLERS FOR BUILDING UP R&D AND INNOVATION IN CHINA

Despite the challenges that we have just discussed, there are many enablers for multinationals aiming to build up R&D and innovation in China. These include the following:

- bringing back Chinese scientists and engineers from abroad
- having well-thought-out policies for hiring and retention
- instilling creativity in the firm's culture
- simplifying and speeding up the innovation process
- maintaining a healthy linkage between headquarters and China
- connecting to Chinese universities and research institutes
- embedding R&D in the Chinese innovation ecosystem
- taking concerted measures to protect intellectual property rights

Bringing back Chinese scientists and engineers

Many highly talented Mandarin-speaking ethnic Chinese scientists and engineers have trained and worked in the United States or in the European Union. By hiring some of them (regardless of passport), a multinational corporation can rapidly build up its capabilities for innovation in China.[4] As mentioned in chapter 1, China has instituted "talents" programs to lure top Chinese scientists home with tax incentives and other privileges.[5]

We met a Chinese scientist, whom we shall call Dr. Li, who was hired by one of the largest European pharmaceutical companies in 2007 to set up its new R&D center in China from scratch. Dr. Li already had experience in building organizations from the ground up. He had been a founding director of the Chinese Academy of Sciences and of a European research institute in Shanghai. Dr. Li returned to China after a prestigious 20-year career as a medical scientist in Europe and the US. He became a member of the European pharmaceutical company's R&D executive team, reporting to its global president of R&D. He has been implementing the company's vision for R&D in China, which entails building an R&D center in Shanghai for the company's worldwide research in an important class of diseases, so that one day not only will medicines be made in China, but medicines will also be discovered by researchers in China. These medicines will then be used by the rest of the world as well as by the Chinese population. Dr. Li was able to develop the company's R&D operations surprisingly quickly—"China fast," in his words. The company now employs more than 400 people in Shanghai, having recruited a lot of home-grown talent and a large number of returnees. Its research capacity now stretches from initial discovery to late-stage development.

DSM has found top-level Chinese scientists very attractive, but has found that in order to recruit them it has to make sure that the projects it does in China are seen as important and that they contribute in building up its R&D competence there. In order to attract these Chinese scientists, DSM is developing technologies for long-term applications so that it will have in China not only a base of fundamental technology but also the supporting technology that will later lead to innovations.

Bringing back ethnic Chinese researchers from abroad also works at lower levels. Matco finds that ethnic Chinese who have studied in the West have a competitive edge over their "trained only in China" counterparts, not only in language skills, but also in self-confidence and motivation, and that they understand and appreciate Western ways and markets. Upon returning to China, they are well placed to lead the development of China as an equal partner in global industrial research and business. Matco has had good experience in recruiting young Chinese researchers studying at leading European universities for master's and PhD degrees and has generally found that such recruits progress faster in their careers.

Policies for hiring and retention

Multinational corporations with enlightened policies for hiring and retention have a better chance of keeping good R&D employees. Our research suggests that Chinese are attracted to the R&D operations of MNCs by the opportunity to learn and develop, the prospect of being given greater responsibility, and the offer of foreign placements. (Of course, salaries and conditions of employment have to be equal to those of competitors.) Although these three factors apply in all countries, potential R&D employees in China have higher expectations for the first two, and a greater hunger for the third, than their counterparts elsewhere. Thus, MNCs have to place greater emphasis on creating an attractive research culture and on providing opportunities for important work. The head of Johnson & Johnson's China R&D told us that, whereas getting technical competence is easy, he looks to hire people who have passion.

The MNC we have called Europa finds that Chinese are keen to work for the company, but that they also want to move on (to other firms, often Chinese) if they see opportunities. Europa hires a lot of people in China but also loses some, which seems to be typical for any company doing business in China. It is important that a multinational have a long-term strategic perspective on building local talent, hiring and developing local people and ensuring that they have opportunities to prepare for running the business in the future. Today, Europa finds that it has not yet achieved the right balance, and that it is particularly difficult to attract local people to top positions. When the company succeeds in engaging real experts—competent people with 20 years' experience in a particular field—it has to make exceptional efforts to nurture them and provide opportunities for growth and recognition.

Bosch finds that to hire successfully is always a challenge in China, but the company benefits from its strong reputation as an employer and from its widespread name recognition. Someone whose résumé includes a stint with Bosch is likely to discover that his or her market value increases. After as short a time as two years with Bosch, some people quit and join another company. But Bosch has done well at retention. In its engineering department, the turnover rate has been below 5 percent every year since 2004—much lower than the turnover rate in the general market for white-collar professionals, which exceeds 10 percent.

Bosch attributes its success in retaining employees to its leadership and to the employment package it offers. At Bosch China, members of the R&D staff can work on significant engineering projects and make use of their capabilities, rather than "being just a postman" who simply passes on messages about problems. Bosch China creates and releases software and other products locally, so people have a sense of ownership. For example, its automotive products factory in Suzhou includes a very advanced, highly automated and integrated manufacturing operation, which is regarded as state-of-the-art and as a pioneering operation of its kind in China. Working on new technologies for such a plant is highly stimulating for a young engineer. Also, Bosch invests heavily in R&D infrastructure in China—for example, its world-class winter and summer vehicle-testing centers. This infrastructure provides an attractive environment for its engineers.

Bosch also offers different paths for development. Because management positions are by nature limited, Bosch has both management career paths and technical specialist paths. Bosch China also sends people to Germany to give them more international exposure. On top of that, the company holds Innovation Day events and gives members of its R&D staff recognition and rewards for filing patents.

Matco recognized the need to recruit and develop young Chinese talent early in its investment planning for China. Even before the decision to build the new lab in China was made, a number of young Chinese were recruited as "industrial postdocs" to work in Matco's laboratories in the UK. Six "talents" were recruited to these positions from leading Chinese universities (notably Tsinghua and Fudan). They spent two years in Europe gaining experience in industrial research and in international teamwork. Matco subsequently hired all six to form the vanguard of the new lab it opened in late 2007.

Another European company recognized the value of delivering international training and development experience and, in 2006, inaugurated a "China College" that recruited a number of "high-flying" graduates from select Chinese universities. After these graduates had been trainedfor 6–12 months, they were sent to the company's home country to work for 18–24 months before being assigned to management positions in China.

A very large energy multinational, which we will call Globular, considers that it is doing well in retaining its R&D personnel, but knows that it should not be complacent and therefore devotes continuous attention to retention. In addition to salary and other components of the employment package, Globular takes into account the special fields of ability of the people it has hired. They are not fresh undergraduates, as in many other companies, but people with PhDs, typically with young families. Globular pays special attention to the particular interests and career needs of such people. In addition, Globular China strives for fairness, transparency, and consistency in in its human-resources policy.

One German company still has many expatriates working in R&D in China (about 25 percent of the R&D employees in the company's China facilities), and doesn't expect that percentage to change significantly, perhaps dropping to 20 percent. Other German companies are talking about the same numbers. But not necessarily all the leaders of its R&D facilities are expatriates—the company is localizing leadership positions. Some Chinese worry about reporting to a Chinese manager, thinking that they would learn more from a German. Having some German staff members report to Chinese will, they believe, be less problematic than having Chinese report to Chinese. And the criteria for promotion are also more transparent in the German company. Some employees

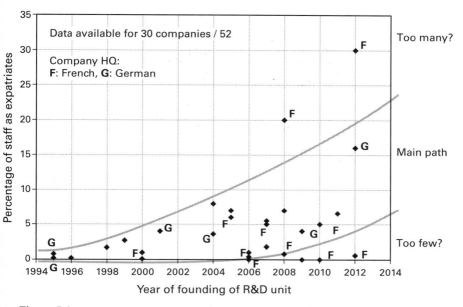

Figure 5.1
Expatriates as percentage of staff.
Source: Dominique Jolly

come from state-owned enterprises and say they left because they did not have the connections (*guanxi*) to progress. They prefer to have a career opportunity with this foreign company, in which success is based on competency and not on *guanxi*.

The Chinese share of a multinational corporation's R&D staff generally increases the longer the corporation has had R&D operations in China. This is evidenced by the data we collected from thirty primarily French and German companies: the older centers on the left side of figure 5.1 have lower percentages of expatriates.

As firms become more deeply implanted in China, they recognize the value of hiring local people for R&D, and they become more experienced at succeeding in both hiring and retention.

Instilling creativity

We have already mentioned the common view in the West and in China that Chinese researchers and engineers lag behind Western ones in creativity. In addition, as "Europa" has found, China lacks a tradition of research *per se*—that is, of knowledge for the sake of knowledge. Chinese businesspeople are, as a generalization, more oriented toward bringing something to the market, rather than taking the time to develop a genuine innovation. This engenders the criticism that in China there is too much focus on action. Europa has learned to work with this focus on action. The company has found that it can't afford to wait for a new development to be 100 percent certain before bringing it to the market. In China, as we saw in chapters 2 and 3, companies believe that 98 percent or 95 percent is good enough, and they have a tendency to launch quickly and then learn from the market exactly what is expected.

Thus, despite the beneficial orientation toward action, a big innovation challenge for multinationals is how to get their Chinese R&D employees to be creative. A representative of one Western company told us that, indeed, some Chinese engineers are more inclined to follow than to create, but that this can be changed by on-the-job training, as Chinese engineers learn quickly and can become very open minded. Another company found that its Hong Kong–educated researchers were more open and creative than its mainland-educated Chinese researchers, but that after a year on the job, in the open atmosphere and style of a Western company, the mainland Chinese researchers adapted to the new way of working.

A Western consultant in China told us that, whereas in the Netherlands it was common for researchers to generate creative ideas by arguing with the boss and with one another, he had found that he could not get Chinese researchers to argue in the same way. There he had to get the boss out of the room, create a group small enough to be manageable, and make sure that the people in the group trusted one another. Another approach that has been tried in China is to have eight people "brainstorm" individually, then meet in pairs to combine their ideas, and then all eight to build on the pairs' results.

Simplifying and speeding up the innovation process

Again and again we heard that Western companies should simplify and speed up the innovation processes that they use in China. For example, IBM China told us that it still needs to get buy-in from the rest of the company before proceeding with an innovation project. Often the review process slows IBM China down relative to local companies. IBM is seeking to come up with a systematic way to let its local unit in China innovate without internally imposed hindrances. Similarly, Nestlé finds that many local competitors are innovative and fast, and Nestlé has to look for ways to compete in China that differ from the way it operates in other parts of the world.

One of our studies focused on innovation speed in China. It was based on a cross-industry qualitative study of 12 selected Western MNCs in Shanghai, supported by extensive interviews with 36 innovation managers, R&D managers, and business managers.[6] We also conducted an in-depth study comparing the time required for innovation processes by "Europa" in China and "Sinco" (a small Chinese manufacturer acquired by Europa in 2008) and by "Chinaco" (a large Chinese competitor). We found that the new-product innovation processes of both Chinaco and Sinco (before its acquisition by Europa) averaged 16 months, and that Europa's process in China averaged 32 months. After Europa fully integrated Sinco, the revised time for the Europa-Sinco process was 27 months. Europa had learned from the acquisition to accelerate its innovation process, though not to the same extent. We recognize, of course that the longer innovation processes of multinationals often yield better results and reduce risks. A company's global reputation might be harmed by the hasty launch of a flawed product. But in China speed is the primary concern in nearly all aspects of business, and Chinese innovation behavior merits close study by multinationals seeking to increase speed.

Probably the most significant change that some multinationals make is to move from sequential steps in the innovation process to parallel steps. Telescoping the process increases the risk of error, but if careful attention is paid to re-thinking and re-engineering each of the steps, and to the protocols for handoff between steps, time can be saved and costly delays can be reduced. In keeping with the recommendations of specialist design companies such as IDEO, multinationals are recognizing the value of rapid prototyping and "failing fast." Because of the size of the Chinese market, there are ways to test a product in a contained region without risking an entire business. And the fast growth of Chinese markets means that the consequences of mistakes can be more easily made up and forgotten than would be the case in longer-established markets.

Linkage between headquarters and China

Maintaining a healthy linkage between the R&D and innovation organizations in the headquarters and in China is essential for developing China's role in a company's global innovation initiatives.[7] Aspects of a healthy linkage include the following practices:

- The headquarters executive to whom the China innovation organization reports is committed to developing the role of China.
- The executive in China is senior enough and capable enough to have the confidence of headquarters.
- Company-wide processes are in place for the effective engagement of China-based executives in global R&D networks and decisions.
- Headquarters has an understanding of and tolerance for China's value to the company's future growth, as well as the value of investing in China R&D.

Bosch acknowledges that this link between China and headquarters is currently weak. Its China R&D unit is entirely self-operating and self-organizing. But that unit's interactions beyond China should increase. Bosch is beginning to set up networks and linkages between its China and European innovation activities activities in the same divisions. For example, capable people from China R&D participate in global meetings to infect others with their understanding of the market.

Connecting via global assignments

Another way to connect with headquarters is to have Chinese researchers working there. Matco has few Chinese doing R&D jobs in Europe, mainly because if they are good they want to work in

China, where the opportunities are seen by them to be better, as China's status in the world has greatly increased in recent years. But Matco's global head of R&D told us that senior Chinese research executives are learning that, if they want to hold down a global job, they have to be prepared to move around the world. The "jade ceiling" that some Chinese researchers believe they face inside the multinationals is not always due to companies' policies.

Connecting via global meetings and visits

Global meetings with participants in China are one way for a corporation's headquarters to connect with China, as are visits by executives from headquarters. DSM has a Global R&D Leadership Team made up of country R&D directors and business-unit R&D directors. DSM's leader of China R&D is a member of that team, which has a monthly teleconference and three or four face-to-face meetings each year to discuss R&D strategy. The meetings are usually held in Amsterdam. The global R&D leaders also come to China two to four times a year. The supervisor of DSM's China R&D heads travels to China at least three times a year. Furthermore, the company's CEO and members of its management board visit China two or three times a year. Within DSM, China has obtained adequate attention at the corporate level, the business level, and the level of China R&D.

In contrast, one of the largest German companies struggles to integrate China into its global R&D effort. Its head of technology and innovation said:

Quite frankly, that is also something we are still working on. ... Ideally we would increase our traveling activity and bring people together more, more often. The management level will travel from time to time, but I am afraid that systematic face-to-face meetings at working level would incur prohibitive travel expenses that we often cannot afford. It depends a little on the general well-being of the company. In good times we find it easier to arrange face-to-face meetings than in economically difficult times, when we have to find other ways. What is essential for our type of activity is to have a global alignment of technology roadmaps. We have many technology fields; we expect each technology field leader to come up with a roadmap that is basically a guide for all research groups across the world. And aligning the team of research group leaders on this one and only global technology roadmap is a very useful exercise.

At DSM the linkage was strong except for the lack of a China person among DSM's 24 corporate-level scientists. This changed in 2015, when two scientists were appointed to DSM's most senior R&D levels—corporate positions. DSM's CTO goes to China about every three months. He meets with the R&D research managers there, and has a lot of email contacts. But he is certainly not the only person from DSM who visits China. In material sciences, for many years DSM hires about six new employees in China per year and brings them to the Netherlands for three months of training. When they return to work in Shanghai, each of them knows how DSM works at headquarters, has a "science buddy" in the Netherlands, and knows people with whom he or she can consult. DSM would like to stimulate the exchange of people. "It makes them feel part of the large organization and that is very important," one senior corporate executive told us. He continued: "This is a deliberate aspect of DSM's philosophy. Put it this way: if you are in a distant location from headquarters (such as China), the tendency to feel disconnected from the main community is very high, and there is a trust level you have to build up, and it works much better if you have exchange of people. R&D people in China also talk to other countries directly. If you are in a distant location then there is a tendency to worry whether you are taken seriously. So bringing people here improves that issue and trust. It also encourages them to respect secrecy."

DSM's corporate scientists are connected to the business, and they have broader scope. Roughly 10 percent of DSM's R&D spending is on long-term R&D. Although this is still connected to DSM's business interests, it is more fundamental, more concerned with developing platforms rather than individual products, and funded by corporate headquarters. For instance, DSM develops new biotechnologies that can have multiple applications in various business fields. DSM has three research councils. One is the Strategic R&D Council, on which business groups are represented. The Strategic R&D Council allocates the money DSM spends on R&D and articulates larger themes, such as with which external parties to collaborate and how to start a large consortium. On the Strategic R&D Council, the vice-presidents of business groups represent

China's interests. (Some of them may be located there, but so far none of them is a Chinese national.) The Science Council is made up of DSM's corporate scientists, who look at the content of the research done (the specific project topics, not just the strategy), but then go a level deeper. Since 2015, one Chinese scientist has been a member of that group. In the R&D Resource Council, DSM looks at the "people issues," such as what kind of talent is needed, how DSM can develop such people rapidly, and how people can be exchanged among China, the United States, and Europe. The R&D Resource Council includes a China representative, an expatriate Westerner living in China. The CTO, who serves as chairman of all three councils, reserves a special budget for collaborations among business groups.

Relocating a business unit's headquarters

Philips has found that one way to connect R&D in China to headquarters is to move the headquarters of a global business to China. Some of Philips' businesses, such as the retrofit LED lamps business, are now run from Shanghai, as a big part of the market is in China, as is the supply chain. All of the key managers of that business are now in Shanghai in order to be close to the retrofit market and its related ecosystem.

Philips does a lot to develop OEM suppliers in Asia for the global LED lamp market. Philips shifted the entire management team of that product category to Shanghai around 2009. There was considerable pressure to make the move and to give the management team sufficient autonomy. So far the effect of that move on Philips' European R&D organization has been more a change in mindset than a restructuring. The difference is that the European teams now work with a remote team headquartered in China. They have to interact daily, so there is a lot of travel, there are a lot of teleconferences, and there are short-term assignments for up to half a year.

The other three enablers

In addition to the five enablers of MNC innovation we have discussed above, there are three others which are important for MNCs to understand and manage. In chapter 6 we will discuss the sixth and seventh enablers: connecting to Chinese universities; and embedding R&D in the Chinese innovation ecosystem. In chapter 7 we will discuss the eighth enabler: protecting intellectual property rights.

WINNING BY REVERSING

We have discussed many ways in which multinational corporations can improve their innovation activities in China to achieve greater success there. But the ultimate winning strategy is to take innovation from China back to the rest of the world by means of the elusive but much sought after "reverse innovation."[8] The best-known example is a portable ultrasound machine that was developed in 2012 by General Electric's Medical Systems subsidiary in Wuxi for the Chinese market and was later marketed in the United States. This GE example of a product from a developing country being transferred effectively to a developed country is well documented, though often considered to be an exception.[9] But in our research we were surprised to find many other examples. Strictly speaking, "reverse innovation" applies only when a product created in a developing country is sold in a developed country, but we will include examples of products developed in China that were sold into other developing economies, as both phenomena run counter to the conventional wisdom about the location of innovativeness.

WHY REVERSE INNOVATION FROM CHINA IS HARD

Reverse innovation from a developing country to a developed country is, *per se*, difficult. For example, DSM finds that its applications in China generally don't result in reverse innovation, because the Chinese market wants lower quality and less sophistication than in their developed markets. In DSM's view, China customers' requirements are very different from the expectations of Western customers. Products with 70 percent functionality and quality can meet local demands, whereas companies in the United States and in Europe are always pursuing a 100 percent quality standard. Because of Chinese consumers' lower spending power, customers are more likely to buy the lower-cost products instead of the expensive "right" ones. Local companies make only "good enough" products for the market; hence DSM also focuses on this approach in China, using incremental innovation to achieve the right price-value combination. Many Western executives in China have told us that Chinese engineers and scientists are very capable up to a certain level, particularly at cost and process innovation. This is their mindset, but they have limited value-based thinking and limited creativity. But this kind of cost and process innovation is what Chinese scientists working in multinationals can add to the latter's capabilities. If products succeed in China, they can probably succeed in India or another large developing country, but perhaps not in the West. At present, only the first steps of reverse innovation from China are under way within many Western companies.

CHINA'S SPECIAL CHARACTERISTICS THAT HELP REVERSE INNOVATION

Reverse innovation from China happens most easily when a product is developed to meet some of China's special characteristics, and those characteristics also happen to apply in some other countries—whether developed or developing. Typically, China needs cheaper, simpler products. Reverse innovation into developed markets usually looks for segments that require lower price or lower functionality, some of which requirements may not have been evident before, as was the case with General Electric's portable ultrasound machine. So this form of reverse innovation is also what we called in chapter 2 "non-customer innovation." At its Suzhou R&D facility, set up in 2010, Philips is developing CT, MRI, and x-ray systems. Even if some of these products are developed primarily for the Chinese market, they may be sold outside China first. That is because these "fit for purpose" products may suit emerging segments in the developed world immediately, while it takes more time and effort to get the needed certification in China.[10]

Another example of China's "good enough" products succeeding in other markets is that of the Chevrolet Sail "supermini" car, developed by Shanghai General Motors, a joint venture of General Motors and SAIC Motors. The latest model, designed and engineered at Shanghai GM's Pan-Asia Technical Automotive Center, is exported to India, to Latin America, to North Africa, and to the Middle East.[11]

Akzo Nobel responds to China's needs for lower-cost products, and some of its products can be "reversed out." Akzo Nobel recognizes that China is now much more than just a high-growth market. China is becoming an exporter of innovative products to the rest of the world. For example, in 2010 Akzo Nobel innovated a low-cost powder coating for buildings. Normally such coatings are made of fluorocarbons that can last 15–25 years, but these are too expensive for China. In response to the cost pressures, Akzo Nobel decided to re-design its resin system to achieve the same effectiveness with substantially reduced cost. Its cost-competitive product has now become very attractive to mature markets.

Innovations from China also can add functionality and serve previously unmet needs in developed countries. Philips' rechargeable LED reading light, which we described earlier, is an example of such added functionality—in this case, that of not disturbing other people nearby. And, as we mentioned in an earlier chapter, other consumer products that Philips developed in China are now being sold around the world.

One big concern that companies have about products that are "reversible" into developed markets is that they may cannibalize their existing business there. The evidence on this so far (admittedly anecdotal) is that this may in fact help companies fend off low-cost competitors from outside their home markets, who would take away their market share anyway. Another benefit is that the "reversed" product will end up satisfying a segment of the market that had hitherto not been able to afford it, thus creating new demand. This is the case with GE's portable ultrasound machines, which enable city doctors to perform diagnoses in remote locations. Another example is provided by a certain European company's food-processing machinery. The company's products are renowned for their quality, long life, and suitability for complex tasks in processing grains and other foods, but those qualities were less important in China than in Europe and the United States. So the company, through acquisitions, developed "good enough" products designed with only the features that were required to suit the Chinese customers' needs. Contrary to its fears, the company found that these products, rather than cannibalize its markets, have created two benefits. One is that customers outside China find the lower-feature equipment suitable for processing animal feed. The second is that some of the company's Chinese customers, seeking to upgrade and differentiate themselves in the Chinese market and aware of the company's quality standards, have purchased the company's premium machines in order to improve the quality of their products.

CHINA AS A LEAD MARKET FOR REVERSE INNOVATION

We identified five reasons why reverse innovation can happens more easily in categories in which China is the lead market.

First, there may be more sophisticated demand in China. For example, because a lot of tea is drunk in China, Philips developed an electric tea-brewing device for China, which it now sells successfully in Europe.

Second, China's internal diversity and its external differences from the rest of the world create opportunities. Nestlé recognizes and uses the strength of the fabled cuisine and culinary art of China, especially in the area of *umami* or *xian* taste. For example, Chinese cooks are expert in cooking chicken soup in such a way as to develop a rich and meaty *xian* taste. The same taste component is also present naturally in tomatoes and in other vegetables. Understanding the science of the *xian* taste, Nestlé R&D China developed a way to capture the *xian* taste in fresh vegetables and created innovative products for other geographic regions. Its Maggi brand of soups and seasonings is one example of "China innovation" deployed to markets in India, Indonesia, and the Philippines.

Third, China is a very fertile ground for innovation because competition is fierce there. Seeking differentiation in the crowded and competitive Chinese market, Nestlé R&D China developed an innovative peelable banana-shaped ice cream product that meets the health requirements of the Nestlé Nutritional Foundation, contains no artificial colorings, and is low in fat and sugar. That innovation, developed in China, was successfully launched in Thailand (under the name Eskimo Monkey) and in several other markets.

Fourth, China may lead the world in the need for a solution. China suffers more from air pollution than any other country. There is a huge demand for air purifiers in cars, in homes, and in offices. Philips' China lab developed an air purifier for cars. This device was developed entirely in China and is now sold around the world. Chinese citizens are so aware of pollution that many of them associate any odor with toxicity, so in 2004 Akzo Nobel developed a paint called Odorless Dulux to cater to their demands. This customer-driven innovation, which was quite successful, has been extended to other Asian countries. Akzo Nobel went further: Recognizing the problem caused by formaldehyde released by furniture, it developed an interior wall paint that absorbs and neutralizes formaldehyde.

Fifth, China may simply be the world's biggest market for a product. China is now by far the world's largest market for new automobiles, with annual sales about 50 percent greater than in the United States. BMW has recognized a special characteristic of China resulting from this: The Chinese spend more time in traffic jams than people anywhere else in the world. Furthermore, most Chinese are less interested in the driving characteristics of a car than in having a comfortable "mobile living room" (our view, not necessarily that of BMW). Indeed, Li Shufu (the founder of the Chinese automaker Geely, which acquired Volvo in 2010) once remarked that "a car is just a sofa with four wheels." Therefore, BMW has made China a major center for the development of in-car entertainment systems. Innovations made at BMW China have been picked up in other markets, and BMW has moved its software team for integrating devices into cars to China.

BMW China is also considering being the Asia hub for some other applications. BMW expects to do more, such as in services. Examples include "Drive Now, Park Now, Charge Now," using an iPad to check the availability of rental cars in some cities, and

booking a parking space in advance. BMW China is also conducting R&D on roaming billing and security and on the renting out of
home parking spaces. BMW could do this kind of experimenting
and learning in Munich, which has a population of 1.3 million,
whereas if it brings this work to Shanghai it can experiment on
a population of 23 million. It is in the large metropolises of
China that BMW can get exposure to novel demands and generate
new ideas.

THE ORGANIZATIONAL REQUIREMENTS FOR REVERSE INNOVATION

Sharing innovations across borders poses many organizational
challenges.[12] These challenges are even greater where China is concerned, because of its great geographic, cultural, political, and other differences from the Western countries in which multinational
corporations are headquartered. Typically, multinationals make no
special organizational effort to transfer innovations out of China.
Instead, they leave that responsibility to the individual business
units, or to the exchanges that occur sporadically as a result of
visits and other forms of communication. This is not enough. At a
minimum, each business unit needs to have people who are looking
at what can be done for, and transferred to, the rest of the world.
Headquarters also need to be actively aware that China can be a
source of reverse innovation. This means not just looking for possible transfers of innovations already made in China. The bigger
potential reward comes from creating innovation projects in China
that have reverse innovation in mind from the beginning. That
means taking a global strategic perspective and ensuring that a
China project team has both inputs from global units and access to
their resources.[13]

CONCLUSION AND RECOMMENDATIONS

As we showed in the previous chapter, multinational corporations
clearly benefit from the *customer* element of the Four Cs framework in China. They face problems in countering the *culture* dimension of the model, and that requires careful attention to their

local R&D strategy and organization. Yet by undertaking R&D in China they can benefit from China's growing market leadership to enhance their capabilities for business beyond China. We recommend that foreign multinationals think systematically about how their strategic objectives in China should be changing. They need to be sure that they align their R&D organization—and, more important, their innovation activities—with the depth of their commitment, using the enablers and processes we have described. Because China is becoming a lead market, developing new *capabilities* in China can pay off with reverse innovations for a company's global business, and generate a great deal of *cash* for investment in further innovation.

6

OPEN INNOVATION IN CHINA

(with Yongqin Zeng)

Having addressed how both Chinese and foreign companies innovate in China, we turn now to "open innovation" (OI),[1] the most progressive kind of innovation in the West, which is being readily adopted in China. Because "open innovation" means interacting with external players, the many special characteristics of these players in China require very specific OI strategies there. OI in China means taking advantage of the many actors in the Chinese innovation ecosystem described in this book: local and foreign companies, government agencies, universities, institutes, consulting companies, and firms' suppliers and customers.[2]

As we argue throughout this book, new ideas with global market implications are continually arising in China. Firms open to tapping local knowledge can gain great advantage by recognizing new opportunities for their international business. In terms of our Four Cs, OI particularly makes use of China's *capabilities* and of elements of what we have called *culture*, and to a lesser extent of *customers*. However, quite a few companies are also integrating *customers* into open innovation.

To research this topic, we conducted detailed interviews with representatives of five innovation-intensive Chinese companies, of twelve foreign multinational companies in various sectors, of two major Chinese universities, of China's Ministry of Education and Ministry of Science and Technology, the Science and Technology Committee of the Shanghai Municipal Government, and the China Academy of Sciences. We also obtained valuable advice from a

leading innovation consulting company and from a Chinese original design manufacturer (ODM).[3]

APPROACHES TO OPEN INNOVATION IN CHINA

China adopted an open-door policy toward technology after 1979
by necessity and it has enjoyed the benefits. Today, the Chinese
government is ambitious in its mission of changing the image of
"made in China" toward "innovated in China," and open innovation has an important role. In May 2015 it announced an ambitious ten-year national plan, "Made in China 2025," to transform
China into a world manufacturing power and OI will be an important element of this plan.[4]

Chinese companies had strong reasons to engage in open innovation. They suffered from many constraints to developing technologies internally, such as lack of equity capital, access to risk
finance, and weaknesses in their internal knowledge base and organizational capabilities.[5] While their innovative ability has evolved
quickly from copying to incremental innovation, as we saw in
chapter 2, most Chinese firms have had to look outside for the
technologies needed. Smaller firms have a stronger need to look
outside for technologies than larger firms, which have deeper
resources.

By contrast, multinational corporations with R&D operations
in China are usually not so constrained by resources. GE, for example, invests $200 million per year in R&D in China, and open
innovation accounts for about 15–20 percent of the total.[6]

There are three common approaches to open innovation in
China and these are used by most of the companies we interviewed, both Chinese and multinational. They involve collaboration with universities and research institutes, with suppliers or
customers in the business value chain, and (through acquisition
or spin-out of innovative technologies) with technical providers
or buyers.

Although the concepts of open innovation used in China are
similar to those in Europe and the United States, we found that
practices in China differed because of variations in culture,

markets, institutions, and technological development, which influence the roles of the different stakeholders in the local ecosystem.

COLLABORATION WITH UNIVERSITIES AND RESEARCH INSTITUTES

Collaboration with academia is perhaps the most common approach to open innovation around the world. Nevertheless, in China it has played very different roles for MNCs and for local companies as China has matured. The use of academic research institutions by Chinese companies appears to be related to the stages of development of a company's innovations and the competitive pressures it faces. A case study of a Chinese automation company concluded that at the stage of basic research a company's better choice is to seek universities and research institutes as collaborative partners, as they usually have sufficient researchers and equipment to conduct laboratory experiments and tests, which the firm lacks. At the second stage, application development, companies may do better to focus on related companies in the same industry, as well as users, as they are more experienced in engineering and use of technology and are more able to help companies to improve their technologies and relevant standards. At the third stage, when firms face international competition, it is better for them to resort to cooperation and support from the government.[7]

As we discussed in the earlier chapters, Chinese firms have benefited greatly from the government-supported innovation ecosystem in their earlier growth, not only when they face international competition. Open innovation is thriving among multinational corporations and larger local companies in China: 95 percent of the interviewed companies have direct collaboration projects with Chinese academic institutions. There are two major forms of collaboration: project-based collaborations to address specific research topics and joint innovation collaboration frameworks with multiple-year agreements, which give flexibility on the topics to be defined by both sides. Examples of the latter are Huawei's collaboration with Jiaotong University and Philips' with Southeast University and Zhejiang University.

Many objectives of open innovation in China are similar to those of multinational corporations in Europe and the United States. Among them are the following:

- to gain extended or complementary innovation resources, ranging from research exploration and concept development to prototypes
- to obtain third-party views on new ideas and technology validations, e.g., clinical research and regulation
- to leverage the company's heavy investment in facilities for measurement and validation through outward OI
- to increase brand awareness through OI with universities, and often to develop talent by teaming up with the firm's human-resources department

The following aspects of open innovation play more important roles for firms operating in China:

- Chinese firms rely more often on academia to do their research and development than do Western companies. Chinese academia has acted in recent years as a primary source of R&D for industry in China, particularly for Chinese companies that were new to innovation. This role is less important today, as more Chinese companies have established their own R&D centers; also, widening the scope of open innovation is no longer a big challenge. Further, there are OEM and ODM companies available to undertake such work. But many smaller firms still rely on outside sources for technology.
- Foreign firms often commence their R&D effort in China by setting up joint labs with Chinese academia and involving scientists from headquarters. This is common among MNCs; examples include Philips, BASF, Unilever, and DSM.
- In China, becoming part of the innovation ecosystem provides a bridge to understanding the country's innovation priorities. Chinese academia has played an essential role in articulating the country's innovation strategy by providing advice on the five-year plans, government R&D policies, and standards. Having good connections to these influential organizations is valuable

in its own right for obtaining ideas from outside the corporation, but it provides the additional benefit of better understanding government priorities; MNCs may even exert some influence in setting standards. Philips, for example, is a member of the Chinese standardization board for lighting. A related benefit is the opportunity to connect through R&D to the mainstream investment priorities that are supported by the government and thus gain early awareness of markets and sectors that will become growth opportunities.

A recent strategic shift, which we emphasized in chapter 1, is that the larger Chinese companies are now setting up R&D centers in Europe and North America. Huawei is well along this road, with 14 foreign R&D centers.[8] A consequence is that local Chinese academics are keen to collaborate with multinational corporations, as they see some of their local clients needing them less. We have argued that MNCs must be more open to innovations arising in China. A few of them have indeed embraced the concept of China as a source of knowledge for global business and are collaborating with world-class Chinese academics on advanced topics (e.g., materials technologies and drug discovery). But MNCs that are still behind the wave can benefit greatly from the research of local institutions, which are often close to the forefront of their fields. Although MNCs have been less active in OI in China than Chinese private companies, they are more capable of overcoming the constraints to OI than are local firms or state-owned enterprises.[9]

The common obstacles encountered by the companies we interviewed were these:

- Mismatch between expectations and delivered results, due to problems of confidence, trust, and competence.
- Poor communication, most often due to cultural differences and language barriers.
- Arrangements for ownership of intellectual property rights. Multinationals are accustomed to obtaining IP rights for projects funded by them, whereas some Chinese universities insist on sharing IP rights.

- Slow and complicated responses from either side, but mainly from the MNC side (owing to the slow approval process, complicated by multiple decision makers in their headquarters). In 50 percent of the interviewed MNCs, OI projects are decided by headquarters, and in a surprising 95 percent of them OI contracts must be approved by headquarters. As we saw in other chapters, many MNCs have not yet improved their internal processes sufficiently to be able to deal effectively with the speed of change in the Chinese market.

Nevertheless, the good practices among the interviewed companies provide a number of recommendations for conducting open innovation in China. They include the following:

- Select the right partners for the company's needs, instead of the best-known institutions (e.g., firms should prefer research institutions or companies that are known to be leading in their field, the leading team at a good university, or scientists who are rising stars. BASF, Philips, Procter & Gamble, the Wanhua Industrial Group, and General Electric have used this approach effectively. One example is Unilever's successful innovation project with two research institutes of the Chinese Academy of Sciences. Unilever had developed a technology for re-mineralizing teeth. By collaborating with the Shanghai Institute of Ceramics (which specializes in ceramic materials for repairing bones) and the Shanghai Institute of Microsystem and Information Technology (which has advanced measurement techniques), Unilever successfully commercialized the technology in its dental-care products.

- Develop and grow the teams from both sides together, with consistent and long-term cooperation. (BASF, Philips, and Wanhua have done this well.)

- Ensure that the collaboration has the best possible project management, with clear strategic objectives, established key performance indicators (KPIs), and regular communications.

- Provide for regular exchanges of staff members during cooperation, since knowledge and ideas move with people. (BASF and Philips are known for this.)

- Be prepared to be flexible on arrangements for IP rights. Aim for a win-win collaboration with sharing of benefits as well as costs, and respect the goals and values of the partner. Most of the MNCs recognize this.

- Empower the R&D entity in China with local decision-making power, as GE, Unilever, BASF, Dow Chemical, GSK, and Philips have done. This requires a conscious decision from headquarters and negotiations about the degree of freedom to act locally.

- Set a deadline to end a collaboration if it isn't working well, as Google and "MNC2" (a disguised name for one of the companies studied) have done. Make sure the collaboration agreement includes the conditions and provisions for a termination process, including rights to intellectual property developed.

BASF'S OPEN INNOVATION WITH CHINESE ACADEMIA

BASF's innovation in China is part of its global activity. It is intended not only for local use, but for global deployment. BASF is becoming a more open organization, and has instituted an overall strategy for open innovation. OI projects are embedded in various innovation activities, and BASF has a professional team to encourage OI and manage the platform for it. There is no fixed budget allocated to OI. Instead, OI is included in the company's overall innovation budget. OI topics are proposed by the local businesses and approved by BASF's global headquarters.

Objectives of BASF's open innovation in China

The objectives of BASF's open innovation work with Chinese academia are to address China's market needs with long-term partners, to incubate new technologies, to create new business models, and to develop R&D talent.

Projects are long-term in outlook, but with targets for the delivery of intermediate results. A project's performance is evaluated by two performance indicators: technical transfers and contribution to launching of new products. There is a flexible system for starting and stopping projects.

The development and organization of OI in BASF China

BASF started its innovation activities in China in 1997 by setting up a Scientific Liaison Office to work with local partners. At that time, open innovation requests for collaboration with locals came from headquarters in Germany, mainly regarding materials and chemistry, and the scientists working on the projects were mostly from BASF in Europe. The role of the local OI team, led by Lian Ma, was to identify the right academic partners and to help define the projects in more detail. The team helped with project definition, contract preparation, and management of the collaboration (e.g., communication, monitoring results, education, and building OI relationships and the network). This was the form of collaboration described above for companies in the early stages of presence in the Chinese market.

However, with the growth in the 2000s of the BASF business into a more entrenched phase in China, BASF established a Campus Asia Pacific in Shanghai in 2012. BASF's OI China team now directs OI efforts and helps the local innovation team to collaborate with academia and industry partners (suppliers and customers) within and outside China. The collaboration has been enriched, from the initial project-based approach, to a strategic partnership and staff exchange in which academic professors work in BASF China labs and the BASF scientists work in the labs of the university partners.

In 2013, BASF took a further step toward strengthening its connections in China's national and regional scientific communities by setting up a Network for Advanced Materials Open Research, led by Sébastien Garnier. An important strategic goal of this network is building up long-term and deep relationships in the universities. It will identify and nurture new ideas with universities to serve the global and the local needs of BASF's business and to identify, develop, and inspire talented people, including PhD candidates and postdocs. The partner institutions include Fudan University, Tsinghua University, the Beijing Institute of Technology, the Chinese Academy of Sciences' Institute of Applied Chemistry,[10] and the Beijing University of Chemical Technology and Engineering.

The Network for Advanced Materials Open Research is responsible for defining the portfolio of projects, the relations with partners, project management, coaching, execution tracking, and networking. The project leaders are expected to direct the technical content. In 2014, nine postdocs and PhD candidates were participating.

Lessons from BASF's open innovation in China

Worldwide, BASF carried out some 1,300 OI projects in 2012, 600 of them with academic partners or with startup companies. In China, BASF executed more than 200 OI projects with academic partners up to 2014, of which 27 were undertaken during 2014.

A good example of a successful OI project at BASF China is an international cross-discipline project on the topic of zeolite catalyst that began in 2007 and involved eight research groups, three of them from China. In the course of this project, 22 papers have been published and 28 patents filed. The project will continue with an orientation towards applications.

BASF's OI team has built up rich experience and competence in the management of open innovation and is now well recognized in the OI community. It has developed many long-lasting and strong partnerships with Chinese academia, and it has learned how best to manage the projects. According to Lian Ma, who built up the OI team for BASF China, it is important to understand the objectives of a mutually beneficial collaboration. Academia's goals are to publish good papers and enhance the inventors' reputations; BASF's goal is to obtain high-quality scientific results that can be transformed into products or processes. Also, trust is built up through consistent long-term relationships. Good project management is necessary (including timely communication and change management and regular reviews, to keep the team from shifting away from the targets), and the appropriate balance of supervision and freedom is critical. Lastly, BASF has developed flexibility toward the terms of arrangements for IP rights with Chinese partners, which also include sharing. According to Lian Ma, "there are few issues in collaboration if you do well the things mentioned above."

PHILIPS' OI COLLABORATION WITH CHINESE INSTITUTIONS

Philips has more than 20,000 R&D employees worldwide, 2,000 of them in China. The milestone of Philips' global transformation from a closed innovation approach to an OI approach came in 2006 with the opening to third parties of Philips Innovation Services, located on the Eindhoven High Tech Campus. Today, Philips considers OI one of the essential elements of an effective innovation system. The High Tech Campus hosts more than 125 companies and institutes and some 10,000 researchers, developers, and entrepreneurs working on advanced technologies and products.

Philips' OI strategy in China

Seeking to become an embedded participant in China's innovation ecosystem, Philips is collaborating with suppliers, customers, academia, startups, and incubators. Philips' innovation activities in China are well connected with its global innovation framework, and R&D done there is expected to deliver results for local and global markets. The role of Philips' OI team in China is to facilitate OI activities there by the following methods:

- developing local OI strategies and portfolios with its businesses
- facilitating and coaching OI activities, the sharing of best practices, and providing training
- developing shared approaches and an information platform
- enhancing interaction with participants in the local ecosystem through consistency in messages and personnel
- developing and managing strategic partnerships (e.g., with Zhejiang University and Tsinghua University)
- building up an OI mindset that values fast integration of external innovation opportunities.

Philips China has been working with Chinese academia since the early 1990s. Apart from project-based collaborations, Philips believes that long-term strategic collaboration with partners in open innovation leads to innovative ideas on selected topics, to co-development of competences and people, to the building of strong trust, to easy communication; and to increased awareness on both sides. A number of innovation centers have been set up in the past 20 years. Four of these are described below.

The Southeast-Philips Display Technical Center

In 1994, Philips set up its first long-term joint innovation center in China with Southeast University (SEU). The Southeast-Philips Display Technical Center, which focuses on display technologies, was expected to build up a leading research team and to serve as a talent-development center for Philips' local business activities. Under a 15-year contract, the center received constant annual funding and a one-time equipment investment from Philips. SEU provided offices, labs, and workers. Projects were defined and reviewed by the center's board twice a year, and the results were shared with both Philips and SEU.

Two of the reasons for the success of the center were its willingness to re-invent itself and its ability to change research topics. Initially the focus was on cathode-ray-tube displays, and many projects were completed (including one having to do with inner-yoke technologies and one concerned with shadow-mask-less tubes). But in the first half of the 2000s, Philips was shifting its attention away from display technologies and toward applications. The focus of the center was re-directed to LCD TV applications in cooperation with Philips Consumer Electronics. Strong contributions were made to the perception of LCD display artifacts (anomalies) and how to minimize them in a television application. This involved work on coding standards, multi-primary color displays, and 3D displays. The expertise that was built up in perception research formed the basis for another change of focus at the end of the 2000s.

Between 1994 and 2010, tens of projects were completed. Some results were applied to products, many papers were published, and some applications for patents were filed. More than 100 graduate students graduated from the center, and many of them went to work for Philips.

In 2010, Philips decided to move out of the display and television industry. Because of the experience that had been gained in perception research, and because of the innovative culture of the people working together at the center, Philips and SEU chose to shift the center's attention to perception research and to the development of LED lighting. Since that shift, Philips Research China and Lighting R&D teams have been playing a major role in this new collaboration. The innovation team at SEU has become a strong group in lighting perception research. More than ten projects have been completed and more than thirty papers published on such topics as flicker perception of LED light sources and glare disturbance from ceiling luminaires in offices, and the results have been applied in product designs.

The Brain Bridge program

The Brain Bridge (BB) program was established by Philips, Zhejiang University, and the Eindhoven Technical University in 2005. (Philips is a leader in innovation on the selected topics, the Eindhoven Technical University is the leading research team in the Netherlands on certain topics, and Zhejiang University is the leading Chinese research team connected to the local community.) It is a phased program, funded by Philips, with five years in each phase. The first phase, focused on consumer electronics, ended in 2010 and the second phase, concerned with perceptual lighting and medical informatics, was completed in 2015. A third five-year phase was scheduled to commence at the end of 2015.

All the projects are defined and reviewed by the BB program's board twice a year. The board consists of the top management of the three parties. The annual board meeting, whose purpose is to review and approve the strategic topics relevant to the mainstream business of Philips and the scientific and technical strengths of the two universities, alternates between China and the Netherlands.

The Center for Biomedical Imaging Research

There have been clinical research collaborations between more than twenty Chinese hospitals and teams from Philips Healthcare China, Philips Business R&D, and Philips Research China. Among the clinical sites, Tsinghua University and Huaxi Hospital are two illustrative examples of co-creation at clinical sites.

The Tsinghua Center for Biomedical Imaging Research (CBIR) was founded in 2010 as part of a 985 Key Discipline Program[11] at Tsinghua University. The CBIR had been using an advanced magnetic resonance imaging (MRI) system and a premium ultrasound machine from Philips in its research. Philips signed a Master Research Agreement with Tsinghua CBIR in 2011. Philips assigned several clinical research scientists to Tsinghua University to co-create new applications for MRI and ultrasound equipment to address liver and cardiovascular disease and other diseases that were highly prevalent in China. Philips' global MRI clinical scientists were involved where needed. Tens of publications and patents were generated by the joint effort between 2011 and 2015, and more valuable results are expected in the coming years.

Co-creating ultrasound liver therapies with Huaxi Hospital

China accounts for 60 percent of the world's liver cancer patients—an example of how China's *customer* differs from those in other countries, stimulating solutions specific to its needs. A team of scientists from Philips Research China and the company's ultrasound business in the United States have been working on ultrasound-based liver therapies with physicians from Huaxi Hospital at Sichuan University. Philips scientists worked side by side with the clinical physicians to understand the needs and to explore possible solutions. The joint effort has transferred to the ultrasound business several technologies that will be implemented in the next-generation ultrasound machine and has published several high-quality papers on liver diseases.

Experience gained from Philips' OI in China

By 2015, Philips China was collaborating with more than twenty universities or institutes and more than twenty health-care clinics. Important reasons for the success of Philips' OI program in China are the following (which have much in common with the recommendations from BASF):

- setting a clear OI strategy and innovation needs aligned with the business strategy

- strong connections to the company's innovation priorities
- having a competent team that can define and execute OI projects with the partners, including clear KPIs, timely communication and feedback, change management, and flexibility within clear boundaries
- creating long-term relations with partners and a win-win approach
- enhancing the connection with the national innovation community
- being part of the ecosystem for crowdsourcing and incubation.

Open innovation is becoming an integral part of Philips' approach to innovation projects. Each project proposal is expected to indicate if open innovation is needed according to the innovation strategy of each business, or as a result of a specific discussion with stakeholders. There is a working package template for each project to clearly define the OI work, if there is any. The regional OI teams are aligned with the global teams, while also addressing local needs.

COLLABORATION WITH SUPPLIERS AND CUSTOMERS

Because of the accelerated pace of change in many industries and markets, companies strive to understand their customers' changing needs at the earliest possible moment. Through feedback mechanisms, in-use field research, and rapid prototyping, customers are increasingly involved in the design of products. Co-creation of innovations entails greater reliance on all these outside sources for new ideas. It is not surprising that the special nature of China's *customers* stimulates a specific response, and this gives a competitive advantage to Chinese firms (as we have seen) but also to MNCs that are well attuned to the need. Similarly, with suppliers, firms have gone well beyond integrating suppliers into their operations planning by involving suppliers directly in the innovation process. No longer are suppliers simply asked to supply according to a company's specifications; now they are expected to develop innovations to the components or the materials—innovations that can then be integrated into their customers' products. Any company operating in China faces a large and rapidly growing market, with numbers of open-minded customers, as well as a well-populated supply chain. As we noted in chapter 3, Chinese customers are relatively forgiving and eager to try new products and services, and there are substantial differences across the country. Openness to ideas from suppliers and customers is an essential way to innovate for those differences. A previous study confirmed the benefits for Chinese firms of "learning by doing" collaborative innovation with suppliers and customers.[12]

Each of the companies we interviewed has direct collaborations with suppliers or customers, and often with both. Since industrial companies often sell to intermediary customers, rather than directly to the end users, many of them are also involving end users in open innovation. For example, DSM is actively working with processors of fish to develop materials suited for the fishing industry in China. Unilever has been working with suppliers of chemicals to develop sustainable new products. The Industrial and Commercial Bank of China, now the world's largest bank in assets and in market capitalization, has been collaborating with a local insurance company to develop new banking products. Philips does significant clinical research in China by having scientists work with doctors and patients in hospitals to explore how best to improve its imaging equipment (MRI, CT, and ultrasound machines). Likewise, Johnson & Johnson has set up a simulated clinical hospital environment in its Suzhou R&D Centre to observe how surgeons behave with patients, one result of which has been the already-mentioned commercialization of a silk-like synthetic suture that suits local surgeons' preferences. Another example of collaboration is the Wanhua Industrial Group, a leading Chinese polyurethanes company, which, after an accident, worked with its competitors to develop heat-proof insulating materials for buildings.

OBJECTIVES OF AND OBSTACLES TO COLLABORATING WITH SUPPLIERS AND CUSTOMERS ON OPEN INNOVATION IN CHINA

The main objectives of firms using collaborations with suppliers and customers in China are broadly similar to those of firms in

Europe and the United States. One of these objectives is to shorten time to market and thus improve the success rate of new businesses by connecting the partners throughout the value chain; another is to meet new needs of customers through early involvement. However, firms in China find that it is more important to deliver quick results. This involves taking advantage of being close to suppliers and customers in the value chain and teaming up with partners to develop comprehensive solutions when the value chain is complex, as Bosch did for the "smart home" and commercial buildings and as IBM did for intelligent systems in cities.

The common obstacles shared by the interviewed companies are the following:

- mismatch of expectations and deliverables between partners and the company
- the overhead costs of managing communications, which reduce motivation
- conflict of interests between the parties (for example, over intellectual property rights)
- leaks of knowledge to competition due to the immaturity of the market and the difficulties of retaining and managing scientists and engineers.

GOOD PRACTICES FOR INNOVATING WITH CUSTOMERS AND SUPPLIERS IN CHINA

Companies (especially Western ones) that are successful in China have developed good practices for conducting open innovation with customers and suppliers. On the basis of their experience, we recommend the following:

- Use project management to establish clear KPIs and regular communications.
- Use staff exchanges to strengthen transfer and retention of ideas.
- Make sure that suppliers are aware that open innovation will add overhead as a price for obtaining the benefits.
- Be prepared, in order to get a deal done, to give in on features that are valuable but not necessary.

- Carefully build long-term trust, which is important to a partnership.
- Remember that a non-disclosure agreement and a contract are necessary tools, but are not a sufficient guarantee of success in China.

Honeywell, DSM, and Philips illustrate good practice on collaboration with customers and suppliers, summarized in the case examples below.

Honeywell's open innovation and collaboration with suppliers

China is Honeywell International's most important market outside the United States. Its revenue in China was $2.4 billion in 2014. It has established four R&D centers in China, employing 2,000 technologists and scientists. The mission of Honeywell International's R&D in China includes the full range of objectives we found in mature MNCs as they have evolved from local cost-based R&D to knowledge-seeking R&D. Thus, Honeywell's R&D mission includes cost reduction, localization of the parent company's products for the Chinese market, local innovation for local needs ("East for East" in Honeywell terminology), as well as locally developed innovations for global markets. A corollary to this is taking advantage of local brain power, and Honeywell's open innovation in China is aimed at participating in the Chinese innovation ecosystem. For Honeywell (China) Co., Ltd. (henceforth referred to as Honeywell China), open innovation includes scouting (discussed below), cooperation with local suppliers and customers, and crowdsourcing, all directed toward maintaining market share in a highly competitive business environment.

Honeywell's strategy and organization for OI in China

Honeywell China has set up a team dedicated to business development and to open innovation. With offices in Shanghai and in Beijing, it is a cross-business group that reports on open innovation to the CEO of Honeywell China and works on both inward and outward licensing. The team explores opportunities for open innovation, for building up links to the technical pool inside Honeywell, and for licensing Honeywell's global technologies to non-competing partners in China. The team is also responsible for partnership management, government relations, and university collaborations. For example, open innovation provided a channel to get certification for an energy-saving project that helped Honeywell in bidding for business in China. It has also enabled Honeywell to explore opportunities to embed its technologies into "eco-city" projects—in which conservation of energy is an important criterion.

Honeywell's collaboration with suppliers

Honeywell has been actively collaborating with Chinese suppliers. Honeywell provides requirements, knowledge, and technical assistance to help Chinese suppliers to develop needed products and to generate their own intellectual property instead of directly sharing Honeywell's proprietary technologies. This simple approach has proved sustainable and has been accepted by Honeywell's Chinese partners and by the Chinese government. There is neither conflict over IP rights in the collaboration nor concern about technical leakage. Honeywell is happy to obtain components and products from Chinese suppliers and integrate them into its solutions, which are then sold to its customers.

For products incorporating mature technologies, which are not considered as "core" technology (essential to the company's competitive advantage), Honeywell has concluded that it can't develop products based on such technologies as effectively as the suppliers. In these cases it is willing to have the products supplied by an ODM or even to buy finished products for resale.

DSM's open innovation in China

In addition to approximately thirty locations where R&D is done, DSM has innovation centers in the Netherlands, in India, and in China (Shanghai). DSM's initial aim in China is to discover innovations that are "local for local," but it expects to develop "local-for-global" technologies in the future. In addition to working on product development and applications development, the innovation centers will support DSM's businesses by tracking market trends, by proactively responding to the needs of customers, and by interacting with the external knowledge infrastructure, such as partners in universities, scientific research institutes, and industry. DSM attempts to use the innovation ecosystem in China to enhance the ability of current products to meet customers' needs.

DSM China doesn't simply copy its innovation center in Europe, but rather emphasizes local autonomy. It has selected certain areas that fit the corporate strategy, including fish farming, duck feeding, and biogas. These were chosen as suitable industries for R&D in China for reasons of local needs and market potential.

DSM is active in open innovation with its Chinese suppliers and customers—currently more often with firms in its supply chain. Because Chinese customers are less patient than those in Europe, the processes of innovation require faster decision making.

Although its R&D center in Shanghai was opened quite recently (in 2012), DSM is beginning to see new product applications developed there through open innovation.

Philips' collaboration with customers and suppliers

China is a major supplier and customer base for Philips. Hence, in seeking the best vendors, Philips' R&D teams have actively reached out to the company's network of suppliers and customers, including those in China. Traditionally, Philips Automotive Lighting has had a dedicated China application lab to design auto lamps with the automotive luminaire companies, and to get feedback that can be used to develop new products. In the consumer area (for example, in the development of its electric tea-maker), Philips worked with potential consumers as well as with the specialized laboratories mentioned earlier.

In addition to the ongoing collaboration with suppliers and customers, a "Product Innovation Forum" was organized in 2013 as a systematic process for attracting outside innovations and selecting suitable ones for support. The forum includes Philips' business units in China, Philips Innovation Services (an in-house Philips service entity), Philips Research China, and Philips Intellectual Property & Standards (IP&S, a service that licenses out innovations from Philips' IP portfolio).

To identify and select candidates for open innovation, Philips uses a three-stage gate process (illustrated here in figure 6.1)

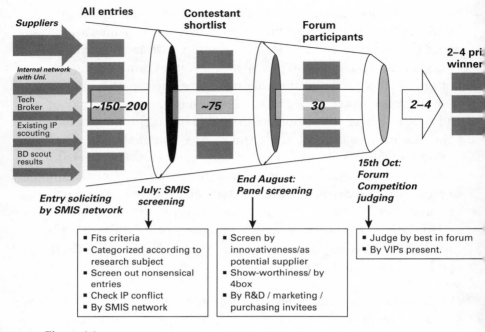

Figure 6.1
Philips' technology submission and selection process for open innovation in 2013.
Source: Philips NV

similar to those used by most companies for internal innovation. Ideas for identified needs are solicited and gathered from outside sources (suppliers, Philips' networks with universities, technology brokers, scouting), then screened to create a short list, then further winnowed in the Product Innovation Forum. The process reduces an initial set of 150–200 ideas down to two, three, or four.

Crowdsourcing within and outside the company
Crowdsourcing is another process that Philips uses in China to find ideas. Philips has an internal crowdsourcing process and started external crowdsourcing a few years ago.

Internal crowdsourcing—InnoTank
The internal crowdsourcing process has several interesting features. The InnoTank Fair provides a platform for Philips China

R&D community to share their creative ideas that are beyond current projects, to inspire an innovation culture, to leverage the brain power of the internal talent, and to enrich the innovation pipeline. This fair has been an annual event since 2011. An InnoTank activity has two phases. The first phase usually lasts for 3–4 months from the call for proposals until the final competition on the day of the InnoTank event. The second phase is concept validation with business owners on selected ideas, which leads to an official project kickoff.

InnoTank 2014 involved 45 teams with 165 engineers or scientists from 13 China R&D organizations and more than 400 visitors. The winners were selected by a jury that consisted of stakeholders from each organization. Three of the winning ideas were further validated with business owners.

External crowdsourcing

In Europe, Philips global has launched a crowdsourcing platform. called SimplyInnovate (http://www.simplyinnovate.philips.com/), that openly invites proposals for new ideas; it also holds a Philips Open Innovation Challenge every year. The Open Innovation Challenge is a contest in which people not employed by Philips can submit their ideas for solving real Philips challenges and can win a chance to pitch their idea during an online award show. Philips China researchers participate in SimplyInnovate and the Open Innovation Challenge, but a Chinese version has not been introduced yet.

HUAWEI'S COLLABORATION WITH CUSTOMERS

As we noted in chapter 2, Huawei is one of the most innovative companies in China. In 2014 it invested more than $7 billion—about 14.2 percent of its revenue—in R&D. Huawei has set up 28 joint innovation centers (JICs) with 14 leading telecom operators, including Vodafone, BT, and France Telecom. In China, Huawei has set up similar centers with China Mobile, China Telecom, and China Unicom. These joint units are quite important for Huawei's success, as the business models of IT (information technology) and

CT (communication technology) are converging and the operating companies need to test new ideas. Although different telecom operators have different needs, sometimes an innovation can be used in the whole sector. For example, the SingleRAN (radio access network)—a single base station that can cover 2G, 3G, and 4G— was implemented by Huawei for Vodafone in 2008 and is now used throughout the telecom sector. Although other suppliers are following suit, the Huawei technology has become the industry standard.

In implementing JICs, Huawei says, it is important to set up the arrangements to take account of many factors. First, two managers should be chosen, one from each partner. The collaborative agreement should be made by the CTO or even the CEO of the telco. Both sides invest. The innovation lab is sometimes located in the telco and sometimes in Huawei. Some telcos set up a demonstration room in which Huawei installs its equipment. The staff usually is about half Chinese and half foreigners and includes 20–40 people from Huawei, mostly engineers. The JICs are not established indefinitely, and a few are closed after a year or two.

In the memorandum of understanding with the customer, Huawei gives the customer a high priority for application of the innovation, but not exclusivity. According to a Huawei executive, "being just one year ahead of other operators is enough for them." Joint development also gives other advantages to the operator. For example, Vodafone makes more use of the Single RAN than any other company.

TECHNICAL SCOUTING

Technical scouting is a broad search for technologies from outside a company to identify technologies with potential value to the company's innovation process. A technology may be exploratory, conceptual, or ready for development. An exploratory technology may be further developed by the R&D center of the company or jointly with the technical provider, a conceptual technology may be taken over by the development team and brought closer to commercialization, and some technologies discovered by scouting may be almost ready for product development. Companies in China use scouting mainly for the purposes of stimulating innovation by combining technology intelligence with business potential assessment and facilitating the sourcing of external technologies. This is typical of China-based companies' greater focus on pragmatic, profitable innovation.

There is a huge pool of technical providers in China, but the needles have to be found in the haystack, so scouting has an important role. In general, Chinese companies have been doing well in technical scouting, and have tended to scout for conceptual or product-ready technologies. In recent years many Chinese companies have built up their own R&D teams and thus have become less dependent on technology scouting once they start to play a leading role in certain fields, as Huawei has done in wireless communications, Wanhua in polyurethanes, and BOE Display Tech Co. Ltd in display technologies. Several companies, including Haier, have chosen to obtain technologies more often from outside the company; for those companies, scouting remains important.

Several multinational corporations (among them Unilever, Procter & Gamble, BASF, and Dow) have dedicated scouting efforts in China. Technical scouting is less used by the heavy industries and the technology-driven companies, such as those specializing in aviation, energy, and large medical equipment, or in fields in which there is high technological complexity or concern about the security of intellectual property (for example, health care and aerospace).

Technical Scouting by Honeywell China

Honeywell does its scouting in China through university professors, small companies, and technology symposiums. There is no dedicated team to do scouting, which is embedded in the mission of the R&D teams. But new technology and disruptive innovations are done in house. Honeywell is accustomed to acquiring companies, so the decision maker and the authority regarding innovation can be in different business fields. For example, in Honeywell's Life Safety business the funding comes from a joint venture, not from headquarters, so the joint venture has more power to make decisions and select products to develop to comply with the Chinese standards. As a result, the joint venture has been growing faster than its Chinese competitors. This is an interesting example of what we recommended in chapter 3: adopting some of the characteristics of local competitors. In fact, Honeywell describes its approach to China as "becoming a Chinese Company."

Technical Scouting by Philips China

There are two forms of technical scouting approaches within Philips: targeted technical scouting and crowdsourcing. To explore and make use of the available technologies within Philips (to avoid "re-inventing the wheel") has become a shared mindset among members of the Philips innovation community. The company's innovation community is very big and it is located at multiple sites. As a result, special effort is necessary to obtain a complete picture of what is available inside the company on specific topics.

Philips Research has a well-established internal system that manages all technical reports published since 1985. In addition, a well-organized research program team keeps track of innovations in each technology domain.[13]

Each Philips project is expected to start by exploring the existing technologies to identify innovation gaps, using either the project teams or technical brokers. Setting clear boundaries is essential when seeking external technology, particularly via technical brokers. It is very important to enhance the culture of open innovation in order to utilize the existing technology and address only the identified gaps. Having the business unit's ownership, investment, and involvement in the scouting activity best ensures the adoption of the results.

BECOMING EMBEDDED IN THE NATIONAL INNOVATION MAINSTREAM

According to Chinese government data,[14] the total R&D investment in China in 2013 was 1,185 billion renminbi (about $162 billion), or 2.08 percent of GDP, slightly higher than the R&D intensity in the European Union (2.02 percent). Government funding was 250 billion renminbi, or 21 percent of the total, and industry investment was 907 billion renminbi, or 76.6 percent of the total.

Two implications of these data are that the Chinese government continues to provide strong support for extending the national innovation system and that business R&D is the mainspring of commercial innovation activity, as it is in the United States and in Europe. So companies need to become embedded in the national innovation mainstream in order to benefit, through open innovation, from the fundamental R&D generated by universities and institutions, and potentially to attract financial support, at the same time working closely with suppliers, customers, and startups.

Despite Chinese government policy, in practice it is often not easy for Chinese stakeholders to reach consensus regarding the value of multinational corporations' involvement in R&D The Minister of Science and Technology and other high officials of the Chinese government recognize the benefit of working with MNCs in the national program. However, mis-alignment between multiple ministries and stakeholders at the execution level means it is difficult for MNCs to participate fully.

We found that several MNCs are making efforts to become embedded in the Chinese National Innovation System. For example, Philips China has made multiple attempts to apply for government projects. A recent case was an application for a so-called 863 Program project[15] in horticulture in 2012. A joint proposal with leading universities in horticulture, it was approved by the provincial and municipal governments but not by the Ministry of Science and Technology. The lesson Philips drew was to prepare early and be well connected to the community, since an application is stronger if it is based on ongoing joint work with the right partners.

For most firms, getting access to R&D funding from China's central government remains problematic. We have not found any examples of MNCs' gaining access to R&D grants from the central government. Rather than push for such funding, MNCs should work with municipal governments, which are more flexible and which have closer connections with individual MNCs, particularly in the city where the MNC's Chinese entity is registered. A number of MNCs have attracted funding from municipal and city governments in that way.

In 2014 there were more than 1,500 MNC R&D centers in China, about 380 of them in Shanghai. Most of them are well connected within their own company locally but rather isolated from the Chinese ecosystem and often from the local government. There are various reasons for this.

First, MNCs were officially allowed to apply jointly for national programs (e.g., 863 Program projects) after many years of lobbying from MNCs. In the meantime, an MNC could be certified as a qualified Chinese innovation organization, though not always as easily as a domestic company. A policy released in March 2015 by China's State Council appears to encourage participation: "Deepen the reform of system mechanism, accelerate the implementation of the strategy on innovation-driven development." In its session 26, the State Council encouraged MNCs to undertake national innovation programs. Time will tell if this means a real change of policy and whether concrete actions will follow from it, but MNCs should now be testing it.

Second, applications by MNCs for R&D projects are being approved by local municipal governments, particularly those of municipalities in which the MNCs are registered—for example, GE and Honeywell have had approval for such projects granted by the Pudong district of Shanghai, where they are registered. The better connected with the community a multinational corporation is, the easier it is for the corporation to gain local support and have its R&D application approved.

Third, multinationals often lack dedicated efforts to become embedded in the local R&D activities. Such efforts would include developing a good understanding of the local government's innovation policies, strong interactions with local technology leaders, institutes, and associations (which form the technical network and ecosystem, and which play a dominant role in proposing innovation strategies in high-priority innovation fields), and early involvement in the definition of innovation topics (6 to 12 months before a call for proposals is issued).

There is also a strategic question to be answered by MNCs' top management: How much effort should be allocated by MNCs to working with the Chinese government? In a European company, there is normally a department dedicated to help its researchers make funding applications and facilitate the interactions with government. However, for MNCs in China there are few dedicated resources available to undertake this role. Specific resources must be allocated to make the above-mentioned activities happen.

Despite the importance of open innovation, MNCs are not yet deeply embedded in the national innovation system of China. We believe they should be making much stronger efforts to become so embedded, as Philips and other MNCs we mention in this chapter are doing, because a new development, Open Platform Innovation, is emerging in China.

Government funding

In China, multinational corporations have difficulty getting government funding for R&D projects, particularly national grants through the National 863 Program (the National High-tech R&D Program) and its successors. Calls for proposals may be announced just a few weeks before submission, which make it impossible for a multinational to submit a proposal in time. Chinese companies have advance warning and are able to prepare. Because of these complications, CTOs of multinationals tend not to make big efforts to apply for funding by China's national government. However, they are more successful with municipal and city governments, which are eager to attract large companies for reasons of employment and tax revenues. Honeywell, for example, has not succeeded in getting R&D grants from the national government, but has obtained grants from the government of Shanghai's Pudong district and from several other local government bodies. The same is true of GE and Solvay.

We recommend that MNCs establish close contacts with local and municipal governments and related research institutions and universities so as to obtain locally oriented funding grants. They should follow the recommendations of an executive at one successful MNC, related to us in an interview:

- Maintain timely understanding of the policy, strategy, and plans of the authorities through online research, a well-maintained network. and third parties.

- Define a company strategy about what to focus on and prepare for.
- Organize applications with the relevant teams and lobbying where needed while going through the process.
- Gain commitment from top management.
- Execute grant projects well to strengthen reputation. Monitoring, self-analysis, reporting. and maintenance are essential.

STRATEGIES FOR PARTICIPATING IN CHINA'S INNOVATION SYSTEM

Companies seeking to take advantage of China's national system of innovation should consider these two points:

- The objectives are to become embedded in the innovation mainstream, to develop in-depth long-term partnerships with important local R&D institutions, to establish trust and respect, to get access to government funding and to gain advanced access to the market.
- The obstacles include the fact that applications by MNCs for participating in national programs, though allowed by policy, are hindered in practice; the fact that an entrant may be expected to share intellectual property rights with local industry partners; the requirement to reveal intellectual property to the government in case of national emergency; and leakage of knowledge to competitors.

We suggest the following solutions, which are based on the experiences of our interviewees in multinational corporations:

- Establish a planned program of actions to increase the reputation of your company's R&D organization in the local ecosystem and the benefits to China of collaboration.
- Understand the national government's strategy and priorities with regard to innovation in China and adjust your company's local business strategy accordingly.
- Connect with and engage local stakeholders (industry experts, local researchers, and officials) so as to become better informed and accepted by them.

- Learn how to deal with local authorities—especially those in your company's registration municipality, whose working culture and perspective may differ from those of your company. Hold regular discussions to gain mutual understanding. Humility and respect are essential.
- Provide help to small and mid-size Chinese companies that need it, and co-create with partners so as to grow along with them.
- Identify your company's unique position in the field, differentiated from competitors.
- Apply initially for projects funded by local governments before making proposals to the central government. Continue to make applications for R&D support even if initially unsuccessful.
- Team up with partners who have established long-term and consistent collaborations.
- Join other MNCs and representative associations in lobbying government at the local and national levels.

These steps require strategic decisions at an MNC's headquarters about the corporation's desired future position in the local ecosystem, about the extent to which it is willing to collaborate with local companies, and about its policies regarding intellectual property. Despite the difficulties, several MNCs have succeeded in gaining support from local governments—for example, Honeywell has received project funding from the Science and Technology Commission of Shanghai, and Rhodia Research China has received funding from the Science and Technology Commission of Shanghai's Minghang district.

In the next section we cite as examples of good practice two other companies that have had some success in obtaining local funding: Solvay and GE China.

HOW SOLVAY GETS SUPPORT FROM THE CHINESE GOVERNMENT

The Belgian chemical company Solvay has been awarded from 5 million to 10 million renminbi per year to support certified R&D ventures, plus a small amount of funding for innovation projects.

Solvay assigned dedicated high-caliber people to work on important steps, which they summarized as follows:

- timely understanding of the policy, strategy, and plans of the authorities, through online research, a well-maintained network and third parties
- defining a company strategy about what to focus on and prepare for
- organizing applications with the relevant teams, and lobbying where necessary during the process
- gaining commitment from top management
- good execution for the grant projects to strengthen reputation: monitoring and self-analysis; reporting, and maintenance.

Solvay successfully applied to be named as a Shanghai Technical Little Giant in 2014. The benefits it gained included 3 million renminbi in support. It was sponsored by the Shanghai Municipal Science and Technology Commission and the Shanghai Municipal Commission of Economy and Informatization.

GENERAL ELECTRIC'S FUNDING FROM GOVERNMENT

Xiangli Chen, president of General Electric's China Technology Center, observed that the provincial model is very similar to that in the United States. Local governments are more open to multinational companies: "In GE for example we have about four projects collaborating with universities that are supported by local governments. Through these projects, we expanded our views and insights, sourced good ideas, and built effective business connections with local partners." Another senior GE manager told us that the company has made it an expectation among local R&D personnel that they will collaborate with outside partners as a normal requirement of their work. As a consequence, all senior technologists are expected to gain the skills needed to develop partnerships, including identifying each party's role in the partnership, understanding each side's interests and concerns, knowing the approval processes from each side, negotiation, and making compromises. The projects, which vary in size from quite small to large, help to make GE a respected partner among local companies and institutions.

OPEN PLATFORM INNOVATION: CHINA'S INNOVATION FUTURE

Recently, as the life cycles of products have become shorter, firms have experienced disruptive technological change. A business can be devastated virtually overnight by better and cheaper products or services launched from unexpected directions. The Internet enables much of this "big bang" innovation.[16] Strategies for dealing with such disruptions are not obvious, but it is likely that firms will involve a broader range of actors in responding and that will require a different approach to open collaboration.

In the past decade there has been a rapid evolution from closed innovation to various forms of open innovation (OI), including innovation by subcontracting, co-creation in various parts of the value chain with customers and suppliers, and the spinning in and spinning off of technologies. This open innovation model involves collaboration with limited partners and has been adopted by many companies in China. However, a new model, platform OI strategy, has established itself as a way of connecting with a broader source of ideas, and doing so more efficiently.

Platform strategies are much more common today among companies that use the Internet as a force for disruption—especially in China, with its millions of small suppliers.[17] In the Open Platform model, a company establishes an Internet-based platform on which it posts requests for solutions to problems. An essential feature of this strategy's success is that the firm sets up an internal process by which proposals are evaluated, filtered, and selected before actions are taken to implement and commercialize the results.

There are two fundamentally distinct approaches to operating a technology platform. One approach is to control the platform and grant access to others, thereby opening up markets for complementary innovations around the platform. The other approach is to give up control, making the platform an open one. Interestingly, according to one study conducted in a developed country, a fully open system appears to be less effective in stimulating new ideas than a controlled platform.[18]

The new wave of innovation is predominantly based on open platforms, and Chinese companies are moving rapidly toward that model. The best-known examples in China are the Haier HOPE platform, the Xiaomi user community (bbs.xiaomi.cn), and the Tencent Open Platform (http://open.qq.com/eng/). The Tencent Open Platform was designed for Tencent's 3 million app developers, serving Tencent's vast community of users (800 million, of whom more than 25 percent are on line at any one time). Tencent's platform offers its developers software tools, including a Business Capability Interface for payment and delivery, round-the-clock assistance, and a Tencent Incubation Center with free offices.

The case studies below offer examples of the diversity of the OI platform approaches that have been adopted in China.

The Haier Open Partnership Ecosystem (HOPE)

Since its establishment in 1984, Haier, a manufacturer of household goods, has become well known in China for product innovation and for closeness to its customers. Reflecting on the need for open innovation, one of its executives said: "Before ... each product line used to focus on its own product and did incremental changes. We didn't see connections among related products. For instance, different lines for kitchen appliances improved features just for themselves; they didn't talk to each other. The end users knew very little about the true value of our products."

In 2010 Haier launched a new product strategy focused on "smart houses." It has since been expanded to "smart communities" and "smart cities." There are a number of aspects to this strategy, including cost reduction, energy use, and sustainability, but a fundamental requirement is delivering value to the customer, not simply technology. This means building intelligence into appliances so as to deliver packages of services, such as entertainment, education, health care, safety, and communication.

Haier was very strong in user interaction, manufacturing, marketing, and distribution. It was relatively weak, in comparison with MNCs in the industry, in technology innovation. Although Haier claimed to spend 4 percent of its revenue on R&D, that wasn't sufficient to support its product strategy. After developing a strong interest in outside sources of innovation, Haier quickly became China's champion of open innovation, with an OI platform active in a broad innovation ecosystem. It claims that more than half of its innovations were made possible by open innovation. "The world is our lab, the world is our talent pool," says Zhang Ruimin, Haier's chairman and CEO.

Haier's major foray into OI was to set up the Haier Open Innovation Center (HOIC) in 2009. Its mission is to explore external technologies and solutions from around the world for all its business units.

The HOIC has two major teams. The Technology to Business (TTB) team is responsible for collecting innovation needs from each business unit. The GRI (Global Resource Integration) team explores external technologies that might be used to meet those needs. The TTB team passes the technical needs to GRI. The GRI reaches out to potential technical providers through its global technology scouting partners, which include technology transfer companies, government agencies, and small startups. The scouting network not only connects Haier's five R&D centers (in China, Germany, the United States, Japan, and New Zealand); it also reaches out to innovators in Israel, South Korea, Singapore, the United Kingdom, Finland, Denmark, and Sweden. The GRI team also recommends technologies to the business teams that might meet the future needs of the business. The business teams are, however, responsible for evaluation and acceptance of candidate technologies.

The HOIC has several supporting teams, including one for business strategy and one for project management; it also has an expert committee. The business strategy team analyses and decomposes the technical needs, then performs preliminary screening of candidate technologies before passing them to the project management team. That team will then interact with the technical providers to adapt the technologies. The HOIC has helped the company's business units to adopt more than 300 technologies since 2008.

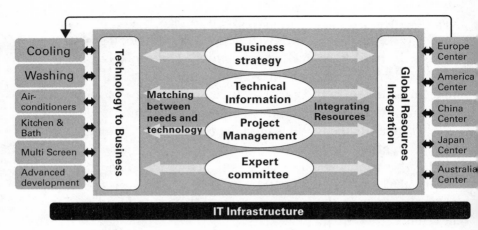

Figure 6.2

The structure of Haier's Open Innovation Center.

Source: Haier Group

The HOPE 1.0 platform, launched in 2013, consisted of two major modules, which mirrored the functions of the HOIC: (1) setting out Haier's needs and (2) collecting technology candidates and interacting with providers. Technical needs could be sent out to everyone who monitored the website. Technical providers could submit solutions online and interact with Haier engineers directly. However, HOPE 1.0 did not attract as many users as had been expected.

In June 2014, Haier launched HOPE 2.0, which included a module for market and technology trends (providing news on technology breakthroughs and industry information) and an Innovation Community. HOPE 2.0 provides services for technology matching and technology transfers to the innovation teams and access to global innovation resources. It also helps technology providers to find suitable partners for commercializing their technologies. The Innovation Community function enables users to carry on discussions and to share information. On average, HOPE 2.0 shortened the time needed to match resources from more than 100 days to fewer than 35 days and doubled the number of needs addressed.

In 2015 the HOPE platform was upgraded again to HOPE 3.0, which is aimed at becoming a leading open innovation platform and ecosystem for the smart home industry. HOPE 3.0 not only explores needed technologies, but also explores new market needs through user interaction and the Innovation Community discussions.

Lenovo's business platform

The computer maker Lenovo has unveiled New Business Development (NBD), an Internet-centric business platform aimed at startups in China. NBD is designed to enable Lenovo's partner startups to make use of Lenovo's software, hardware, sales channels, and other resources while utilizing their own technologies and concepts to design new products and services. Peter Hortensius, Lenovo's CTO, commented:

> We also think that the transformation in the marketplace to an internet-centric business model creates interesting new opportunities for larger companies like Lenovo to partner with smaller companies focused on unique, innovative concepts. And we can use the internet to get better insights, target hot new opportunities, and meet customer demands incredibly quickly. We will continue to develop and unleash our own innovative products across a wide range of categories. At the same we want to be a company that helps fuel innovation in the industry and bring new ideas and interesting products to customers.[19]

The first wave of smart devices to be launched since the introduction of NBD included the New Glass smart glasses, the New Smart air cleaner, and the Newifi smart router. There are two models of smart glasses, designed for two different types of customers in China. The first, dubbed M100, is meant for industrial users and was developed in collaboration with the US-based company Vuzix. The second was specially designed, in collaboration with Ceyes Company, for Chinese consumers. Both types run Chinese operating systems and are adapted to the Internet environment in China. The Newifi smart router, jointly developed by Lenovo and the China-based D-Team, is equipped with special applications designed to secure privacy and to foil stealing or hacking.[20]

Lenovo is working on an Open Innovation 2.0 platform, opening opportunities for companies worldwide to collaborate.

Xiaomi's open platform for customers

Xiaomi leapt to prominence with a competitively priced smart phone, launched in 2011, that incorporates its Android-based MIUI firmware. Xiaomi gained a reputation in China for involving its customers in co-design of its products through its open innovation platform. Now the world's third-largest maker of smart phones, it was valued at $45 billion in 2014 after an equity round that raised $1 billion.

Xiaomi's open platform (http://dev.xiaomi.com/) consists of platform services and a community of more than 3 million "Mi Fans."[21] Xiaomi created its open innovation ecosystem to enable seamless interaction of stakeholders and users in the entire product process (product specification, design, development, internal testing, iterative release, external testing). It is another successful example of the Open Innovation platform concept. The main characteristics are the following:

- Xiaomi provides open platform services, which enable Mi Fans to develop applications.
- The platform is user-oriented instead of product-oriented. Through the Internet, Xiaomi built up a community that enables easy and instant interaction between Xiaomi teams and Mi Fans. Xiaomi can instantly and widely collect feedback; it listens carefully to Mi Fans and swiftly incorporates their feedback into improved products.
- Because Xiaomi's products are co-developed with Mi Fans, Mi Fans have a strong sense of ownership of the products. The users become not only co-creators but also promoters.
- All of Xiaomi's employees, including top management, have access to the latest feedback from all users via the Xiaomi community.

CONCLUSION

In the current industrial revolution, the new platform is the Internet in conjunction with mobile access to information and communication. The Internet platform creates the opportunity for open innovation to extend to a vast army of potential suppliers, no longer tied to a fixed place, to customers, and to a community (such as social media) beyond the company's immediate stakeholders. It has reduced even further the barriers to competition and has made possible disruptive innovation from many sources. Open-platform-based innovation is increasingly being adopted by both leading companies and startups.

China's opening its doors to foreign investment and trade in 1979 changed the world's supply chains, to the benefit of global consumers. The pattern of China's economic development is now entering a new era, shifting from *chufang* (extensive growth) to *jieyu* (intensive growth). The Chinese government is ambitious in its mission to change the image of "made in China" toward "innovated in China," and is beginning to benefit from the world's largest innovation ecosystem, which is increasingly an open platform. China is in a strong position to be a leader in the next wave of open innovation, described by some as "Open Innovation 2.0."

The term "Open Innovation 2.0" is used by the European Commission (the European Union's executive body) to describe an EU initiative to foster an interconnected ecosystem of participants from business, government, and society, with the goal of promoting greater and more collaborative outcomes.[22] Though this initiative is high on promise, it is notably sketchy on practical details, and it is too soon to say whether Europe is inventing a new phenomenon that deserves to be characterized as "OI 2.0." But as opportunities to innovate expand widely through the growth of open platforms, China is in a strong position to become a global leader by drawing on its large and dynamic ecosystem.

The examples of Haier, Lenovo, and Xiaomi show us that it is essential for innovation-oriented companies in dynamic economies to make use of the many external innovation resources that are available worldwide. Companies with internally focused innovation strategies will be left out in the coming years, even if they are now technically dominant. An open innovation platform will be a major asset of leading companies, and active participation in China will be essential.

Open innovation is an important strategy for tapping the two main factors contributing to the capabilities of China's companies: *customer* and *culture*. Open innovation has now been embraced by local companies that want to increase their access to innovative ideas from suppliers and sources of technology. Because of the creation of science and technology parks, national technological institutes, and university research centers, getting science and engineering support for new business ideas is easier than it was in the past. The examples cited above demonstrate that Chinese companies are developing new capabilities, now being built around OI platforms, which will be differentiating assets in domestic competition and in markets beyond China. Open innovation in China has also helped multinational corporations to gain access to the *customer* and begin to penetrate the wider *culture* ecosystem. Multinationals that have implemented OI in China are better placed to succeed locally and to tap new knowledge. To get the most benefit from investing in innovation in China, however, a multinational must have a very clear strategy for dealing with one of the most vexing aspects of the *culture* factor: protection of intellectual property. We turn to that in the next chapter.

7

PROTECTING INTELLECTUAL PROPERTY IN CHINA: LEGAL PROVISIONS AND STRATEGIC RECOMMENDATIONS

(with Maja Schmitt)

Some multinational corporations hesitate to enter China because of concerns about loss of intellectual property.[1] This concern is even more valid when it comes to innovating or conducting R&D in China. There is encouraging news on this front: the framework for protection of intellectual property in China is improving, and there are more and more instances of firms' successfully taking legal action. China's government is paying more attention to this issue and has recently made several announcements and taken several actions, including increasing the number of IP courts. Nevertheless, it is important to adopt a strategic approach from the outset as well as a legal approach. In this chapter we consider both approaches.[2]

CHINA'S LEGAL SYSTEM FOR INTELLECTUAL PROPERTY RIGHTS[3]

Intellectual property rights have been acknowledged and protected in China since 1979. The legal framework is built on three national laws and on other legislation. The National People's Congress passed three national laws: the Patent Law, the Trademark Law, and the Copyright Law. The Standing Committee of the National People's Congress, the State Council, and various ministries have passed related regulations.

Relevant Laws
Patent Law
Seeking to encourage invention and to promote the development of science and technology, China acceded to the Paris Convention for the Protection of Industrial Property in 1984, then to the Patent

Cooperation Treaty in 1994. China has amended its Patent Law three times, in 1992, 2000, and 2009 to comply with its international obligations. Patents in China are granted by the State Intellectual Property Office (SIPO). There are three types of patents: invention patents, utility model patents, and design patents. Administrative enforcement is handled by provincial or municipal intellectual property offices. The fourth amendment was made available for consultation in April 2015. The new law also allows for punitive damages to be awarded with higher penalties for willful infringement.

Trademark Law

China's Trademark Law, meant to guide administration of trademarks and protect trademark owners' exclusive rights and maintenance of quality of products or services bearing the registered trademarks, is administered by the China Trade Mark Office (CTMO). Only registered trade and service marks are protected in China. There is no common-law protection for unregistered trademarks, except for "well-known" marks.

Copyright Law

China has acceded to the Berne Convention, which was enacted to protect the copyright of authors in their literary, artistic, and scientific works and to encourage the creation and dissemination of works. In most cases, the copyright term is the life of the author plus 50 years, but for cinematographic and photographic works and works created by a company or organization the term is 50 years after first publication.

Other legislation

Many pieces of legislation have been passed to improve China's system of IP rights, including the Regulations on Customs Protection of Intellectual Property Rights and the Law Against Unfair Competition of China. The latter prohibits the unauthorized use of registered trademarks, infringing on trade secrets, the illegal use of well-known goods or names of other people, and other misleading and deceptive conduct.

There are some notable differences between China's Trademark Law, Patent Law, and Copyright Law and the laws of Western countries. For instance, China's Trademark Law is characterized by a first-to-file rule, which stipulates that a trademark is granted to the party that files first rather than the party that first uses the trademark. This practice, combined with the necessity of registering Chinese translations in addition to original names, results in expensive conflicts for multinational companies seeking to enter the Chinese market. China's Patent Law is characterized by a first-to-file rule as well. Despite these legal differences, the Chinese legislation for the most part conforms to standards set by the World Trade Organization.

THE DEVELOPMENT OF INTELLECTUAL PROPERTY RIGHTS IN CHINA

From the 1980s through the 1990s, China was undergoing rapid reform and development. Benefiting from participation in the global economy, China for the first time seriously attempted to strength its recognition of intellectual property rights. As a result, China joined the World Intellectual Property Organization and passed the Trademark Law of the People's Republic of China (in 1982) and the Patent Law of the People's Republic of China (in 1984). After its accession to the World Trade Organization in 2001, China amended its IP laws in line with its commitments. Since 1995, China has enforced its patent, trademark, and copyright protections through both administrative procedures and criminal forms of adjudication. However, because of administrative reluctance to pass along cases to the judiciary, the majority of cases are handled by administrative processes. Unlike litigation, administrative decisions don't award monetary damages to victims of infringement. Local administrative agencies also tend to be underfunded and, since counterfeiting is often important to local economies, to be lax about enforcement.[4]

Although China now has many laws protecting intellectual property rights (IPR), enforcement lags greatly in practice. But that is gradually improving as it becomes more and more in the interests of Chinese companies and the Chinese government to enforce

IPR. In its twelfth five-year plan the national government indicated its desire to shift the structure of the economy from low-productivity manufacturing to a balanced economy with a stronger service sector and a focus on scientific innovation. Protection of IPR is an important element of this transition.

The year 2005 was a milestone in the implementation of the IP strategy. It marked the country's resolution to strengthen protection of IPR. Recently, the general office of the State Council of China announced The Further Implementation of the National Intellectual Property Strategy Action Plan (2014–2020). This Action Plan defined the guiding ideology, main goals, and action steps for implementation of the National Intellectual Property Strategy for the years 2014–2020. The main goals are for China to increase significantly its creation of IP, enhance the utilization of IP, and improve its capability to protect and manage IP by 2020.

The Action Plan defines twelve expected targets related to intellectual property rights. In accordance with the requirements of encouraging creation, effective utilization, legal protection, and scientific management, the government will focus on strengthening the utilization and protection of intellectual property rights and on creating a favorable legal, market, and cultural environment, and "will strive to build an IP power, an innovative country, and a well-off society."[5] The Action Plan puts forward four major actions to implement IP strategy. The first is to promote the creation and the utilization of intellectual property. The second is to strengthen protection of IP rights. The third is to strengthen management of those rights. The fourth is to expand international cooperation in the area of IP rights. A major step in implementation of the Action Plan was the opening in 2014 of three courts dedicated to intellectual property—one in Beijing, one in Shanghai, and one in Guangzhou. Expert observers anticipate that these courts will quickly gain technical expertise and specialization, thereby improving China's enforcement of IP laws.[6] As with many other aspects of the law in China, it remains to be seen how effective the implementation of these steps will be.

A STRATEGIC APPROACH TO PROTECTING INTELLECTUAL PROPERTY IN CHINA[7]

Protecting a company's intellectual property depends on the appropriability regime for intellectual property in a country and on the structure of the industry in which the company operates.[8] Whereas both factors are often assumed by companies to be beyond their control, under some circumstances a company can modify them to its advantage.[9] In China, where the system for protecting intellectual property is still evolving, multinational corporations have limited opportunity to influence the government to strengthen the appropriability regime through changes to the law or more stringent enforcement. (One example of a successful approach was Microsoft's persuading the Chinese government to install authentic Windows software on government-purchased computers.)

Changing where value is captured
An alternative to changing the IP regime is to change the locus of where value can be captured. This can take the form of reshaping a firm's value chain so as to capture value at a point that is less vulnerable to China's IP regime. The firm reshapes or segments its value chain to keep the IP-sensitive parts outside China's jurisdiction, making it difficult for copycats to reverse-engineer them. A more radical approach is to reshape the industry[10] by integrating the company's operations in China into a network of complementary assets owned by the company or contractually outsourced to others. Apple has been successful with this approach because of the close integration of its overall product design into the design and specifications of major components. Because individual suppliers have difficulty discovering how those components are integrated, Apple has been able to capture most of the value created by its innovations and to protect the IP from copying.

Other strategies to protect intellectual property in China
Some companies set up an R&D center in China to focus on a research domain in which the company doesn't currently have

a large body of intellectual property. If a company establishes a close collaboration with one of its partners using one of the modes described above, with a mutual interest in utilizing the findings, each party has an incentive to avoid leakage. And if the field is new to the first company, it is less likely to require inward transfers of existing IP. For example, the major energy company for which we have used the pseudonym Globular funds a number of R&D projects in collaboration with Chinese universities and research institutes, most of them in fields concerned with alternative energy, in which the company has limited existing IP at stake.

Another important strategy is for MNCs to patent in China intellectual property that may have been patented elsewhere if they have any intention of using it in China. Because patents are national rights, this is essential for protection. Failure to patent in China can result in a Chinese competitor's learning about the technology (perhaps from published US patents) and then freely exploiting what it has learned in the local environment.

A third strategy is for MNCs operating in China to take greater than usual care to employ well-established practices of IP protection, such as protecting inflows and outflows of sensitive classes of material, monitoring access to important labs and restricting the use of laptop computers and mobile phones. This strategy also includes the use of secrecy agreements with employees and suppliers and restricted-access rights to internal databases. An executive of one German company told us: "The IT department makes of course every effort to keep our data safe. Just like any other big company, we encounter the occasional attempt to break into our system, therefore we try to be careful. This being said, we certainly don't want to establish an internal wall between Germany and China. This would be very counterproductive to our practical collaboration, and send the wrong message to our Chinese co-workers." But it is more acceptable to monitor workers in China than it is in the West. Most Chinese companies go much further than Western ones in monitoring and controlling the use of various devices. In some firms no mobile phones are allowed in or out of a building, USB ports on computers are blocked, and employees are under constant surveillance. Thus, it is not unacceptable for a multinational to institute such practices in China.

A fourth practice that we observed is splitting R&D into modular tasks, allocating some tasks to headquarters, and allocating some other tasks to a group in a China R&D center.[11] Although this requires close collaboration between headquarters R&D and the China R&D center, it can provide protection, as the research can be compartmentalized. One major German technology company usually makes sure that a number of important components are kept out of China. The problem is that there is not much else that this company can do. The Chinese co-workers need an understanding of the complete assembly to work effectively and safely. Therefore, it doesn't make sense to hide too much data from them. The company's German head of China R&D has his own rule of thumb: Decide what you *don't* want to share with your Chinese colleagues, and share the rest freely.

In China, as in other countries, a company has to decide whether it wants to keep a certain piece of intellectual property as a trade secret or to obtain a patent. Keeping the IP as a trade secret can be the better option in cases where it is embodied in operating procedures and processes that are difficult to observe from the outside. For example, the Dutch company Royal DSM has a product called Dyneema, a very strong polyethylene fiber used in anti-missile systems and in marine ropes. Producing Dyneema involves some "kitchen" secrets so sensitive that DSM doesn't move that knowledge outside its home base. Most of these secrets are in the hands and heads of the DSM scientists who operate the Dyneema manufacturing processes. Those scientists stay in the Netherlands.

DSM told us that it has the same rules in China as in the rest of the world. Different rules in China would be interpreted as a signal of distrust.

One way to improve innovation globally is to be more open about sharing existing knowledge, and that can also reduce the duplication of effort. The dilemma is this: a company must accept either the risk that ideas will leak out or the risk that the company will innovate less that it otherwise would. Which of those two risks is higher? That is difficult to say. DSM feels that the balance is in favor of facilitating local innovation. But the company is careful about allowing access to important IP at an early stage in an individual's career, preferring to wait until a level of trust has been built up.

A fifth strategy, some executives told us, is to have highly motivated employees who want to have long careers with the company. Of course a company can't stop an employee from leaving and going to work for another competitor, but a well-thought-out retention policy can help. However, Western companies should be well aware that Chinese employees are generally not as loyal to companies as Western employees. A German head of China R&D told us: "The Chinese staff do not have the same feeling towards the company that I would have and they do not care about the 100-plus-year history of German engineering. However, they are loyal to their boss. So if your R&D managers have a good relationship with them, that probably will reduce the risk of information being stolen. But there is no guarantee."

Legal aspects of protecting intellectual property in China[12]

When considering intellectual property in China, it is important to distinguish between IP in the form of know-how or trade secrets and IP that is registered by means of patents, trademarks, design rights, or copyright. If IP is registered in China, there are laws in place to protect the IP rights (subject to the aforementioned caveats about enforcement). But know-how and trade secrets must be kept secret, both inside and outside China. If secret information becomes publicly available anywhere in the world, it is available for all to read and use. It is difficult in all countries to take effective legal action once secret information is stolen.

For IP that is to be protected by patents in China, the main issues to consider are the following.

Why file IP cases in China ?

The Netherlands recently celebrated 100 years of patent law, whereas China has had patent law only since 1984. However, intellectual property is now part of the Chinese government's strategy, and the laws and procedures for dealing with it are continually being improved. In 2013, China's patent filings under the Patent Cooperation Treaty (PCT) accounted for about 10.5 percent of the world's PCT filings, and the Chinese companies ZTE and Huawei were number one and number four worldwide in PCT filings in 2011 and 2012.[13]

In the past few years there have been, on average, 4,500 court cases involving intellectual property per year. Of these, 75 percent have concerned trademark and copyright issues. Every year there are about 100 patent-infringement cases. The monetary damages awarded in such cases are still relatively small (on average, the equivalent of $ 74,000) but there are moves to increase damage awards under a new draft of the fourth amendment to the Chinese patent law. More than 60 percent of cases concern injunctions to stop an infringement action. Enforcement can be difficult in China, but it isn't easy in Europe or the United States. To obtain a winning judgment, it is necessary to be creative and fully exploit all of the defendant's weak points. In short, patents are long-term investments, and companies that don't apply for them quickly will not be ready when China's patent laws and enforcement procedures mature.

Getting the right people to create IP in China

The following practices are important:

- Create a good connection with top innovators in your company to coach and teach others in critical thinking. (There is no shortage of highly qualified people, but how many are really innovators?)

- Hire for innovative potential. (It is too easy to focus on language skills rather than critical thinking skills. To compensate for deficiencies in language skills, a company can hire translators.)

- Lobby educators to change their style of educating young people to include critical thinking. (Education in critical thinking is now occurring at some of China's top universities, but not yet at many other levels of the Chinese education system.)

- Contract with local institutions for "local for local" R&D and perhaps for "local for global' projects.

- Make it a priority for members of your R&D staff to get to know local customers and their needs.

Protecting trade secrets

Loss of a trade secret is difficult to prove—a company must not only show that something was a secret, but also that it was stolen and that the company suffered damages. Thus, it is obviously best not to let your secrets out. Follow the four rules of protecting trade secrets:

- Create an inventory of what you have.
- Assess its value.
- Mark as a trade secret.
- Keep it safe.

Other ways to protect trade secrets include the following:

- Consider also holding secret documents in the Chinese language, which may aid in proof and enforcement.
- Form a local team of employees from your IP office, your security staff, and the relevant business unit, to identify trade secrets and to provide physical and virtual protection for them. Segregating of duties and limiting access are important; encoding formulas and lists of raw materials may also help.

One European multinational conducts quite a lot of open innovation in China but is not particularly worried about the loss of intellectual property. Its head of China R&D told us: "There is always the odd case of someone leaving with the crown jewels. But the last person to do so at this company was an Englishman. That has helped me when people raise concerns about Chinese scientists walking away with our secrets. I cite that example. Indeed, I think this fear has been caused by Europeans and Americans trying to protect their home base. The best way to prevent people from stealing our secrets is to treat them really well."

Knowledge of potential infringement

Becoming quickly aware of infringement is important. Helpful actions include improving your knowledge of the local landscape, including intelligence about competitors, applications and products. Also, IP searching should be done in Mandarin on Chinese websites and databases to identify risks and spot opportunities. Searches in English rely on translations, which can be faulty and can miss relevant filings. The phonetic tool Pinyin is valuable for pronouncing Chinese but can't be used for searches.

Filing IP cases in China

The total costs of filing IP cases in China are comparable to those in Europe. The fees of the State Intellectual Property Office are quite low, but local agents who do the filing and the administration are expensive.

Deciding whether to seek IP protection in China through a direct national filing or through a PCT filing is a matter of strategy and cost. If the invention in question was made outside China and protection is required in many countries, PCT is often used. If protection is required in only a few countries, a series of direct national filings, including with the SIPO in China, may be appropriate. If the invention in question was substantially made in China, a patent application must be filed first in China to comply with China's legal provisions. There is an assumption that filing via PCT means the invention is of a higher originality, but there is no proof for that—filing in itself is not a measure of quality. There is more time available for review than when filing in a single jurisdiction, but this may not be no advantage when seeking to be protected in China.

A Western company should consider make use of utility model patents[14] in China; they can provide protection quickly, at low cost, with only a low requirement for originality. In addition, they are also difficult to revoke, and they can be a major obstacle for competitors. There is also a real risk that a local competitor may register a Western company's existing technology in China by means of a utility patent, then proceed to sue the foreign company for infringement if it attempts to exercise the technology there. The lesson is to apply for a Chinese utility patent for any technology developed elsewhere if it is planned to use that technology in China.

Trademark protection is necessary as a backup in cases of patent infringement and is very helpful in providing evidence. A brand name can also be filed in Chinese characters, but it is important to look not just at the phonetic translation but also at the meaning of the characters. It took Coca-Cola a long time to arrive at the Chinese name *kekou kele* ("delicious and happy"). Another good example is BMW, which is translated as *baoma* ("precious horse").

Prosecution

Court cases and patent offices suggest that interpretation of the law in China is in line with that in Europe. Patent claims must be well supported by extensive examples, as claims may be limited to the scope of the examples. First invalidation challenges are made before a Patent Re-examination Board (PRB) level, and it is important to win at that level. Only 10–15 percent of decisions are reversed by higher courts.

Inventor Reward Remuneration Policy

Updates to the Chinese patent law are expected, including changes to the Inventor Reward and Remuneration Rules. These may affect how the inventor is remunerated and what rights inventors have in the event that an invention isn't commercialized by the company that employed the inventor. It is therefore advisable to put in place clear policies and administrative procedures to ensure that all ideas are recorded and each is allocated a specific status, and to make appropriate payments.

Agreements

The following procedures are useful:

- Have a "gatekeeper" policy for your Chinese R&D sites and train employees in how to avoid giving government officials more information than they must.
- There are a number of subsidies and tax breaks available to local companies, some of which require filing patents or owning intellectual property in the name of the local entity.

- Agreements should be suitable for possible enforcement in China. International arbitration is, in theory, enforceable, but enforcement is unlikely to happen in practice; thus, it is better to conform to Chinese or Hong Kong law. And agreements should be bilingual.

- Ensure that the company's name is also given in Mandarin. The pinyin (phonetic) name doesn't have legal effect; it is a company's name as given on its "chop" (seal) that defines the legal entity. Signatures have limited legal effect in China, whereas a chop has the legal effect of a signature.

- In contract research, improvements are not automatically owned by the contractor. Unless separate payment is stipulated, they are owned by their developers.

- Customers in China are becoming more aware of IP issues and may ask sales forces to include "freedom to operate" statements in purchase agreements.

But agreements go only so far in China. A representative of a German auto company told us that it sets up non-disclosure agreements but never knows whether they are worth the paper. The important things are how much intellectual property the company brings to China and how to protect it. Makers of premium automobiles are successful in Germany, the aforementioned person told us, not because the companies built up walls, but because of competition and innovation. Success in China for a multinational corporation will not be possible without technological innovation. The way to stay ahead of competitors, especially Chinese ones, is to be faster at innovating than they are.

Enforcement

The Chinese government intends to evolve China into an "innovative country" by 2025. Protection of intellectual property for both local and foreign firms will assume greater importance in achieving this goal. But can IP rights be enforced? This is a major concern for all multinational corporations operating in China. Patents that are published in the European Union and in the United States can be read and copied wherever they are not locally in force. As noted, some Chinese players register utility patents for IP copied from foreign firms. Therefore, to defend a position in China a multinational corporation must have its own intellectual property registered in China, both for purposes of enforcement and for purposes of negotiation with other parties, such as licensees. The important points are as follows:

- IP law, civil law, and criminal law can be used to enforce IP rights.
- There is anecdotal evidence that foreign plaintiffs have been more successful than domestic plaintiffs.
- Local legal support is required for collection of evidence and for enforcement actions.
- Collecting evidence is difficult, and evidence must be collected in the right jurisdiction in the right way.
- In what jurisdiction the legal action occurs matters greatly. There are some 122 IP courts in China, but those in Shanghai and Beijing are considered more fair to multinational corporations than most of the others. The relative influence a company has with the local government in a specific jurisdiction may also affect proceedings.
- No reliable data are available on successful enforcement of judgments, but it appears to be difficult.

TRUSTING CHINESE PARTNERS

Perhaps the fear of loss of intellectual property rights in China is worse than the reality. We close this chapter with the example of how the major MNC we have been calling Globular handles IP issues with its many innovation partners in China, including universities and research institutes.

Globular says it has little fear of loss of IP in China. The company has a continuous focus on protecting IP there, but that is also its approach everywhere. Globular has found a *modus operandi* for protecting IP, which begins with a very careful understanding of what Globular needs. It has found that there is often less need for exclusivity than might have been expected. Speed is more important than exclusivity. As a result, there is room for flexibility with its partners in China. Globular has participated in joint ventures around the world for decades, and has learned that it doesn't want to rely solely on legal agreements. What is needed is a proper relationship. Globular doesn't form a partnership with every potential partner, but it invests in each partnership it does establish. This entails clarifying and agreeing the terms of the relationship and continually reassessing the progress and responding to problems.

In a strategic partnership with an innovation partner, Globular establishes a framework agreement that serves as an overarching guidance document that covers everything the parties want to do together. So for individual, specific R&D projects Globular doesn't have to go through discussions of intellectual property, legal issues, or even financial matters. It simply has to follow the framework agreement, which has the necessary IP arrangements built in.

Globular's most telling comment may be this one: "The Chinese are very pragmatic people." We interpret that as meaning that most Chinese employees and or partners will cooperate and protect their employer's or partner's intellectual property so long as the mutual interests are aligned. The task for the company is to create and maintain that alignment.

Another company that has developed an effective approach to dealing with intellectual property relationships with Chinese partners is General Electric, which has extensive R&D facilities in China. A senior manager told us that GE has made it an expectation among local R&D personnel that they will collaborate with outside partners as a normal requirement of their work. Many of the projects are quite small; however, in each case, intellectual property is managed by agreement between the two parties, and the agreement is carefully prepared in advance. Clauses in the agreement cover such matters as what parts of the technology will be shared and what parts will be allocated to one partner or the other, provisions for licenses and royalties, and resource contributions. Because GE has had extensive experience with a variety of partners, it is able to ensure mutually satisfactory arrangements.

CONCLUSION AND RECOMMENDATIONS

Dealing with issues of IP rights in China is really difficult, particularly because of the still-developing state of the rule of law. Of our Four Cs, *culture* has the greatest effect on intellectual property rights in China. First, the long-time culture of illegal copying sets up the problem of defending IP rights. Second, the subordination of courts to the Communist Party means that institutional weaknesses and politics can easily trump legality. Third, the clear ambition of the Chinese government to make China technologically independent encourages companies, especially state-owned ones, to push the boundaries of IP rights. But, as we have described, China has increasing interest in protecting its own developing IP rights, and as a consequence there is steady improvement in enforcement there. By carefully using the frameworks and tools in this chapter, both foreign and Chinese companies can increase their ability to protect their own intellectual property.

8

LESSONS IN LEADERSHIP AND STRATEGY FROM CHINA

(with Lin Xu and Yi Ta Chng)

In previous chapters we explained the first two phases in the development of China's innovation capabilities in terms of two of our Four Cs: *customers* and *culture*. *Customers*, with their scale, richness, dynamism, idiosyncrasies, and diversity, provided fertile ground for the flowering of innovativeness. *Culture*, with China's entrepreneurship, deep understanding of customers, visionary leadership, and relentless drive, coupled with the ambition and investment of the government, provided the seeds and nutrients for innovation to take root and flourish. In this process, foreign investment—both from Western multinational corporations and from ethnic Chinese firms outside China—played an early and decisive role after the opening of the country in 1979.[1] Yet despite their early dominance in bringing new products and processes to an eager market, MNCs have had to cede their leadership in many fields, as local companies have developed their own *capabilities*. Some MNCs have concluded that the rewards in China are not worth the trouble, and the slowdown that occurred in mid 2015 has lent some credibility to that view, which we argue here is nonetheless mistaken. In this chapter we will endeavor to offer compelling reasons for MNCs to ride out the unsettled weather and to learn valuable lessons from being in China.

Chinese companies imitated, adapted, experimented, and learned to innovate incrementally with "fit for purpose" solutions on the way to achieving world standards and entering into the most recent phase: the ambition to become MNCs in their own right through entry into foreign markets. Their ability to do so will rest on the other two factors we identified: *capabilities* and *cash*. We have already identified the nature and the sources of Chinese companies' capabilities. In this concluding chapter, we will go beyond R&D and innovation to discuss the leadership and strategy lessons companies can learn from China. We have a new, perhaps shocking, idea: *Multinational corporations can now learn from China to improve their activities in the rest of the world.*

We say this because of our Four Cs (the unique characteristics of China's customers and culture, the capabilities of local companies and the cash that now fuels their global ambitions) and because confronting Chinese companies on their home turf is the best way for a multinational corporation to gain the capabilities, and indeed the cash, needed to confront them in its home market. Tackling your competitors in their home market exposes your capabilities to the same forces they have faced and dealt with successfully, many of which aren't visible on the surface in China and are quite invisible from a company's home environment. Competing in China gives multinational firms experiences similar to those of their competitors and develops new capabilities that, we argue, make them fitter to compete globally. Yes, there are obstacles in the way of foreign companies competing in China, but a significant number of MNCs have coped and indeed flourished, recognizing the value of the vast Chinese market and the learning they can take to the rest of their business worldwide. Procter & Gamble is well aware of this imperative; it has been active in China for 30 years. P&G took a lesson from the challenges it faced and overcame in Japan in the early 1980s, when tough local competitors were on the point of pushing P&G out of the country. Ed Artzt, P&G's chairman, made a historic decision to stay in Japan and to commit the necessary resources. His reasoning was this: "Compete with them in their own backyard, for you will eventually have to compete with them at home. ... We cannot afford to be anything but successful there."[2] Learning from Japan enabled P&G to succeed in China, where today it is known for three of the top five consumer brands despite great differences in customers and culture.

China is too big a market to ignore. Surprisingly, like Japanese companies in the 1980s, Chinese companies can provide other firms with ideas about management, business models, and leadership that they need in order to hold onto their home markets and to succeed globally. From the 1960s to the 1980s Western companies ignored the radical management ideas of Japanese firms, such as *kanban*, Total Quality Management, and Just-in-Time. They may now be in danger of missing new ideas from China. Although China has not yet devised revolutionary management ideas that have proved as universally powerful as Japan's, the potential is there, as we will see from the following summary of what is unique about the China managerial environment and what leaders—both Chinese and Western—can learn from it.

The first reason for the bold claim above is that unique characteristics make China a complicated environment and hence a valuable field for learning. In chapter 1 we explained how China's demand characteristics now favor conducting innovation there. We identified many of the unique characteristics of China's environment there and in other chapters. Here we want to draw attention to the particular features of China's environment that provide opportunities for MNCs to learn and respond. These fall under the headings of our first two factors: *customers* and *culture*. Participating in the pressures and the opportunities of this dynamic ecology provides companies with a breeding ground for new learning and new capabilities that can change a company's global strategy, as it has done for Chinese companies. Figure 8.1 illustrates the connections between *customers* and *culture* and *capabilities*. Figure 8.2 shows the connections between *capabilities* and *cash,* which has made possible the third innovation phase discussed in chapter 1.

CUSTOMERS: UNIQUE CHARACTERISTICS OF CHINA'S MARKET

China's customers have many characteristics and behaviors that are unique, and diverse within China itself.

In today's China, customers and users behave quite differently from those in the rest of the world. Fast to mature and fast to adopt new trends, and often e-savvy, they have a "forgive and forget" mentality, and their changing tastes often create micro-niches. China's young people, in particular, don't fit the old stereotype of

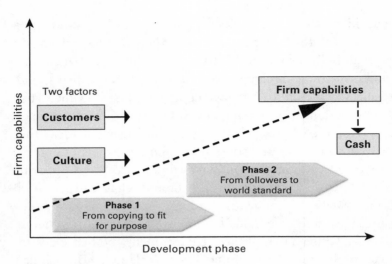

Figure 8.1

The first two phases of innovation in China.

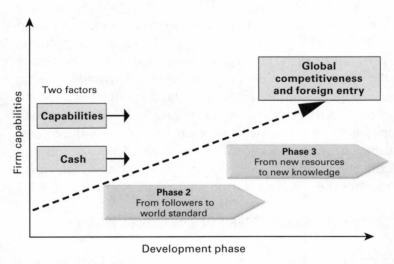

Figure 8.2

The third phase of innovation in China.

placid conformists. They are diverse in their social and political values, care about their peer group yet embrace personal expression, are materialistic yet idealistic, and may have contradictory nationalistic and international tastes. These Chinese tastes and behaviors matter, because they can be early signals of trends emerging in other markets, including Western ones.

In the mid 1980s Toyota thought that China's citizens would not be able to afford to buy cars for fifty years, so it turned down the government's invitation to establish manufacturing in China. Like Toyota, perhaps no one could have predicted that Chinese consumers would get as rich and mature as quickly as they have. Only thirty years ago, as we discussed in chapter 4, multinationals in all sectors exported models to China from home without needing to pay much attention to local market characteristics. Now, however, increasingly mature consumers in every sector in China choose carefully among products and services, selecting those that resonate with their own tastes, lifestyles, and cultural heritages. Coca-Cola and McDonald's were successful at selling Western culture to the Chinese, but Mattel has found the same task less easy for its global icon, Barbie. Children and their parents prefer the home-grown Xi Yang Yang, an educational animated sheep, to the post-adolescent American doll. A recent McKinsey report showed that the new generation of Chinese luxury consumers are demonstrating increasing preference for products with Chinese values over those with Western ones.[3]

Today, Chinese consumers are seen as among those fastest to adopt new products and applications. According to the market-research firm Nielsen, China is one of the top three markets for new, fast-moving consumer products. Though Chinese consumers often enthusiastically embrace newness, perhaps their most notable characteristic is their passion for Internet-related and mobile-phone-related products and services. Chinese consumers do so much with their smartphones that they usually carry phones with the largest screens in the world—many of them designed and made by Chinese rather than foreign companies. This obsession with mobile phones has led one city (Chongqing) to institute a separate lane for pedestrians walking while using mobile phones.[4]

At the same time, as first-generation or second-generation consumers, the Chinese are more forgiving and forgetful than Western consumers, so mistakes don't have the long-term consequences they would have in the West. In chapter 3 we described how the numerous defects of the Chery QQ car did not stop it from becoming a best seller in China. In contrast, in earlier times, Italy's Fiats and (even worse) Yugoslavia's Yugos never recovered from their quality problems when introduced into the US market. MNCs operating in China are concerned about how a mistake in the Chinese market might affect their reputations worldwide. They are right to worry, but this can inhibit their ability to meet market demands as rapidly as local firms. A representative of one MNC told us that because of reputation concerns it had taken his company nearly two years to get headquarters' approval for a product that created a new consumer category in China. If MNCs can learn to innovate at the speed expected by their Chinese customers and practiced by local Chinese competitors, and if they can embed the practice into their worldwide processes, that capability should prove a major benefit everywhere they operate.

China's Market: Dynamic, Different and Diverse

China's market has a speed of change and a diversity that are unprecedented. Between 1978 and 2015, China's urbanization rate increased from 17 percent to 55.6 percent, every new city dweller increasing his or her consumption by a factor of 10. It took Britain (with an urbanization rate of 82.6 percent), the United States (81.6 percent), and Japan (93.5 percent) many more years to achieve such growth in consumption. Average income levels in China, in current US dollars, rose from under $1,000 in 2000 to $7,594 by 2014.[5] On a Purchasing Power Parity basis, the average in 2014 was $13,216. (The US average was $54,629.) But this average hides huge variations. China's overall Gini coefficient in 2014 was 0.47 (a less equal income distribution, compared with the OECD average of 0.32).[6] There is a sizable top segment of consumers who are big spenders by global standards, as one third of the country's wealth is held by 1 percent of its citizens. Thus, there are many examples of extreme consumption behavior. For example, Carl

Zeiss sells million-dollar diamond-encrusted eyeglasses only in China, and many of the buyers are men, not women. In the mass market, Haier has introduced a range of major appliances that have Swarovski crystals embedded in their front panels. MNCs that don't have an ear firmly to the ground miss the opportunities in China's myriad of niches. And a niche in China can be the size of the whole market in some Western countries.

All companies can learn from such extremes of consumer tastes. In an earlier era, Japanese companies learned from the Japanese preference for products that were "light, short, small, and thin" as well as of the highest quality, and went on to produce worldwide successes such as the Honda Accord and the Sony Walkman as well as the refined consumer products that P&G had to compete with. In China, the preference seems to have been for products that are large and showy, although there is an increasing shift toward discretion among the most sophisticated wealthy Chinese consumers. This taste may not appeal to most consumers in developed markets, but may well appeal to the top echelons in other developing markets, and often to aspiring consumers in the developed world. Echoing Japanese consumers' insistence on the highest standards of quality, Chinese customers in the high-price segments have a strong desire for authenticity and for respected brands. Witness the Chinese visitors thronging the boutiques of Paris, London, and New York in search of authentic luxury goods.

At the other end of the income scale (the "bottom of the pyramid"), China has hundreds of millions of consumers. Those consumers need a different kind of innovation, which we called in chapter 1 "good enough" or "fit for purpose" innovation. We showed in chapter 1 that Chinese companies' success in satisfying these large segments bred innovative capabilities that they then applied to creating and filling other segments. Companies that can stretch their capabilities to serve the entire income range in China are, like an athlete with a varied training program, building robust capabilities for global success. Design firms such as IDEO tell of the value of learning from "extreme users" who, though not representative of the current average user, are indicators of future trends as tastes becomes more discerning. In Europe, Philips developed a range of new kitchen implements by working with the renowned chef Jamie Oliver. Its China business introduced the first garment steamer by observing the Chinese aversion to traditional ironing. A purely Western mindset would have dismissed that opportunity as "extreme."

In addition to income diversity, there are many cultural and behavioral differences across the different regions of China. Significantly different user habits come from deep cultural beliefs, ethnic diversity, and the histories of the different regions. The regions are not static, as there is a continual flux of migrants seeking employment in distant provinces, despite the restrictions of the *haikou* system. With this widespread dynamism, it is not surprising that consumer markets are moving fast, a huge proliferation of alternatives emerging almost as soon as a new product is created. For example, in the much warmer southern regions, such as Guangdong province, consumers want washing machines that take smaller loads for more frequent washing of soiled clothes; in northern regions they want high-capacity machines for less frequent washing. Haier has responded by creating a small washer for the southern market. Geographic differences also affect business-to-business markets. For example, the diversity of China's ground conditions and climates has stimulated Sany, a manufacturer of construction equipment, to develop many more models for each application than do its foreign rivals. Sany is broadening its market reach while at the same time stretching and expanding its capabilities, which are valuable for other developing markets, such as Thailand and the Philippines.

In southern China, owing to influence from Hong Kong, official and business dinners are celebrated with cognac. For reasons of cost and authenticity, hosts often purchase cases of the expensive brandy in wholesale stores before an event. This has resulted in a more developed wholesale sector, and the food and beverage industry in that region is more progressive, adopting BYOB (bring your own bottle) practices not broadly seen in other parts of the country. Being aware of these subtle differences requires being present and engaging closely with the full variety of people and locations.

The fast growth of China's economy, the large empty market spaces, and the diversity make it easy to succeed with new ventures. Local entrepreneurs recognize that there are plenty of "white space" opportunities, and plenty of room for "blue sky" thinking about different business models and practices. For example, a popular local hotpot restaurant chain, HaiDiLao, rewards its restaurant managers who have found innovative ways to make waiting for tables more bearable: They provide massages and manicures. Contrast this with a typical Western fast-food franchise that focuses on standards, "quality" control, and limited service. The Western retailers B&Q and IKEA entered China to create a home do-it-yourself market. IKEA quickly understood the Chinese lack of experience with DIY and preference for having tradesmen do work in the home. It shifted its focus to providing ideas and aspiration for its customers (encouraging families to visit the stores as an outing), and it now organizes workers to go to their homes to assemble purchased items. B&Q, however, stuck to its low-service-retail-center format (yet with too many unproductive employees), and its profitability declined as a result.

In chapter 3 we explained how differently Chinese companies innovate. Not surprisingly, they are also becoming very creative in design and business process. In fact, some of the most creative ideas seen in China today are coming from Chinese companies. The fast-rising Chinese mobile phone maker Xiaomi, whose open-innovation practices were discussed in chapter 6, has created a highly innovative business model that enables it to match or exceed competitors' product attributes at lower prices.[7] There are three main reasons for this. First, by using online sales channels exclusively, Xiaomi cuts costs by an estimated 30 percent. The second reason is Xiaomi's unique product strategy. While one of its biggest competitors, Apple, is famous for concentrating on one smartphone at a time, another major rival, Samsung, caters to the mass market by offering a large number of phones under different names, with a complicated set of pricing strategies. Xiaomi's product strategy takes salient elements from both competitors. It sells only a few models at a time, but with a very fast software update schedule, so that customers feel that that its phones are upgraded often. The software of Xiaomi's own Android-based operating system allows these regular upgrades (which are based on feedback from its loyal customers) and a higher degree of phone customization, a capability that differentiates Xiaomi noticeably from competitors. By comparison, Xiaomi's two Asian competitors produce a large variety of smartphone models, but they provide software updates for only a select few products. Third, Xiaomi's innovations in value-chain management also help hold down costs and increase revenues. Xiaomi also uses its smartphone as a conduit for introducing paid software and application programs. In the short time since Xiaomi was founded, its customers have downloaded applications about a billion times. Aside from generating an additional revenue stream, the apps keep customers attracted to its platform. Though Xiaomi's apps platform is not an original innovation in itself, Xiaomi's ecosystem involves customers in developing additional applications, games, and other services, thereby helping Xiaomi to grow very rapidly.

CULTURE: CHINA'S INTENSE COMPETITORS

Intense competition breeds winners with superb capabilities, one of the factors Michael Porter identified in his pioneering study of the sources of national competitive advantage.[8] Silicon Valley is the prime example of competition's fostering strong and innovative companies. Now it is China's turn to be the breeding ground of world-beating competitors, for reasons that fit well with Porter's analysis. Most world-leading companies are competing in China, and they face local companies that have developed world-class capabilities as they have evolved quickly through the three phases of growth we described in chapter 1. Local firms involved in exporting and importing business learned quickly, despite not having large R&D departments in their early stages. Some attribute this to the greater ease of copying in the digital age, so that initial absorptive capacity was not an impediment.[9] Their speed may also have been due in part to the more widespread availability of technology.

Local firms also benefited from spillovers of technology from MNCs in China. Since 2005, many local companies have become as competitive as the best MNCs—and quite often even better. Some have emerged as world-class in their sector. Among them is Lenovo, founded in 1984, which acquired IBM's PC business at the end of 2004 and has since become the world's biggest PC maker by volume.[10] Others companies have achieved global leadership through the rapid growth and the vast scale of what has become the world's largest market. Galanz became the world's largest manufacturer of microwave ovens in 1995. Mengniu surpassed the Italian firm Parmalat to become the world's biggest seller of ready-to-drink milk in 2010, even though China doesn't have a strong dairy tradition. Indeed, many Chinese were lactose intolerant, but the nutritional value of milk was promoted by the government and Mengnui seized the opportunity. As we described in chapter 2, Huawei has combined investment in innovation and domestic scale to become a world leader, as has Haier. These companies achieved their dominance not through luck or government support, but through fierce and vigorous competition, led by innovation. Their size today provides the resources and cash for continuing investment in innovation, as well as overseas expansion, as exemplified by Huawei, Haier, and Lenovo. Yes, it is true that in some cases government helped with cash through grants for R&D or plant investment, with protective actions, or with local procurement policies. But leaders of successful Chinese companies unfailingly speak of the fierce competitive environment and the necessity to innovate continually to stay in place. Dan Breznitz and Michael Murphree described the behavior they observed among local firms in global supply chains as the "Red Queen" phenomenon: running fast simply to stay in place.[11] Our conversations with many Chinese executives confirm that this is the norm in Chinese private and public corporations, small and large.

While many of the successful Chinese companies followed the path we outlined earlier—from copying to incremental innovation, to "fit for purpose," they have also moved through the "world standard" phase and are now actively seeking new knowledge. This is driven in part by their global aspirations but also by the increasing incomes and sophistication of Chinese consumers, with their voracious appetite for high-quality goods and services. As we emphasized in chapter 1, China's corporate landscape has evolved to the point of having the capacity to satisfy these new demands through innovation-based competition. Business organizations are greatly shaped by their customers. (Japanese firms are renowned for their obsession with quality and detail, under the pressure of their demanding customers.) Michael Porter saw demanding customers as another of the forces shaping the competitive advantage of a country, through the pressure on its firms to respond. And in responding successfully, they develop the capabilities to innovate for demanding customers all around the world.[12] Thus, the fact that Chinese consumers enthusiastically embrace newness forces companies in China to differentiate themselves constantly in a Darwinian struggle for survival. It is also an enduring characteristic of Chinese companies, as we showed in chapter 3, that they do *everything* fast, not just innovation. They are quick to innovate because they know their customers deeply and are intent in looking for new needs, they quickly allocate a lot of resources to the problem, and they quickly test prototypes in the market. This fierce and fast competition has created the world's biggest Petri dish for breeding world-class competitors.

Our Four Cs framework attributes the foreign expansion of Chinese companies to their home-grown capabilities and to the cash generated by local success, which enable them to acquire brands, technology, and market share in new markets. A number of other local innovators that have triumphed in China have already become world leaders through technological innovation. Envision Energy in wind turbines and Himin Solar in household solar panels are among the best-known examples. Another group of Chinese innovators have been active in the era of Internet and mobile technologies, in which China has already achieved huge scale. Tencent, which began in China by copying the pioneering Israeli-designed ICQ, has introduced a range of innovative services for local Internet users' needs. It was the first company to offer cloud storage for Internet cafés, and it created the widely popular WeChat mobile text and voice messaging service. The innovative features of WeChat made it the world largest stand-alone mobile phone messaging application as ranked by monthly active users. Without any promotion, WeChat reached 200 million users within eight months of its launch, and quickly spread to thirty countries.

Tencent, now the world's third-biggest Internet company, has embarked on international expansion, and it entered the United States in 2014.[13] Foreign customers who have experienced its services want the same in their home countries. In the US market, WeChat is offering stiff competition for Whatsapp. Tencent's US executives say that WeChat offers sharing of IDs, "handset shakes," QR code scans, radar scans to incorporate groups, and that it also offers built-in text voice, group chat, video calls, and photo sharing. WeChat also offers a certified secure messaging service. One of the first communication services from China to tap an international customer base, it claims more users outside China than at home. And in January 2015 Tencent became the first private online bank in China with the launch of its Webank.

Alibaba—long dominant in e-commerce in China, already the world's largest e-commerce company, and one of the most valuable since it was listed on the New York Stock Exchange—is now going global. It will be able to build on its capabilities in designing and operating multiple e-commerce platforms in China and on its experience in working with global brands and in helping thousands of individuals to become e-commerce entrepreneurs. Alibaba is also crossing industry boundaries to disrupt the finance industry. It is now one of the world's pioneers in e-payments, so much so that Spain's Santander, one of the world's largest banks, is seeking to partner with Alibaba and other Chinese companies to learn how to develop online platforms for financial services, not just for China but for the world. Alibaba opened its personal wealth management fund, Yu'e Bao, in 2013. In June 2015 it launched MyBank, an online bank which is aimed at serving small companies that have difficulty getting service from the large traditional banks. The capabilities that underpin this expansive new business include Alibaba's experience with millions of small entrepreneurs on its e-commerce platforms and its Alipay payments service and its deep Internet and digital technology expertise. Alipay has become international by offering non-Chinese sellers a collection service for Internet payments from Chinese buyers, conversion to foreign

currency, and remittance overseas—activities that usually are re-
served for banks.

The success of these companies outside China is a wake-up call
to multinationals, which are beginning to see China as a source of
global competitive advantage. Though many MNCs still stick to
the outdated view of China as no more than an outlet for global
products and services developed at home, there has been a substantial shift toward innovation in China for the Chinese market, as we
showed in chapter 4. This new approach is starting to pay off. Per-
nod Ricard China, for example, gets the majority of its revenues
from market-specific innovations, and Kraft Foods China earns
more from products launched in the past three years in China than
from any other market in the world.

Although China is a proving ground for honing a firm's innovative capabilities, taking the China opportunity seriously in the
face of fierce and innovation-based competition means that both
foreign and Chinese companies have to focus continually on
deepening unique and sustainable capabilities. How can this
be done?

CAPABILITIES: WHAT TO LEARN FROM CHINA

How should companies exploit the unique characteristics of
China? We propose five major lessons that companies should learn
from China and implement as strategies:

- Bold experimentation and rapid iteration to identify and create
  innovation opportunities and ensure agility.
- Innovation through creative adaptation—innovating by focusing on the needs of local markets.
- Developing the ability to find and rapidly exploit opportunities
  to create new categories.
- Focusing on "lean value" by designing simple products that target very specific needs, avoiding anything superfluous, and providing only what is necessary.
- Developing mixed teams and global leaders—China's current
  business environment presents a great setting for companies to

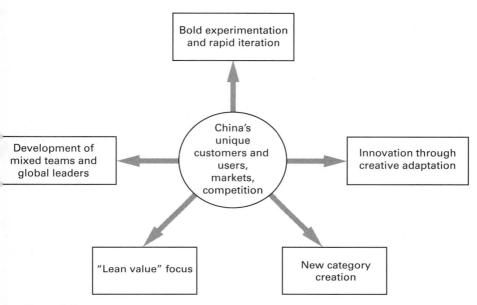

Figure 8.3
Learning from China.

manage mixed teams with diverse backgrounds and to cultivate future global leaders.

Bold experimentation and rapid iteration

Local innovation is often written off as imitation. But, although it is controversial to say this, for China uniqueness in innovation is not as important as opportunism. Coca-Cola's 15-million-renminbi launch of Vitamin Water was usurped by Nongfu Spring's launch of its nearly identical and lower-priced (5 renminbi a bottle) Victory Vitamin just a few months later. A few months after that, Coca-Cola reduced the price of Vitamin Water to 6 renminbi. In 2009, Coca-Cola imitated Wahaha's Nutri-Express (a 2-billion-renminbi "milk smoothie drink" business that had been built from scratch in 2005) by launching Minute Maid Pulpy Super Milky, created by the company's Global Innovation Technology Center in Shanghai, at a slightly lower price. Within three months of that launch, Minute Maid Pulpy Super Milky (Guo Li Nai You) was on sale in more than 300 cities as a result of an intensive campaign that brought into play Coca-Cola's global strengths in distribution, advertising, and sales. Though that innovative imitation has been a great success, Wahaha is still the market leader by far. It is worth considering how much stronger Coca-Cola's position might be if there had not been a four-year gap after the launch of Nutri-Express. When large new markets are being quickly created by local competitors, multinationals have a great chance to do well if they follow quickly and make use of their global advantages. We do not, however, see such fast moves as often as we would expect. For example, no Western multinational has yet entered the booming market in traditional herbal cooling drinks, which is worth 30 billion renminbi.

Often, in order to succeed in the Chinese market, a company must to be brave enough to experiment and willing to make mistakes. For example, GlaxoSmithKline's R&D center for neurological diseases in China (a center with a global mandate) spends much less time deciding which drug compounds to test than the company's Western R&D centers do. Instead, it tests three times as many compounds—something it can afford to do in China, taking a lead from one of the ten strengths of Chinese firms. Chinese companies—particularly private, non-state-owned ones—are usually quite fearless. They are not ashamed of imitation, seeing it as learning from others. Many (perhaps most) large Western and Japanese companies seem to have forgotten such fearlessness, having been made cautious by low rates of growth and heavy regulation in their home countries. They fear that they have too much to lose by taking a more aggressive stance in China. Representatives of several multinational corporations told us that product launches in China were delayed by slow decision making at headquarters. Sometimes decision making is slow because of headquarters' uncertainty about the importance of the Chinese market, sometimes because of worries about reputation, and sometimes because of insufficient delegation to the executives of the local operation. Yet China is a low-risk market for bold actions because of its fast growth, even at the lower 7 percent rate experienced since 2014. Western MNCs have to find organizationally acceptable ways to take risks in China and to do so speedily.

China favors the brave. Procter & Gamble has a $3 billion hair-care business in China today thanks to a few risks it took in the 1990s. The first risk was to be the first company to market hair-care products aggressively outside the developed markets of Guangzhou, Shanghai, and Beijing, investing heavily in advertising in secondary markets before internal distribution chains were set up and before applications to track and analyze sales data were available. The second risk was to invest heavily in sampling, by offering reluctant retailers free products to sell, to gain their confidence and support for P&G's expansion. These bold moves, coupled with a good understanding of the specific product characteristics needed for Chinese hair, enabled the company to grow sales in this category and establish a leadership share that it still holds more than twenty years later.

Innovation through creative adaptation

Many innovative successes in China result from turning a nuanced understanding of local culture into a creative adaptation for a new category or consumer need. For local companies, the creativity is often due to the strong intuition of an important individual in the organization—usually the founder. This approach is very effective while that individual remains in place, as is more common in Chinese companies than in multinationals. On the other hand, multinationals, with their well-articulated routines and processes, should be better placed to make local creativity an entrenched capability. Exactly how this is done is less important than how much support it is given. Retaining creative locals in important positions is a valuable step, while keeping seasoned foreign executives in place for a long assignment in China is also desirable. It is also sensible to reduce the geographic breadth of responsibility capable executives often have, for whom continual travel limits their attention span and effectiveness in any one country.

Sometimes, the whole approach to how business is done must be changed for China. Innovative business models are frequent among new Chinese companies, as we saw in earlier chapters, and cut-and-paste transfer of business models by multinationals can fail. In 2003, Eachnet (eBay's acquired operation in China) had taken 90 percent of China's nascent online consumer-to-consumer business. However, the basic elements for e-commerce in China were missing, such as a credit-card system, a logistics network, Internet penetration, and an e-commerce user base. In contrast, as we described in chapter 2, Jack Ma, who had started Alibaba as an online platform for business-to-business suppliers in 1999, decided to enter the consumer-to-consumer market in 2003 by launching Taobao ("treasure hunt") with a focus on rapid growth. With two business-model innovations, Taobao increased the market from 2 billion renminbi to more than 30 billion in three years, and changed the landscape of the whole retail business in China. Ma's first innovation was to eliminate transaction fees in order to encourage trial (not viable in the long term without advertising, but an effective short-term tactic). Second, in order to overcome the twin problems of an undeveloped credit-card infrastructure and conservative Chinese attitudes toward online purchasing, Taobao introduced an online payment system (Alipay) in which an escrow service was a central feature. A defeated eBay closed its China operation a year after Taobao entered the market. Taobao's revenues are now four times those of eBay, with Alipay an established and fast-growing separate business.

The need for creative adaptation is apparent in Best Buy's failed experience in China. Best Buy, long a dominant electronics retailer in the United States, arrived in China in 2006 with the expectation that it could transform the Chinese electronics retail business. All nine of its branded stores had been closed by 2011 and in December 2014 it announced its intention to sell the 184 outlets it had gained in 2006 through its acquisition of the Chinese retailer Five Star. Its service-centered retail model, based on owning the sales environment and acting as a trusted impartial intermediary between brands and consumers, simply did not work for its Chinese audience. It is not that Chinese customers don't *like* impartial advice, caring employees, and a pleasant environment; it is that they don't *value* them enough to pay an extra 100 renminbi for a camera. Best Buy found that the margin it added to its products to pay for training employees and offering them generous compensation packages was a deterrent to its would-be customers in China. Best Buy also underestimated the strength of the popular Chinese pastime of tracking down a good bargain. Chinese customers enjoyed going to Best Buy and chatting with employees to decide their desired purchase, but they also enjoyed the satisfaction of going over to the local outlets GOME and Suning to actually lay down (significantly less) cash.

In contrast with Best Buy, GOME and Suning, each with more than a thousand stores across China, have dominated the Chinese market by acting more like curators, renting space to selected brands, which then own the sales interaction with the customers directly (training, supplying, and shouldering the cost of their own employees). GOME and Suning also leave up to their suppliers interior decoration (something that Best Buy found added significantly to its costs). "We spent three to four times more (than the local players) on our staff and interior decorating," a former Best Buy manager commented. With its limited number of stores making it impossible to negotiate for the lower wholesale prices that local competitors enjoyed, Best Buy found itself with very high operational costs, which it had to pass on to consumers. In contrast, GOME's and Suning's long-term marketing efforts centered on cost advantage. Best Buy failed to understand China's very specific customer conditions and the well-developed capabilities of its competitors. The former head of Best Buy Asia commented: "What we learned, very crucially, is that in China you cannot make revolutionary change. You have to work at the pace of the Chinese consumer."

Although maturing consumers in China have begun to appreciate good service, it is not yet seen as more desirable than a better price. And what is considered good service in China differs quite a lot from Western norms. Yi Ta Chng and Lin Xu are currently helping a Western retail client in China to figure out how to transform its organization into one that offers Chinese-style service. Properly understanding the customer, the culture, and the whole ecosystem in which the business must function can lead to an innovative and workable business model.

The International Hotels Group (China's leading hotelier, with nine well-known brands worldwide) recognized that none of the multinational hotel chains had a specific brand that recognized the differences in service needs arising from China's cultural differences. They created a new hotel brand, Hualuxe, aimed at meeting these preferred Chinese requirements. Launched in 2015, it emphasizes the importance of the "hosting and banqueting" experience, offering late-night dining opportunities, and recognizing hierarchy among its customers—the latter idea being an alien one for Westerners. This new business has been set up initially for expansion throughout China. Eventually it will roll out globally, as Chinese are expected to make up 25 percent of all global travelers within the next ten years. Success in China with a China-designed customer value proposition should lead to long-term growth outside China for this company.

Chinese companies have already started to apply creative adaptation outside China. In chapter 3 we described Haier's insight into the behavior of US consumers to create a three-temperature refrigerator (initially to store ice cream); we also discussed Huawei's insight into foreign customers' needs for base stations that occupied less space on high-rent office floors. Goodbaby has innovation centers in three countries that not only provide intelligence that is used in adapting Goodbaby's products to each country's tastes but also to exchange ideas and experience, for application in each other's markets. And Four Dimension Johnson has developed a business model for its cash-in-transit vehicles that uses low-cost labor in China to produce mass-customized cabins, which are shipped to Europe for final assembly and sale.

Reverse innovation out of China by multinationals, which is creative adaptation with global applications, is a test of how well a company has absorbed the lessons of innovating in China. In chapter 5 we described several examples from companies as diverse as Akzo Nobel, BMW, General Electric, General Motors, and Philips. Whereas the low growth of Western and developed Asian markets has tended to dampen their home companies' creativeness, China's rapid development and diversity create an environment for mature-market companies to reinvigorate their creative spirits.

Recognizing the opportunity for a new business model requires not only appreciation for local culture based on local presence but also sensitivity in corporate management to accept and support a different concept of service in a different market. There can be twin benefits: not only success in the Chinese market, but also the opportunity for reverse innovation into the rest of the world.

Creation of new categories

In China's market, new and often surprising product and service categories are frequently being created. As was noted above, Wahaha, the leading beverage company in China, released Nutri-Express, a blend of juice and milk, and created an entirely new sector that has attracted many followers. Bubble tea (milky tea with chewy arrowroot starch "bubbles") had become popular across China through cafés and beverage kiosks, but it was Xiang Piao Piao, a local beverage startup, that created the market for instant bubble tea for on-the-go and in-home consumption in 2005. Its Zhen Zhu Nai Cha ("pearl milk tea"), sold in a café-style cup with a straw, was made with softer coconut starch bubbles to simulate the long brewing process of original arrowroot. The café association enabled Xiang Piao to charge a premium over the prices of other convenience beverages. By 2011 this new category, with multiple participants, had sales of 10 billion renminbi. It is a Chinese example of creating a new space in a crowded market. "Bubble tea" shops are appearing in the West as an exotic new idea; why not a foreign launch of a similar product by a multinational?

For many companies, new category creation is a strategic priority. But executing it well requires a deep commitment to local culture. In addition to different habits, there are other differences that come from deeper cultural beliefs and history. For instance, China has a concept of the "inner heat" of the body. In Chinese thinking, specific foods affect your internal balance either by warming you up (black tea, alcohol, red meat, etc.) or cooling you down (green tea, most green vegetables, duck meat, etc.). Too much inner heat is considered unhealthy and is thought to lead to a wide range of illnesses, from skin problems to serious organ dysfunction. Unfortunately, the spicy and greasy foods and high alcohol consumption associated with Chinese business dining make "inner heat" inevitable. The Guangdong-based JDB Group addressed this problem when it brought a traditional herbal cooling drink from Guangdong to the national market. Wong Lo Kat was launched in 1995. After ten years, sales in the sector had grown to more than 20 billion renminbi ($3 billion). Soda-based drinks are also believed to increase "inner heat," and JDB, by communicating Wong Lo Kat's functional superiority, has stolen drinkers away from soda in droves.

Changing the way a customer experiences a product or a service can also carve out new space. Hsu Fu Chi took this approach to confectionery. Instead of selling whole blocks, it lets consumers create their own selections from a wide range of choices and buy by weight. This pick-and-mix approach is a familiar habit in traditional marketplaces everywhere in China, where consumers have always valued touching and selecting products themselves. Hsu Fu Chi brought this model to the modern confectionery setting, and the format tempted people to purchase. The company also maintains direct interaction with customers through dedicated retail sales counters. It soon became one of the biggest confectionery companies in China, and in 2011 it attracted a $1.7 billion offer from Nestlé for a 60 percent share.

An increasingly important way to develop new categories is to segment the market geographically, which at first may seem less attractive to companies accustomed to greater homogeneity in the US market or in Japan. Although competition in first-tier and second-tier Chinese cities is increasingly intense, there are more than 100 cities in China with populations exceeding a million, and their development will fuel growth in the coming decades. Many multinationals are now attempting to establish firm foundations in third-tier and fourth-tier cities which they hadn't previously considered high priorities (one of Best Buy's mistakes). The problem is that many local companies are already well established there. Huawei was the first of many local companies to use the famous Chinese strategy of "encircling cities from the country."[14] It effectively used its influence in rural areas for subsequent expansion to first-tier cities.

Some multinationals have done well in lower-tier markets. For instance, to avoid head-to-head competition with other hypermarket chains that had taken root in first-tier cities, the Sun Art Retail Group, a partnership between RT Mart (Taiwanese) and Auchan (French), has aggressively expanded to lower-tier cities. Entering China in 2011, Sun Art became the biggest Chinese hypermarket chain in sales, bypassing Wal-Mart and Carrefour. Procter & Gamble has innovated with single-serving shampoo sachets in lower-tier cities where lower incomes limit purchase quantities. In the pharmaceutical industry, in order to develop the market outside first-tier cities, Western corporations have changed their sales model, bypassing middlemen and sending their own sales agents into local hospitals.

According to the American Chamber of Commerce in China, in 2010 most American enterprises were already planning to focus their investments in the lower-tier cities. Success in lower-tier cities, however, is not guaranteed for Western companies. Local brands are often strong, and market conditions often differ from big city experience. Wahaha's Future Cola has a bigger market share than either Coca-Cola or Pepsi outside the first-tier and second-tier cities, so if global competitors are serious they may have to behave tactically like local challengers. And this isn't simply a battle of price; Future Cola has built an emotional advantage with a nationalistic positioning as "Chinese people's own cola."

As we noted earlier, Chinese consumers are increasingly sophisticated and are taking on some of the habits and behaviors that are seen in developed markets. However, this process should not be confused with "Westernizing." Chinese consumers retain an attitude that is rooted in their cultural heritage. If anything, as they grow more sophisticated, they increasingly prefer locally relevant products and services. This is a warning sign for established companies that global best practice may not guarantee innovation success and that there are always competitors ready to step in with a more relevant offer. On the other hand, if multinationals foster a deep understanding of consumers and the local market dynamics, and are able to harmonize that knowledge with their global experience and technological knowhow, they will have the basis for culturally powerful innovations.

Some of the new product categories created for the Chinese market, such as Nestlé's peelable banana ice cream, can be exported to the rest of the world. On the other hand, success in China can sometimes blind a Chinese company to differences in consumers' tastes abroad. Few Chinese companies can yet boast of an internationally recognized brand. For example, Shanghai Jahwa, a major Chinese cosmetics company, has struggled to penetrate Western markets with its locally admired Herborist brand, which is promoted with references to herbal ingredients used in traditional Chinese medicine. Western consumers don't yet appear to value the "made-in-China" association for products associated with health and beauty, or food. By contrast, Shanghai Tang (originally a Hong Kong company, now owned by Switzerland's Richemont, the world's second-largest luxury goods company) has become a successful clothing brand by re-interpreting the style of 1920s Shanghai in a modern idiom.

The lesson from these experiences is that it may be more important for a multinational to export the China-inspired mindset of constantly seeking novelty to its people than to emphasize a product's origin in China. "China-for-global" products that have been celebrated as exemplars of "reverse innovation" depend for their appeal outside China not on their China-specific origins but on their suitability to address needs that are universal. These may take the form of lower-cost, more efficient, or more diverse ways of filling a need (as in the cases of GE's portable ultrasound devices and Four DImension Johnson's CIT vehicles) or may satisfy universal needs in a novel way (as in the cases of Nestle's peelable banana ice cream and Tencent's WeChat). Being present in China offers multinationals exposure to the dimensions of customers and culture in that still fast-growing country, as well as a needed appreciation of the capabilities of their competitors.

Focusing on "lean value"

The time when Western companies could automatically command a price premium in China is coming to an end. The gap in quality and the perception of quality is narrowing, with Chinese consumers increasingly choosing local brands on the basis of preference as well as cost. Meanwhile, multinationals have often been less eager than the locals to reach the masses with "good enough" products and services that offer "lean value" by focusing only on desirable benefits and eliminating unimportant costs. For example, it took Procter & Gamble China years to get its headquarters to agree to launch Crest toothpaste as a mid-price brand in China. But once launched, Crest went on to become the leading toothpaste in China. The potential of the 300-million-strong emerging middle class is often discussed optimistically, but China still has a long way to go before it will have a Western-style middle class with significant discretionary income. And there are wide disparities of disposable income between cities (in Shanghai, disposable income averaged 46,000 renminbi in 2014) and rural regions (in the poorest province, Tibet, disposable income averaged 10,700 renminbi in the same year). The average for China as a whole in 2014 was 20,170 renminbi ($3,280). For many aspiring members of the middle class, commitments to housing and other living costs leave little discretionary income.

Thus, despite the appearance of wealth visitors see when they confine themselves to the centers of the larger cities, the majority of Chinese have only modest amounts of cash to spare for things beyond the necessities of daily life. And the many problems consumers face in air and food quality, health, education, domestic housing, and insurance clamor for innovative answers. For these reasons, multinationals should consider seriously the potential of products and services that are "fit for purpose," using their substantial R&D resources to create solutions for the many needs of consumers who want reasonable value for modest outlays. In-car air purifiers, garment steamers, low-intensity book lights, formaldehyde-absorbing interior paint, low-cost cardiac monitors, and ultrasound machines are all examples of multinationals' ingenuity at work for such needs.

The broader market is not going to be captured by developing only premium products. IKEA, seeing its purpose in China as reaching the "many people" with good quality and design, has, on ideological grounds, rejected the common Western temptation to focus on premium segments in China. As IKEA opens stores across China, it is aggressively focused on refining its already lean model to stimulate volume growth in the mass market. For example, a simple but durable dinner plate sold by IKEA costs 2.90 renminbi (50 US cents). That is one fourth the price of the cheapest pack of disposable white paper napkins at City Shop, a premium hypermarket in Shanghai and Beijing catering to higher-income customers and expatriates.

Multinationals from developed countries, as they seek constant differentiation in their home markets, usually opt for "feature inflation," which results in price inflation and value deflation. Chinese consumers don't want to pay for over-featured products and services. Thus, China provides an excellent training ground for implementing management ideas that are current, if not deeply entrenched, in the West. Multinationals can benefit greatly from operating in this laboratory, in which their efforts will be strongly tested. China is an excellent proving ground for practicing design thinking and lean manufacturing.

Developing mixed teams and global leaders

Fast change, innovation, and mixed teams are watchwords of today's corporate leaders, and China provides a great place for cultivating leadership qualities. An excellent example is Procter & Gamble. In the late 1980s and the early 1990s, Procter & Gamble was a leader in recruitment at top universities in China and was able to attract some of the best rising talent in the country. To effectively train and retain these bright new hires, P&G brought in some of its best people from its newly built organizations in Asia—not people from the United States and Europe, although that would have been easier. The result was a culturally and ethnically diverse group of middle managers who formed a culture of entrepreneurship and creativity based on a strong understanding of evolving Chinese culture. By picking its best employees from Hong Kong, Singapore, India, Japan, the Philippines, and Taiwan, Procter & Gamble demonstrated a level of confidence in doing business with "Asian" insights. This was coupled with well-established business practices introduced by peers from the United States and Europe. The combination of the best from East and West created a ten-year period of unparalleled growth for P&G. Senior leaders in the region were enthusiastic yet rigorous supporters of innovative practices. These leaders included A. G. Lafley, Robert McDonald, and Dimitri Panayotopoulos. Lafley and McDonald eventually became CEOs of P&G. Panayotopoulos, the former head of P&G China, rose to the position of vice-chairman.

Taking an enlightened approach to the opportunity to learn in China has paid off well for Procter & Gamble, not only for the China business, but more broadly. P&G's hair-care business in China was based on enhanced conditioning shampoo technology from the United States, an understanding of the importance of low-price sachets from Southeast Asia, and supply-chain efficiencies learned from Japan. Its skin-care business in China was driven by an understanding of how to create multi-step regimens from Japan and by experience with the distribution of laundry detergents in Europe. The lack of previously existing models in China and the absence of dominating cultural groups allowed ideas to germinate and allowed young Chinese managers to influence and shape the creation of a China-centric operating model.

Today's successful executives must have multicultural skills to become future global leaders. China's current business environment presents a great chance for companies to cultivate mixed teams with members from diverse backgrounds. But China offers much more to the development of managers than a diverse working environment. It teaches important lessons about speed in decision making, customer intimacy, dealing with intense competition, lean operations, and design thinking. This experience, if absorbed by enough capable people, will allow for learning in China to be transferred back to headquarters and the rest of a multinational company's operations.

LEARNING TO LEARN IN CHINA

What is so powerful about Procter & Gamble's experience is that P&G recognized from the beginning that it should allow learning to happen—that it should view learning from diverse experiences as its most important priority. In order to learn what they must learn, companies must actively plan to learn, which includes learning from locals, learning how to "play Chinese," and, in a reversal of the conventional learning pattern, learn from Chinese companies' experiences at home and abroad. (Remember, from chapter 6, Honeywell's goal of "becoming a Chinese company.")

We have identified two major principles for multinational companies seeking to learn from China and to exploit what they learn elsewhere:

- Plan proactively to learn from China and apply the lessons.
- Learn from the best Chinese companies' distinctive characteristics, such as risk taking, speed of action, lean value (fit for purpose), and identification of new customer needs.

Actively planning to learn

Learning cannot be left to chance: it must be deliberate and planned. Some companies, among them Procter & Gamble, have learned in China's market; many others have not. Many Japanese companies believed that they knew Chinese culture well, so they made less of an effort to learn about the idiosyncrasies of China's market than they might have. Some Western companies adopted an attitude of superiority. In contrast, the more enlightened Western MNCs felt that they knew very little about the market and the culture, and from the beginning planned well to learn from China.

Part of the learning challenge for multinationals is to make a deliberate shift away from outdated attitudes. There is no longer any place for arrogance or complacency. Years ago the China head of a leading Western telecom company put it this way: "Huawei is only in the position it is because it copies us multinationals and lives off government subsidies." Recently that Western telecom company was driven out of the market as Huawei stepped into the lead in China and overseas. Although today executives aren't likely to be so casual in dismissing Chinese capabilities, other negative attitudes are still present in subtler guises. We were recently with a global CEO visiting China who, hearing about local competitors, implored his team to focus primarily on competition from the big multinationals. In contrast, the more experienced CEO of another diversified multinational corporation told us that, whereas in the US market he had only a few big competitors, in China he had "scores—even hundreds." Market comparisons between countries often hide the real situation. Many global multinationals celebrate a double-digit growth rate in China because it is impressive in comparison to other markets. However, it is easy to forget that some local Chinese companies have been growing at triple-digit rates, and they regard a 50 percent growth rate as normal. Another corporation had envisioned becoming the top multinational in its sector in China, but multinationals already held no more than a shrinking 20 percent of that sector. We urge the leaders of multinational corporations to remember the Red Queen: your company's 30 percent annual growth in China could mean a decreasing market share.

Learning from the locals

It is important for corporate leaders to learn from the best Chinese companies' distinctive characteristics. China is the most important market in the world, and it is bustling with exciting local companies fighting to dominate the fast-growing domestic market. Throughout this book we have used examples of these local innovators to illustrate the scale and the diversity of innovation in China. However, our real purpose is to offer through these examples a potentially new set of rules for business. The best Chinese companies are clever innovators that often surpass current Western best practices; they use rapid iteration and bold imitation, an aggressive appetite for competition, and insightful product positioning. Companies that want to innovate in China successfully need to take on these characteristics. They also need to relearn these characteristics for markets outside China, even in their home countries.

A TIMELY OPPORTUNITY

To take advantage of China's market dynamics, companies have to think beyond current market boundaries and reach past existing demand. With rapid evolution of the market bringing new phases of competition, innovation success in China is increasingly dependent not on perfecting products within a defined market space, or even on providing "fit for current needs," but on strategically redefining that space, answering questions such as these: How can we develop new categories that take advantage of fast change? How can we meet emerging needs from newly developed regions? How can we develop business models that differ from the past and can accelerate success? And what can we take beyond China—to other rapidly developing countries and to our home markets? Visionary local companies and multinationals have redrawn their strategies by thinking expansively about what customers want now and what they will want in the near future, what products and services they should provide for those needs, where they will produce, what they will sell, where they will sell it, and how. These should be timeless questions for every company, but they are not regularly included in the strategic process. Learning from China can provide the stimulus to do so.

China-specific innovation is no longer an optional activity for Western companies with operations in China. Over the years, the best Chinese companies have learned how to progress toward a dominant position through their innovative capabilities. It is now time for multinationals to start learning from the local competitors. Companies will have to undertake reforms for this difficult task: prioritizing nimbleness, fostering an innovation culture, thinking expansively about opportunities, getting deeper under the skin of local culture, and even imitating some of the behavior patterns of local companies.

However, let us not forget that the global resources of multinational corporations give them a huge advantage over local firms. Despite domestic strength, global expansion is a new phase for most Chinese companies, and their path to success is not easy. Meanwhile, multinationals have rich banks of products and expertise that they can apply in locally powerful ways. For instance, when local firms bring successful innovations to the market, multinationals can use their accumulated expertise to introduce improvements swiftly, taking a leaf from the Chinese playbook by copying and improving.

Most important, what has been learned in China can and should be deployed in other markets. We have already observed this in examples of reverse innovation from China. Consider also that Minute Maid Pulpy Super Milky, which was created for China in 2004, became Coca-Cola's first billion-dollar global brand to originate in an emerging market. More broadly, with Western nations facing uncertain economic changes, the lessons learned through navigating China's dynamic competition landscape are powerful forces for innovating in a world where the fight for market share is intensifying rapidly.

A CALL TO ACTION

Around the time this book is published, China's National People's Congress is expected to meet to approve its thirteenth five-year plan. At the time of writing, the details had not been announced; however, we expect that the plan will continue the emphasis on innovation, but in a context of broader changes to the economic and institutional elements of China's mixed economy. A number of statements hinted at the need to address deeper issues. In November 2014, Premier Li Keqiang said that China should "continue to take development as the top priority, put emphasis on reform and innovation ... restructuring, streamlining administration and delegating power to lower levels ... and opening up to the outside world."[15] In a statement issued May 27, 2015, President Xi Jinping said that China should "maintain economic growth, transform the growth mode, optimize industrial structure, promote innovation, step up agricultural modernization, reform institutional mechanisms, boost coordinated growth, strengthen ecological progresses, safeguard people's living quality and improve support for the poor."[16] Both of these statements indicate that, in order for China to continue to raise the living standards of its people, institutional and structural changes will be necessary. They imply that serious attention will be paid to the enabling conditions for innovation and growth.

At the time of writing, China was experiencing a slowing of growth, which had been expected, but which caused concern around the world. Its stock markets were shaken, and there were fears of more serious effects. We write with this awareness, but also with the expectation that the government will take offsetting fiscal measures, injecting investment funds into the economy as it did during the Global Financial Crisis of 2008. In doing so, it will have to balance measures with immediate effect, such as infrastructure investment, with the more systemic policies that will be called for in the thirteenth five-year plan. An important objective of the next plan will be to move China's industrial base up the value chain toward more sophisticated, less labor-intensive, higher-value-added sectors. This was the motivation for the release in 2015 by the State Council of a plan titled Made in China 2025. Drafted by the Ministry of Industry and Information Technology, this is an ambitious plan to transform China into a leading manufacturing power by the year 2049.[17] Emphasizing quality of output rather than volume, it aims to raise domestic added value to 70 percent of output by 2025. Although the proposal singles out ten sectors for priority attention (as previous plans have done),[18] much of it calls for broad changes in the industrial structure, in the microeconomic environment, in the conditions of competition, and in other areas of importance to entrepreneurship and strong enterprises, including education.

These ideas are consistent with the findings of several studies of the sources of competitive advantage in countries. Michael Porter's work placed emphasis on four microeconomic factors in a "diamond of competitive advantage," with little role for government. Increasingly, however, the consensus is that government has an important role alongside business in developing a country's innovative capacity by investing in infrastructure and in financial and human capital and by implementing policies that encourage entrepreneurship and competition. Other studies find that government has a critical role in investing in innovation capital, but that this is a necessary but not sufficient condition; it must also encourage an innovation-oriented environment.[19]

It seems, therefore, likely that the thirteenth five-year plan will signal an important, perhaps crucial, shift in direction toward reforms of institutional and microeconomic policies in which greater liberalization and competition could open opportunities not only for local companies but also for multinationals. China can continue to benefit from multinationals' resources, skills, and innovative capabilities if the environment encourages them to commit to a deeper presence. We earnestly hope that this book will be read in such an environment.

At the same time, we emphasize the message of the previous seven chapters. China has achieved a remarkable level of innovative capability in a short period of time. Its businesses will move from incremental innovation to radical, breakthrough innovation as they move into the third phase of their growth. To counter them both in China and in the markets of the advanced economies, leaders need to plan actively to learn from China's experience. Corporate and regional leaders of Western, Japanese, and Korean companies should actively push their China subsidiaries to act fearlessly on the five strategies we have set out above. Corporate leaders should actively seek to create and deploy organizational processes and cultures that transfer such experience to the rest of their operations around the world. Leaders of companies that operate in China, and leaders of those that do not, should turn their attention from preoccupation with their traditional markets to ensure that their companies learn the lessons of innovating in China, for China, and for the world.

Many centuries ago, the world learned from China. For the past hundred years, however, China has been patiently learning from the world. It is now time for the world to learn from China again. Multinational corporations should "seize the day" (*bǎ wò jīn rì*). That is the most urgent priority for every CEO.

NOTES

Chapter 1

1. Joel Mokyr, *The Lever of Riches* (Oxford University Press, 1990).

2. See, for example, Richard McGregor, *The Party: The Secret World of China's Communist Rulers* (Harper Collins, 2011); Juan Antonio Fernandez and Laurie Underwood, *China CEO: Voices of Experience from 20 International Business Leaders* (Wiley, 2006), chapter 8.

3. See Regina M. Abrami, William C. Kirby, and F. Warren McFarlan, *Can China Lead? Reaching the Limits of Power and Growth* (Harvard Business Review Press, 2014).

4. Ming Zeng and Peter J. Williamson, *Dragons at Your Door: How Chinese Cost Innovation Is Disrupting Global Competition* (Harvard Business School Press, 2007).

5. Dan Breznitz and Michael Murphree, *Run of the Red Queen* (Yale University Press, 2011).

6. See, especially, Xiaolan Fu, *China's Path to Innovation* (Cambridge University Press, 2015); Yifei Sun, Max von Zedtwitz, and Denis Fred Simon, editors, *Global R&D in China* (Routledge, 2008).

7. Anil K. Gupta and Haiyan Wang, *How to Get China and India Right* (Jossey-Bass, 2009).

8. Shaun Rein's book *The End of Copycat China: The Rise of Creativity, Innovation, and Individualism in Asia* (Wiley, 2014) is about individuals and policy rather than companies. Yinglan Tan, in *Chinnovation: How Chinese Innovators Are Changing the World* (Wiley, 2011), offers examples but only limited strategic advice.

9. Vijay Govindarajan and Chris Trimble, *Reverse Innovation: Create Far from Home, Win Everywhere* (Harvard Business Review Press, 2012).

10. Alibaba's platforms (Taobao, Tmall, and Juhuasuan) enabled 8 million small entrepreneurs to set up online businesses, serving 231 million active buyers. Source: Group Holding Ltd., Form F-1 Registration Statement, Securities and Exchange Commission, Washington, May 6, 2014.

11. See Joanna Lewis, *Green Innovation in China: China's Wind Power Industry and the Global Transition to a Low-Carbon Economy* (Columbia University Press, 2013); Kelly Sims Gallagher, *The Globalization of Clean Energy Technology: Lessons from China* (MIT Press, 2014).

12. The Ten-Thousand Talents Program was launched in August 2012 with the goal of fostering more than 10,000 talented Chinese people, including 100 world-class scientists (*China Daily*, 2013). This program is different from the Thousand Talents Program, which was launched in 2008 with the aim of recruiting talented people with from all around the world to extend their careers in China. The recruitment number had reached 4,000 in 2013 (Chinese Talents, 2013/12, original is in Chinese, translated by the authors' assistants).

13. PricewaterhouseCoopers, Tax Preferential Policy for R&D Activities in China, 2012.

14. Breznitz and Murphree, *Run of the Red Queen*.

15. See, for example, Loren Brandt and Eric Thun, "The fight for the middle: Upgrading, competition, and industrial development in China," *World Development* 38, no. 11 (2010): 1–20.

16. Xiaobo Wu, Rufei Ma, Yongjiang Shi, and Ke Rong, "Secondary innovation: The path of catch-up with 'Made in China,'" *China Economic Journal* 2, no. 1 (2009): 93–104.

17. Qingdao Haier Investor Relations, October 21, 2013 (http://www.haier.net/en/investor_relations/haier/).

18. Authors' estimate, based on Heritage Foundation, China Global Investment Tracker Dataset (http://www.heritage.org/research/projects/china-global -investment-tracker-interactive-map).

19. José F. P. Santos and Peter J. Williamson, "The new mission for multinationals," *Sloan Management Review* 56, no. 4 (2015): 45–54

20. Héctor Hernández et al., 2014 EU Industrial R&D Investment Scoreboard. Joint Research Centre—Institute for Prospective Technological Studies, European Commission, Luxembourg.

21. Including Chinese companies having a corporate registration in the Cayman Islands or Bermuda.

22. The abbreviation PCT refers to applications made through the Patent Cooperation Treaty process, which facilitates the filing of patent applications in multiple countries by making a single application that conforms to certain standardized requirements in any one of the 148 PCT contracting states, or directly with the WIPO. An international search process is initiated, and the applicant gains time before entering into the national phase, when it seeks approval from specific countries. The decision to grant a patent in each country and the administration of patents remain national prerogatives. Approximately 10 percent of worldwide patent applications are filed through the PCT process.

23. World Intellectual Property Organization, March 19, 2015 (http://www .worldipreview.com/news/huawei-tops-list-of-pct-filers-8066).

24. Royal Dutch Shell, the leading investor in R&D among Western oil and gas companies, invested $1.3 billion.

25. Barry Jaruzelski, John Loehr, and Richard Holman, "The Global Innovation 1000: Navigating the digital future," *strategy+business*, issue 73, winter 2013.

26. Thompson Reuters, 2013 Top 100 Global Innovators, 2013.

27. Barry Jaruzelski, Volker Staack, and Brad Goehle, "The Global Innovation 1000: Proven paths to innovation success," *strategy+business*, issue 77 (2014). (On March 31, 2014, Booz & Company merged with PwC to form a consulting unit within PwC called Strategy&.)

28. *Forbes*, "The world's most innovative companies," August 13, 2014 (http://www.forbes.com/innovative-companies/list/).

29. The Forbes Innovation Premium is "a measure of how much investors have bid up the stock price of a company above the value of its existing business based on expectations of future innovative results (new products, services, and markets). Members of the list must have $10 billion in market capitalization, spend at least 2.5 of revenue on R&D and have seven years of public data."

30. Baidu, Henan Shuanghui Investment and Development, Tencent Holding, Tingyi Holding, Hengan International Group, and Inner Mongolia Yili. (Kweichow Moutai and China Oilfield were on the 2013 list but not the 2014 one.)

31. For an example, see Regina M. Abrami, William C. Kirby, and F. Warren McFarlan, "Why China can't innovate," *Harvard Business Review* 92, no. 3 (2014): 107–111.

32. For a survey of these reforms and China's economic development, see Lyn Denend and Bruce McKern, The Business Environment of China: Challenges of an Emerging Economic Superpower, Case Study IB-57, Stanford Graduate School of Business, 2009.

33. George Yip and Bruce McKern, "Innovation in emerging markets—the case of China," *International Journal of Emerging Markets* 9, no. 1 (2014): 2–10.

34. See Denis Simon and Cong Cao, *China's Emerging Technological Edge: Assessing the Role of High-End Talent* (Cambridge University Press, 2009).

35. National Science Foundation, Science and Technology in the World Economy, Science and Engineering Indicators 2014, appendix, table 2-39. More recent data weren't available at the time of publication, but the numbers have certainly increased. See http://www.nsf.gov/statistics/seind14/index.cfm/appendix/tables.htm.

36. In 2013 the number of Chinese returning from abroad totaled 353,500 out of a total of 3 million who have gone abroad since 1979. Source: Xinhua News Agency, February 22, 2014 (http://news.xinhuanet.com/english/china/2014-02/22/c_133135494.htm).

37. See also Chunlin Zhang, Douglas Zhihua Zeng, William Peter Mako, and James Seward, *Promoting Enterprise-Led Innovation in China* (World Bank, 2009).

38. Alibaba Group Holding Limited, Form F-1 Registration Statement, Securities and Exchange Commission, Washington, May 6, 2014. Updated from Company website.

39. Vijay Govindarajan and Chris Trimble, *Reverse Innovation: Create Far from Home, Win Everywhere* (Harvard Business School Press, 2012).

40. Orit Gadiesh, Philip Leung, and Till Vestring, "The battle for China's good-enough market," *Harvard Business Review* 85, no. 9 (2007): 81–89.

41. The program is described in The National Medium- and Long-Term Program for Science and Technology Development (2006–2020), State Council, People's Republic of China.

42. For a detailed discussion of China's development strategy, see *China 2030: Building a Modern, Harmonious, and Creative Society* (World Bank, 2013).

43. P. Zhou and L. Leydesdorff, "The emergence of China as a leading nation in science," *Research Policy* 35, no. 1 (2006): 83–104.

44. Junying Fu, Rainer Frietsch, and Ulrike Tagscherer, Publication Activity in the Science Citation Index Expanded (SCIE) Database in the Context of Chinese Science and Technology Policy from 1977 to 2012, Discussion Papers Innovation Systems and Policy Analysis no. 35, Fraunhofer Institute for Systems and Innovation Research, 2013.

45. Authors' estimate, based on National Science Foundation, National Center for Science and Engineering Statistics (September 2013); Battelle Memorial Institute estimates of other funding sources, in Battelle Memorial Institute and *R&D* Magazine, *2013 R&D Funding Forecast*, 2012.

46. M. M. Keupp, A. Beckenbauer, and O. Gassmann, "How managers protect intellectual property rights in China using de facto strategies," *R&D Management*, 39, no. 2 (2009): 211–223; X. Quan and H. W. Chesbrough, "Hierarchical segmentation of R&D laboratories in China," *IEEE Transactions on Engineering Management* 57, no. 1 (2010): 9–21.

47. State Council, People's Republic of China, The National Medium- and Long-Term Program for Science and Technology Development (2006–2020): An Outline (English translation, 2006), p. 8.

48. Ibid., p. 9.

49. Ibid, p. 10.

50. Marina Mazzucato, *The Entrepreneurial State: Debunking Public vs. Private Sector Myths* (Anthem, 2013).

51. Haiyang Zhang and Tetsushi Sonobe, "The development of science and technology parks in China, 1988–2008," *Economics* 5, no. 6 (2011) (doi:10.5018/economicsejournal. ja.2011–6; http://dx.doi.org/10.5018/economics-ejournal.ja.2011-6).

52. Albert Guangzhou Hu, "China's technology parks and regional economic growth," in proceedings of the Fourth International Conference on the Chinese Economy, Clermont-Ferrand, 2003.

53. We thank one of the anonymous MIT Press reviewers for suggesting this section.

54. World Bank, World Development Indicators, 2014.

55. National Bureau of Statistics of China, Communiqué on National Expenditures on Science and Technology in 2013, October 23, 2014.

56. There is a discrepancy of 1.4 percent in the National Bureau of Statistics data, so these figures don't add up precisely.

57. Converted to US dollars at the average 2013 exchange rate of 0.1613. Source: Oanda.com.

58. Organization for Economic Cooperation and Development, Main Science and Technology Indicators, June 10, 2014 (http://www.oecd.org/sti/msti). The OECD estimated China's R&D intensity to be 1.984 percent in 2012 and that of the European Union to be 1.978 percent. The differences are no doubt insignificant.

59. About 59 percent of US government R&D spending is defense-related. Since some of that has spinoffs for commercial business (e.g., Apple's iPhone), our estimate includes $10 billion of the research component of defense R&D.

60. World Bank, World Development Indicators, 2014.

61. Fu et al, Publication Activity in the Science Citation Index Expanded (SCIE) Database in the Context of Chinese Science and Technology Policy from 1977 to 2012.

62. QS Quacquarelli Symonds, QS World University Rankings 2014 (http://www.topuniversities.com/university-rankings/world-university-ranking).

63. Mazzucato, *The Entrepreneurial State.*

64. Authors' calculation, based on Battelle Memorial Institute and *R&D* Magazine, *2013 R&D Funding Forecast*, 2012.

65. Thomas Barlow, Innovation in America: A Comparative Study, United States Studies Centre, University of Sydney, 2008.

66. Abrami et al., "Why China can't innovate."

67. Stephen L Sass, "Can China innovate without dissent?" *New York Times*, January 21, 2014.

68. For example, the low participation of foreign researchers in patents granted in China, noted below.

69. Anil K. Gupta and Haiyan Wang, "Beijing is stifling Chinese innovation," *Wall Street Journal*, September 1, 2011 (http://www.wsj.com/articles/SB10001424053111904583204576541732014359842).

70. PricewaterhouseCoopers, Tax Preferential Policy for R&D activities in China.

71. Gross domestic expenditure on R&D by sector of performance and source of funds, OECD StatExtracts (http://stats.oecd.org/Index.aspx?DataSetCode=GERD_FUNDS). The figure of 4.4 percent of the total GERD is not specified in the OECD statistics.

72. Li Keqiang, Report on the Work of the Government, delivered at Second Session of Twelfth National People's Congress. Source: Xinhua News Agency, March 5, 2014.

73. Jessica Morrison, "China becomes world's third-largest producer of research articles," *Nature*, February 6, 2014 (http://www.nature.com/news/china-becomes-world-s-third-largest-producer-of-research-articles-1.14684).

74. SCImago,SJR—SCImago Journal & Country Rank, 2012 (http://www.scimagojr.com).

75. Ibid.

76. There are big differences here from the National Science Foundation's data, which show the United States' share as 30.7 percent and China's as 13.6 percent in 2012. See National Science Foundation, Science and Technology in the World Economy, Science and Engineering Indicators 2014.

77. "Looks good on paper," *The Economist*, September 28, 2013.

78. Anil K. Gupta and Haiyan Wang, "China as an innovation center? Not so fast," *Wall Street Journal*, July 28, 2011.

79. State Intellectual Property Office of the PRC, Annual Report 2013, appendix 1: Statistical Data (http://www.sipo.gov.cn/).

80. US Patent and Trademark Office, US Patent Statistics, Calendar Years 1963–2013.

81. State Intellectual Property Office of the PRC, Annual Report 2013, appendix 1: Statistical Data (http://www.sipo.gov.cn/).

82. Interestingly, nine of the top ten design patent applications were from non-Chinese companies. Source: World Intellectual Property Organization, PCT Yearly Review, Geneva, 2013.

83. World Intellectual Property Organization, *PCT Yearly Review*, Geneva, 2013.

84. For an explanation of the PCT process, see note 22 above.

85. OECD Factbook 2014: Economic, Environmental and Social Statistics (http://www.oecd-ilibrary.org/economics/oecd-factbook-2014_factbook-2014-en).

86. Alan Marco, Richard Miller, and Jay Kesan, Perspectives on the Growth in Chinese Patent Applications to the USPTO, working paper 2014-1, Office of Chief Economist, US Patent and Trademark Office, Alexandria, Virginia, 2014.

87. Ibid., p. 14.

88. For more details, see World Intellectual Property Organisation, PCT—The International Patent System (http://www.wipo.int/pct/en/).

89. World Intellectual Property Organization PCT Yearly Review 2014: The International Patent System. Geneva, 2014.

90. Ibid. No other Chinese company was in the top 50.

91. World Intellectual Property Organization, PCT Yearly Review 2014.

92. World Intellectual Property Organization, PCT Yearly Review 2013. The proportion of foreign investors was lower for both Japan and South Korea.

93. World Intellectual Property Organization, World Intellectual Property Indicators 2013.

94. Stuart Anderson, "40 percent of *Fortune 500* Companies founded by immigrants or their children," *Forbes*, June 19, 2011.

95. Gupta and Wang, "Beijing is stifling Chinese innovation."

96. High-technology products are defined as products with high R&D intensity. Data are in US dollars as of this writing.

97. IHS Global Insight, Science and Engineering Indicators 2012, World Trade Service database, 2011, appendix, tables 6-26–6-31.

98. Authors' calculations, based on IHS Global Insight, Science and Engineering Indicators 2012.

99. Robert Koopman, Zhi Wang, and Shang-jin Wei, "Estimating domestic content in exports when processing trade is pervasive," *Journal of Development Economics* 99, no. 1 (2012): 178–189; Hong Ma, Zhi Wang, and Kunfu Zhu, Domestic Value-Added in China's Exports and Its Distribution by Firm Ownership, US International Trade Commission working paper 2013-05A, 2013.

100. World Intellectual Property Organization, World Intellectual Property Indicators 2014.

101. McKinsey Global Institute, The China Effect on Global Innovation, July 2015.

102. "Fast and furious. Chinese private firms are embracing innovation," *The Economist*, September 12, 2015.

103. A book published in 2013 by Jossey-Bass (Seung Ho Park, Nan Zhou, and Gerardo R. Ungson, *Rough Diamonds: The Four Traits of Successful Breakout Firms in BRIC Countries*) uses a framework of four Cs quite different from the one we have developed. In that work, four phrases beginning with the letter C are used to explain the success of a selection of privately owned firms from four countries (China, Russia, Brazil, and India). The four Cs of Park et al. are characteristics that they have identified as internal strategies or behaviors of these firms that do not explicitly include external variables: "Capitalizing on Late Development," "Creating Inclusive Market Niches and Segments," "Crafting Operational Excellence," and "Cultivating Profitable Growth." Park et al. make some specific reference to features of Chinese companies in their ninth chapter, and they identify three sets of factors that are in some respects similar to the ten distinctive characteristics of Chinese companies we identify as elements of our *capabilities* factor. Those three sets of factors are "Early Success," "Core Competences," and "Growth Management."

Chapter 2

1. Eden Yin and Peter Williamson, in a paper titled "Rethinking innovation for a recovery" (*Ivey Business Journal* 75, no. 3, 2011: 1–6), offer a 2 × 2 matrix pertaining to innovation in China that considers incremental process and product in-

novation, radical process and product innovation via basic R&D, cost innovation and application innovation, and business-model innovation. See also P. Williamson and M. Zeng, "Chinese multinationals: Emerging through new global gateways," in *Emerging Multinationals in Emerging Markets*, ed. R. Ramamurti and J. V. Singh (Cambridge University Press, 2009).

2. Ming Zeng and Peter J. Williamson, *Dragons at Your Door: How Chinese Cost Innovation Is Disrupting Global Competition* (Harvard Business School Press, 2007).

3. Yin and Williamson, "Rethinking innovation for a recovery."

4. Ibid.

5. Peter Williamson, BROAD Group: Chinese Innovation in the Air, case study 311–115–1, Cambridge Judge Business School, 2011.

6. See also S. Roy, K. Sivakumar, and I. Wilkinson, "Innovation generation in supply chain relationships: A conceptual model and research propositions," *Journal of the Academy of Marketing Science* 32, no. 1 (2004): 61–79.

7. Liang Haishan, Haier Supply-chain Management (company presentation, Supply Chain Conference, 2004).

8. See also Rajesh K. Chandy and Gerard J. Tellis, "Organizing for radical product innovation: The overlooked role of willingness to cannibalize," *Journal of Marketing Research* 35, no. 4 (1998): 474–487.

9. http://www.4gspeed.net/articles/share/211418/

10. See also Rosanna Garcia and Roger Calantone, "A critical look at technological innovation typology and innovativeness terminology: A literature review," *Journal of Product Innovation Management* 19, no.2 (2002): 110–132.

11. See also Peter Skarczynski and Rowan Gibson, *Innovation to the Core: A Blueprint for Transforming the Way Your Company Innovates* (Harvard Business School Press, 2008), pp. 111–114.

12. Booz & Company, Benelux Chamber of Commerce, CEIBS Center on China Innovation, and 21st Century Business Review, An Emerging Innovation Power: 2013 China Innovation Survey, 2013); Strategy& and CEIBS Center on China Innovation, China's Innovations Going Global: 2014 China Innovation Survey, 2014.

13. http://www.haier.net/en/about_haier/haier_strategy/

14. Tarun Khanna, Krishna Paelpu, and Philip Andrews, Haier: Taking a Chinese company global in 2011, case study 9-712-408, Harvard Business School, p. 3.

15. "Who's afraid of Huawei?" *The Economist*, August 4, 2012 (http://www.economist.com/node/21559922).

16. According to Huawei's 2014 annual report.

17. http://enterprise.huawei.com/ilink/en/bout-huawei/newsroom/press-release/HW_062703?KeyTemps=Awards

18. See also Huawei R&D and Innovations (Huawei corporate presentation, 2013); David de Cremer and Jess Zhang, "Huawei to the future," *Business Strategy Review* 25, no. 1 (2014): 26–29.

19. Alibaba Group Holding Ltd., Form F-1 Registration Statement, Securities and Exchange Commission, Washington, 2014. Updated from Company website.

20. Victor Luckerson, "China's Alibaba finds riches on Wall Street," Time.com, September 19, 2014 (http://time.com/3404714/alibaba-ipo-jack-ma-wall-street/).

21. Robert D. Hof, "eBay's patient bid on China," *BusinessWeek Online*, March 15, 2004 (http://www.businessweek.com/magazine/content/04_11/b3874019.htm).

22. Mike Butler, "Alibaba considering Alipay spin-off," *Yahoo Finance*, November 11, 2014 (http://finance.yahoo.com/news/alibaba-considering-alipay-spin-off-132555779.html).

23. Alibaba, *Ma Yun's Speeches* (in Chinese), Hongqi Press, 2010, p.161.

24. Its full name is Jiangsu Yuwell Medical Equipment and Supply Co., Ltd.

25. Changjiang Securities, Maintain Stable Growth, Blood Sugar Meter Business Becomes the Power of Future Development, December 5, 2012.

26. "Fast and furious: Chinese private firms are embracing innovation," *The Economist*, September 12, 2015.

27. Ibid.

28. In 2012 and 2013, this survey included the collaboration with the Benelux Chamber of Commerce and the Wenzhou Chamber of Commerce in China. In 2014, the German Chamber of Commerce replaced the Wenzhou Chamber. See each year's report: Innovation—China's Next Advantage? 2012 China Innovation Survey, joint report by Booz & Company, Benelux Chamber of Commerce, CEIBS Center on China Innovation, and Wenzhou Chamber of Commerce; An Emerging Innovation Power: 2013 China Innovation Survey, joint report by Booz & Company, Benelux Chamber of Commerce, CEIBS Center on China Innovation and 21st Century Business Review; China's Innovations Going Global: 2014 China Innovation Survey, joint report by Strategy& and CEIBS Center on China Innovation. The survey response counts were 110 in 2012, 264 from 1,500 sent in 2013, and 386 from 2,000 sent in 2014.

29. Booz & Company, Benelux Chamber of Commerce, CEIBS Center on China Innovation, and 21st Century Business Review, An Emerging Innovation Power: 2013 China Innovation Survey, 2013.

30. Strategy&, China's Innovations Going Global: 2014 China Innovation Survey.

31. See also P. Williamson and M. Zeng, "Chinese multinationals: Emerging through new global gateways," in *Emerging Multinationals in Emerging Markets*, ed. R. Ramamurti and J. V. Singh (Cambridge University Press, 2009).

Chapter 3

1. "Joyoung beats multinationals and became industry leader" (http://homea.people.com.cn/n/2013/0220/c41390-20542830.html).

2. For a discussion of the "good enough" market, see Orit Gadiesh, Philip Leung, and Till Vestring, "The battle for China's good-enough market," *Harvard Business Review*, September 2007: 2–11.

3. Sea-jin Chang and Sam H. Park, "Winning strategies in China: Competitive dynamics between MNCs and local firms," *Long Range Planning* 45, no. 1 (2012): 1–15.

4. http://baike.baidu.com/view/10036350.htm

5. www.carsurvey.org

6. See http://en.wikipedia.org/wiki/Chery_QQ

7. M. Zeng and P. J. Williamson, *Dragons at Your Door: How Chinese Cost Innovation Is Disrupting Global Competition* (Harvard Business School Press, 2007).

8. Gadiesh et al., "The battle for China's good-enough market."

9. Clayton Christensen, *The Innovator's Dilemma: Why New Technologies Cause Great Firms to Fail* (Harvard Business School Press, 1997).

10. Zeng and Williamson, *Dragons at Your Door*.

11. http://washersearch.co.uk/haier-washing-machine.html; Dan Wang, "Haier shakes up the stubborn European consumer world," *Global Entrepreneur* 19 (October 2012): 26–28.

12. Peter J. Williamson and Eden Yin, "Accelerated innovation: The new challenge from China," *MIT Sloan Management Review* 55, no. 4 (2014): 27–34.

13. Ruxiang Jiang, "China's hard-work culture: Today an advantage, tomorrow a weakness," HBR Blog Network, 2011 (http://blogs.hbr.org/cs/2011/12/chinas_hard-work_culture_today.html).

14. Nils Behnke and Norbert Hueltenschmidt, Changing Pharma's Innovation DNA, Bain & Company, 2010.

15. Ruxiang Jiang, "China's hard-work culture."

16. "Learning from wolves to fight lions," *China Daily*, September 1, 2010 (http://www.chinadaily.com.cn/bizchina/2010-09/01/content_11241465.htm).

17. Zhanghong Zhou, "Huawei's secrets," *Fortune China*, December 2012.

18. Williamson and Yin, "Accelerated innovation."

19. M. Wade, Y. Fang, and W. Kang, Tencent: Copying to Success, case study 3-2274, IMD Business School, 2011.

20. Ibid.

21. Glenn Leibowitz and Erik Roth, "Innovating in China's automotive market: An interview with GM China's president," *McKinsey Quarterly*, February 2012.

22. Ibid.

23. Tian Wei, "China's electric cars lag behind in global race," *China Daily*, October 23, 2012 (http://www.chinadaily.com.cn/cndy/2012-10/23/content_15837888.htm).

24. Industrial and Commercial Bank of China, ICBC Annual Report for Brand and Corporate Culture 2011.

25. Mansour Javidan and Nandani Lynton, "The changing face of the Chinese executive," *Harvard Business Review* 83, no.12 (2005) (http://hbr.org/2005/12/the-changing-face-of-the-chinese-executive/ar/1).

26. Lynn S. Paine, "The globe: The China rules," *Harvard Business Review*, June 2010: 103–108 (http://hbr.org/2010/06/the-globe-the-china-rules/ar/1).

27. See "Warren Buffett cried in a BYD vehicle," *Bloomberg Business Week* 2 (2013): 88–92. BYD stands for "build your dream."

28. As ranked in the 2009 Hurun China Rich List.

29. See Williamson and Yin, "Accelerated innovation."

30. Thomas M. Hout and Pankaj Ghemawat, "China vs the world: Whose technology is it?" *Harvard Business Review*, December 2010 (http://hbr.org/2010/12/china-vs-the-world-whose-technology-is-it/ar/1).

31. Ibid.

32. Guangyu Li and Jonathan Woetzel, "What China's five-year plan means for business," *McKinsey Quarterly*, July 2011(https://www.mckinseyquarterly.com/Strategy/Innovation/What_Chinas_five-year_plan_means_for_business_2832).

33. "China's first bullet train exported to Europe rolls off line," *People's Daily Online*, July 9, 2015.

34. http://www.nea.gov.cn/2012-01/21/c_131370764.htm; http://www.nea.gov.cn/2012-08/02/c_131755182.htm

35. http://www.goldwind.com.cn/web/about.do?action=story

36. Raymond Vernon and L. T. Wells, "International trade and international investment in the product life cycle," *Quarterly Journal of Economics* 81, no. 2 (1966): 190–207.

37. Also see Williamson and Yin, "Accelerated innovation."

38. "Made in China 2025 plan unveiled to boost manufacturing," Xinhua News Agency, May 19, 2015.

39. Scott Kennedy, "Made in China 2025," Center for Strategic and International Studies, 2015 (https://csis.org/publication/made-china-2025).

Chapter 4

1. See also Denis Fred Simon, "Whither foreign R&D in China: Some concluding thoughts on Chinese innovation," *Asia Pacific Business Review* 13, no. 3 (2007): 471–480; Yifei Sun, Maximilian Von Zedtwitz, and Denis Fred Simon, "Globalization of R&D and China: An introduction," *Asia Pacific Business Review* 13, no. 3 (2007): 311–319.

2. Dominique Jolly, Bruce McKern, and George S. Yip, "The next innovation opportunity in China," *Strategy+Business* 80, autumn 2015: 16–19.

3. Courtney Fingar, "China passes US in race for FDI in research and development," *Financial Times*, July 22, 2015.

4. Raymond Vernon and L. T. Wells, "International trade and international investment in the product life cycle," *Quarterly Journal of Economics* 81, no. 2 (1966): 190–207.

5. Lars Hakanson and Robert Nobel, "Foreign research and development in Swedish multinationals," *Research Policy* 22, no. 5–6 (1993): 373–396; Alexander Gerybadze and Guido Reger, "Globalization of R&D: Recent changes in the management of innovation in transnational corporations," *Research Policy* 28, no. 2–3 (1999): 251–274; Tony S. Frost, "The geographic sources of foreign subsidiaries' innovations," *Strategic Management Journal* 22, no. 2 (2001): 101–123.

6. John Hagedoorn, Danielle Cloodt, and Hans van Kranenburg, "Intellectual property rights and the governance of international R&D partnerships," *Journal of International Business Studies* 36 (2005):175–186; Ito Banri and Wakasugi Ryuhei, "What factors determine the mode of overseas R&D by multinationals? Empirical evidence," *Research Policy* 36 (2007): 1275–1287.

7. Maximilian von Zedtwitz, "Managing foreign R&D laboratories in China," *R&D Management* 34, no. 4 (2004): 439–452.

8. Guo Bin and Jing-Jing Guo, "Patterns of technological learning within the knowledge systems of industrial clusters in emerging economies: Evidence from China," *Technovation* 31, no. 2–3 (2011): 87–104.

9. Paul Almeida and Anupama Phene, "Subsidiaries and knowledge creation: The influence of the MNC and host country on innovation," *Strategic Management Journal* 25, no. 8–9 (2004): 847–864.

10. Ming Zeng and Peter J. Williamson, *Dragons at Your Door: How Chinese Cost Innovation Is Disrupting the Rules of Global Competition* (Harvard Business School Press, 2007).

11. Dan Breznitz and Michael Murphree, *Run of the Red Queen* (Yale University Press, 2011).

12. "Wages in China," *China Labour Bulletin*, June 2013 (http://www.clb.org.hk/en/content/wages-china).

13. R. McKinnon, "Wage increases: The win-win answer on China trade," *Wall Street Journal,* July 29, 2010.

14. M. von Zedtwitz and O. Gassmann, "Market versus technology drivers in R&D internationalization: Four different patterns of managing research and development," *Research Policy* 31 (2002): 569–588; B. McKern and G. Yip, "Innovation: The key to China's structural transition," in New Champions in Innovation, report published by World Economic Forum and *Harvard Business Review China*, 2012.

15. Orit Gadiesh, Philip Leung, and Till Vestring, "The battle for China's good-enough market," *Harvard Business Review* 85, no. 9 (2007): 81–89.

16. Jeffrey R. Immelt, Vijay Govindarajan, and Chris Trimble, "How GE is disrupting itself," *Harvard Business Review* 87, no. 10 (2009): 56–65.

17. "Testing GM's shock absorbers," *The Economist*, May 1999; K. Walsh, *Foreign High-Tech R&D in China: Risks, Rewards, and Implications for US-China Relations* (Henry L. Stimson Center, 2003).

18. Raymond Vernon, "The product cycle hypothesis in a new international environment," *Oxford Bulletin of Economics and Statistics* 41, no. 4 (1979): 244–267.

19. Peter J. Williamson and Eden Yin, "Accelerated innovation: The new challenge from China," *MIT Sloan Management Review* 55, no. 4 (2014): 27–34.

20. M. W. Peng and D. Y. Wang, "Innovation capability and foreign direct investment: Toward a learning option perspective," *Management International Review* 40, no.1 (2000): 79–93; O. Gassmann and Z. Han, "Motivations and barriers of foreign R&D activities in China," *R&D Management* 34, no. 4 (2004): 423–437.

21. Fingar, "China passes US in race for FDI in research and development."

Chapter 5

1. We had help in a few of these interviews from Wim Vanhaverbeke and Nadine Rooijakkers of Hasselt University, and also benefited from their ideas.

2. See also Maximilian Von Zedtwitz, "Managing foreign R&D laboratories in China," *Research Policy* 34, no. 4 (2004): 439–452; Maximilian Von Zedtwitz, Sascha Friesike, and Oliver Gassmann, "Managing R&D and new product development," in *The Oxford Handbook of Innovation Management*, ed. Mark Dodgson, David M. Gann, and Nelson Phillips (Oxford University Press, 2014).

3. This issue was first identified by Raymond Vernon in *Sovereignty at Bay: The Multinational Spread of US Enterprises* (Basic Books, 1971). For a more recent discussion, see Ravi Ramamurti, "The obsolescing 'bargaining model'? MNC-host developing country relations revisited," *Journal of International Business Studies* 32, no. 1 (2001): 23–39.

4. See also Maximilian von Zedtwitz, "Initial directors of international R&D laboratories," *Research Policy* 33, no. 4 (2003): 377–393.

5. See note 12 to chapter 1.

6. This study was led by Hester B. Boomgaard as part of her thesis work for an Executive Master of Finance & Control at Maastricht University, advised by Bruce McKern and George Yip and by her mentor at Maastricht University, A. G. van Riel.

7. Guido Reger, "Coordinating globally dispersed research centres of excellence— the case of Philips Electronics," *Journal of International Management* 10, no. 1 (2004): 51–76.

8. See Vijay Govindarajan and Chris Trimble, *Reverse Innovation: Create far from Home, Win Everywhere* (Harvard Business Press, 2012).

9. Jeffrey Immelt, Vijay Govindarajan, and Chris Trimble, "How GE is disrupting itself," *Harvard Business Review* 87, no. 10 (2009): 56–65.

10. One Chinese company that is successful in this field, Mindray, also launches new equipment first in the US market, but it does so because gaining approval from the regulatory authorities there greatly strengthens its credibility among hospitals and medical practitioners in the Chinese market.

11. Steven Veldhoen, Anna Mansson, Bill Peng, George Yip, and Bruce McKern, 2013 China Innovation Survey: An Emerging Innovation Power, Booz & Company, Shanghai, 2013.

12. Francesca Sanna-Randaccio and Reinhilde Veugelers, "Multinational knowledge spillovers with decentralised R&D: A game-theoretic approach," *Journal of International Business Studies* 38, no. 1 (2007): 47–63; Jaeyong Song and Jongtae Shin, "The paradox of technological capabilities: A study of knowledge sourcing from host countries of overseas R&D operations," *Journal of International Business Studies* 39, no. 2 (2008): 291–303; José Santos, Yves Doz, and Peter Williamson, "Is your innovation process global?" *MIT Sloan Management Review* 45, no. 4 (2004): 31–37; Steven D. Eppinger and Anil R. Chitkara, "The new practice of global product development," *MIT Sloan Management Review* 47, no. 4 (2006): 22–30; Dimitris Manolopoulos, Klas Eric Söderquist, and Robert Pearce, "Coordinating decentralized research and development laboratories: A survey analysis," *Journal of International Management* 17, no. 2 (2011): 114–129.

13. On how to create global products, see George S. Yip, *Total Global Strategy: Managing for Worldwide Competitive Advantage* (Prentice-Hall, 1992), chapter 4.

Chapter 6

1. Open innovation has been defined as follows: "Open Innovation means that valuable ideas can come from inside or outside the company and can go to market from inside or outside the company as well." Henry Chesbrough, *Open Innovation: The New Imperative for Creating and Profiting from Technology* (Harvard Business School Press, 2003), p. 43.

2. Important as OI is, very little was known about the phenomenon in China, with a few exceptions. Notable here is the work of Xiaolan Fu, who, in her comprehensive analytical study of innovation in China, analyzed the determinants of open innovation in Chinese companies. (See chapter 7 of her book *China's Path to Innovation*, published by the Cambridge University Press in 2015.) Other work bearing on OI includes a study by S. Zhu and D.You of human capital and social capital (both internal and external) in Chinese high-tech firms. Zhu and You found that these three elements were positively related to innovation performance, and that integration of a firm's human capital and the external social capital also had a positive effect. See S. Zhu and D. You, "An empirical research on the influence of intellectual capital on innovation performance at the background of open innovation," *Journal of Xiangtan University* 37, no. 4 (2013): 72–76.

3. An ODM is a designer and maker of finished products that are then branded and sold by another company.

4. Xinghua News Agency, Made in China 2025 Plan Unveiled to Boost Manufacturing, May 19, 2015 (http://www.xinhuanet.com/english/).

5. Fu, *China's Path to Innovation*.

6. Interview by the authors, GE China, 2013.

7. J. Chen and P. Wang, "Selective open innovation: Based on the case of SUP-CON group," *Soft Science* 25, no. 2 (2011): 112–115.

8. *Asia Today International*, August/September 2012: 8.

9. Fu, *China's Path to Innovation*.

10. Part of one of the thirteen regional branches of the Chinese Academy of Sciences.

11. See note 15 below for an explanation of the key R&D programs.

12. Y. Chen and W. Ye, "The interaction between internal R&D and external knowledge sourcing: The study on innovation strategy of STI and DUI industries," *Studies in Science of Science* 31, no. 2 (2013): 266–285.

13. Likewise, Akzo Nobel has developed "communities of practice" to formalize and reinforce the existing informal networks of knowledge among its 4,000 scientists and technologists and to facilitate sharing of knowledge and practice. See https://www.akzonobel.com/innovation/rd_organization/.

14. Xinhua News Agency, October 23, 2014.

15. The 863 Program (formally the National High-tech R&D Program), implemented during three successive five-year plans, is aimed at boosting China's overall high-tech development, R&D capacity, socioeconomic development, and national security. It focused initially on five sectors, to which two others were added. It was preceded by the Key Technologies R&D Program, initiated in 1982 and implemented through four five-year plans. It was followed by the National Basic Research Program of China (the 973 Program), which is intended to strengthen basic research by developing human resources. It official goal is described by the Ministry as follows: "a contingent of scientific talents will be trained and a number of high-level national research bases will be established to upgrade the primary innovative capacity of the nation." The 973 Program was supported by funding in the tenth five-year plan. See http://www.most.gov.cn/eng/programmes1/200610/t20061009_36223.htm.

16. Larry Downes and Paul Nunes, *Big Bang Disruption: Strategy in the Age of Devastating Innovation* (Penguin Portfolio, 2014).

17. Weiru Chen and Zhuoxuan Yu, *Platform Strategy: Business Model in Revolution* (CITIC Press, 2013).

18. Kevin Boudreau, "Open platform strategies and innovation: Granting access vs. devolving control," *Management Science* 56, no. 10 (2010): 1849–1872.

19. Lenovo Unveils Internet-centric Business Platform in China Aimed at Start-ups. Lenovo News Release, Beijing, July 24, 2014 (http://news.lenovo.com/article_display.cfm?article_id=1804).

20. Ibid.

21. Xiaomi Open Platform: http://dev.xiaomi.com/.

22. European Commission, Open Innovation 2.0 Yearbook 2014, p. 149.

Chapter 7

1. Anil K. Gupta and Haiyan Wang, "Safeguarding your intellectual property in China," *Bloomberg Businessweek*, May 20, 2011; M. M. Keupp, A. Beckenbauer, and O. Gassmann, "How managers protect intellectual property rights in China using de facto strategies," *R&D Management* 39, no. 2 (2009): 211–223.

2. We do not seek to provide a complete guide to protecting IP; rather we provide an overview and recommendations for best practice, based on the experience of MNCs in China. For an excellent in-depth discussion of managing intellectual property rights in China, see Oliver Gassmann, Angela Beckenbauer, and Sascha Friesike, *Profiting from Innovation in China* (Springer, 2012). See also Andrew Mertha, *The Politics of Piracy: Intellectual Property in Contemporary China* (Cornell University Press, 2007). For a very useful short article, see David Llewelyn and Peter J. Williamson, "China's IP protection minefield: Separating fact from fiction," *Intellectual Asset Management*, no. 69 (2015): 34–40.

3. This section is based on research conducted in 2015 by Gary Liu (Lü Hui), an MBA student at CEIBS.

4. http://jolt.law.harvard.edu/digest/patent/chinas-ip-reform-state-interests -align-with-intellectual-property-protection-again

5. http://jolt.law.harvard.edu/digest/patent/chinas-ip-reform-state-interests -align-with-intellectual-property-protection-again

6. http://www.spruson.com/china-new-ip-court-system-starts-first-ip-court -beijing-3/

7. This section is based on work done by Dominique Jolly of SKEMA Business School with Bruce McKern and George Yip.

8. David J. Teece, "Profiting from technological innovation," *Research Policy* 15, no. 6 (1986): 285–305.

9. David J. Teece and Gary P. Pisano, "How to capture value from innovation: Shaping intellectual property and industry architecture," *California Management Review* 50, no. 1 (2007): 278–296.

10. Ibid.

11. See also X. Quan and Henry W. Chesbrough, "Hierarchical segmentation of R&D process and intellectual property protection: Evidence from multinational R&D laboratories in China," *IEEE Transactions on Engineering Management* 57, no. 1 (2010): 9–21.

12. This subsection is based primarily on Maja Schmitt, "Intellectual property protection in China from a multinational company perspective," in *China Strategies* (Apex Asia Media, 2015). The author is IP Director for DSM China.

13. See http://english.sipo.gov.cn/laws/annualreports/2013/ (the 2014 report was not available at the time of writing) and http://www.wipo.int/ipstats/en/wipi/.

14. In China, the term "utility model patent" means something different from what "utility patent" means in the United States (that is, an original invention), and "utility model patent" means a new application of existing knowledge. The criteria

for originality are much less stringent, and the duration is restricted to ten years. For more on this, see http://www.wipo.int/sme/en/ip_business/utility_models/utility_models.html and http://english.sipo.gov.cn/laws/annualreports/2013/. A good source of statistics is http://www.wipo.int/ipstats/en/wipi/.

Chapter 8

1. For a short summary of the early development, see Lyn Denend and Bruce McKern, The Business Environment of China: Challenges of an Emerging Economic Superpower, Case Study IB-57, Stanford Graduate School of Business, 2009.

2. Paul H. Stoneham and Michael Yoshino, Procter & Gamble Japan (C), Case Study 9-391-005, Harvard Business School, 1991.

3. McKinsey online, 2011 (https://solutions.mckinsey.com/insightschina/).

4. Allegedly copied from a trial in Washington, and later copied by the city of Antwerp.

5. World Bank, Economic Development Indicators, 2105 (http://data.worldbank.org/indicator/).

6. Angel Guerria, Setting the Stage for China's 13th Five-Year Plan: The OECD Contribution, OECD, Beijing, 2015.

7. This section is based on analysis by Gong Jiong, formerly of the Accenture Institute for High Performance and now at the University of International Business and Economics in Beijing.

8. Michael E. Porter, *The Competitive Advantage of Nations* (Free Press, 1990).

9. Xiaohui Liu and Trevor Buck, "Innovation performance and channels for international technology spillovers: Evidence from Chinese high-tech industries," *Research Policy* 36, no. 3 (2007): 355–366.

10. Although trailing Apple and Samsung in revenue by a large margin.

11. Dan Breznitz and Michael Murphree, *Run of the Red Queen* (Yale University Press, 2011).

12. Porter, *The Competitive Advantage of Nations*.

13. Rebecca Fannin, "Tencent's recent hire pushes WeChat mainstream in the US—Watch out, WhatsApp," *Forbes*, March 2014 (http://www.forbes.com/sites/rebeccafannin/2014/03/18/tencents-recent-hire-pushes-wechat-mainstream-in-the-us-watch-out-whatsapp/).

14. One of Mao's successful military strategies.

15. "China holds meeting on 13th five-year plan," *China Daily*, September 5, 2014(http://news.xinhuanet.com/english/china/2014-09/05/c_133621684.htm).

16. "President Xi outlines position on 13th five-year plan," Xinhua News Agency, May 28, 2015 (http://news.xinhuanet.com/english/2015-05/28/c_134279414.htm).

17. "Made in China 2025 plan unveiled to boost manufacturing," Xinhua News Agency, May 19 2015 (http://www.xinhuanet.com/english/).

18. The "ten key sectors" are new information technology, numerical control tools and robotics, aerospace equipment, ocean engineering equipment and high-tech ships, railway equipment, energy saving and new energy vehicles, power equipment, new materials, medicine and medical devices, and agricultural machinery. Source: Xinhua News Agency.

19. See, for example, Jeffrey L. Furman and Richard Hayes, "Catching up or standing still? National innovative productivity among 'follower' countries 1978–1999," *Research Policy* 33, no. 9 (2004): 1329–1354.

SELECTED BIBLIOGRAPHY

Abrami, Regina M., William C. Kirby, and F. Warren McFarlan. "Why China can't innovate." *Harvard Business Review* 92 (3) (2014): 107–111.

Abrami, Regina M., William C. Kirby, and F. Warren McFarlan. *Can China Lead? Reaching the Limits of Power and Growth*. Boston: Harvard Business Review Press, 2014.

Almeida, Paul, and Anupama Phene. "Subsidiaries and knowledge creation: The influence of the MNC and host country on innovation." *Strategic Management Journal* 25 (8–9) (2004): 847–864.

Barlow, Thomas. *Innovation in America: A Comparative Study*. United States Studies Centre, University of Sydney, 2008.

Boudreau, Kevin. "Open platform strategies and innovation: Granting access vs. devolving control." *Management Science* 56 (10) (September 2010): 1849–1872.

Brandt, Loren, and Eric Thun. "The fight for the middle: Upgrading, competition, and industrial development in China." *World Development* 38 (11) (2010).

Breznitz, Dan, and Michael Murphree. *Run of the Red Queen: Government, Innovation, Globalization, and Economic Growth in China*. New Haven: Yale University Press, 2011.

Bullinger, Angelika C., Matthias Rass, Sabrina Adamczyk, Kathrin M. Moeslein, and Stefan Sohn. "Open innovation in health care: Analysis of an open health platform." *Health Policy* 105 (2) (2012): 165–175.

Chandy, Rajesh K., and Gerard J. Tellis. "Organizing for radical product innovation: The overlooked role of willingness to cannibalize." *Journal of Marketing Research* 35 (4) (November 1998): 474–487.

Chang, Sea-jin, and Sam H. Park. "Winning strategies in China." *Long Range Planning* 45 (1) (2012): 1–15.

Chen, J., and P. F. Wang. "Selective open innovation: Based on the case of SUPCON group." *Soft Science* 25 (2) (2011): 112–115.

Chen, Weiru, and Zhuoxuan Yu. *Platform Strategy: Business Model in Revolution*. Beijing: CITIC Press, 2013.

Chen, Yufen, and Weiwei Ye. "The interaction between internal R&D and external knowledge sourcing: The study on innovation strategy of STI and DUI industries." *Studies in Science of Science* 31 (2) (2013): 266–285.

Chesbrough, Henry W. *Open Innovation: The New Imperative for Creating and Profiting from Technology.* Boston: Harvard Business School Press, 2003.

Christensen, Clayton M. *The Innovator's Dilemma: When New Technologies Cause Great Firms to Fail.* Boston: Harvard Business School Press, 1997.

Development Research Center of the State Council of PRC and World Bank. *China 2030: Building a Modern, Harmonious, and Creative Society.* Washington: World Bank, 2013.

Dodgson, M., and L. Xue. "Innovation in China." *Innovation: Management, Policy and Practice* 11 (2009): 2–5.

Dodgson, Mark, and David M. Gann. "Technology and innovation." In *The Oxford Handbook of Innovation Management*, ed. Mark Dodgson, David M. Gann, and Nelson Phillips. Oxford University Press, 2014.

Dodgson, Mark, David M. Gann, and Nelson Phillips. "Perspectives on innovation management." In *The Oxford Handbook of Innovation Management*, ed. Mark Dodgson, David M. Gann, and Nelson Phillips. Oxford University Press, 2014.

Downes, Larry, and Paul Nunes. *Big Bang Disruption: Strategy in the Age of Devastating Innovation.* Penguin Portfolio, 2014.

Eppinger, Steven D., and Anil R. Chitkara. "The new practice of global product development." *MIT Sloan Management Review* 47 (4) (2006): 22–30.

Fernandez, Juan A., and Laurie Underwood. *China CEO: Voices of Experience from 20 International Business Leaders.* Singapore: Wiley, 2006.

Frost, Tony S. "The geographic sources of foreign subsidiaries' innovations." *Strategic Management Journal* 22 (2) (2001): 101–123.

Fu, Junying, Rainer Frietsch, and Ulrike Tagscherer. Publication Activity in the Science Citation Index Expanded (SCIE) Database in the Context of Chinese Science and Technology Policy from 1977 to 2012. Fraunhofer ISI Discussion Papers Innovation Systems and Policy Analysis, No. 35, 2013.

Fu, Xiaolan. *China's Path to Innovation.* Cambridge University Press, 2015.

Furman, Jeffrey L., and Richard Hayes. "Catching up or standing still? National innovative productivity among 'follower' countries 1978–1999." *Research Policy* 33 (2004): 1329–1354.

Gadiesh, Orit, Philip Leung, and Till Vestring. "The battle for China's good-enough market." *Harvard Business Review* 85 (9) (2007): 81–89.

Gallagher, Kelly Sims. *The Globalization of Clean Energy Technology: Lessons from China.* Cambridge: MIT Press, 2014.

Gao, J., and G. Jefferson. "Science and technology take-off in China? Sources of rising R&D intensity." *Asia Pacific Business Review* 13 (2007): 357–371.

Gao, J., X. Liu, and M. Y. Zhang. "China's NIS: The interplay between S&T policy framework and technology entrepreneurship." In *Science and Technology*

Based Regional Entrepreneurship: Global Experience in Policy & Program Development, ed. S. Mian. Cheltenham: Edward Elgar, 2011.

Garcia, Rosanna, and Roger Calantone. "A critical look at technological innovation typology and innovativeness terminology: a literature review." *Journal of Product Innovation Management* 19 (2) (2002): 110–132.

Gassmann, Oliver, Angela Beckenbauer, and Sascha Friesike. *Profiting from Innovation in China*. Berlin: Springer, 2012.

Gerybadze, Alexander, and Guido Reger. "Globalization of R&D: Recent changes in the management of innovation in transnational corporations." *Research Policy* 28 (2–3) (1999): 251–274.

Govindarajan, Vijay, and Chris Trimble. *Reverse Innovation: Create Far from Home, Win Everywhere*. Boston: Harvard Business Review Press, 2012.

Gu, S., and B. A. Lundvall. "Policy learning as a key process in the transformation of the Chinese innovation system." In *Asia's Innovation Systems in Transition*, ed. B. A. Lundvall, P. Intarakumnerd and J. Vang. Cheltenham: Edward Elgar, 2006.

Guo, Bin, and Jing-Jing Guo. "Patterns of technological learning within the knowledge systems of industrial clusters in emerging economies: Evidence from China." *Technovation* 31 (2–3) (2011): 87–104.

Gupta, Anil K., and Haiyan Wang. *Getting China and India Right: Strategies for Leveraging the World's Fastest Growing Economies for Global Advantage*. Hoboken: Jossey-Bass, 2009.

Hagedoorn, John, Danielle Cloodt, and Hans van Kranenburg. "Intellectual property rights and the governance of international R&D partnerships." *Journal of International Business Studies* 36 (12) (2005): 175–186.

Hakanson, Lars, and Robert Nobel. "Foreign research and development in Swedish multinationals." *Research Policy* 22 (5–6) (1993): 373–396.

Hernández, Héctor, Alexander Tübke, Fernando Hervás, Antonio Vezzani, Mafini Dosso, Sara Amoroso, and Nicola Grassano. *2014 EU Industrial R&D Investment Scoreboard*. Luxembourg: Joint Research Centre—Institute for Prospective Technological Studies, European Commission, 2014.

Hu, M. C., and J. A. Mathews. "China's national innovative capacity." *Research Policy* 37 (2008): 1465–1479.

Immelt, Jeffrey R., Vijay Govindarajan, and Chris Trimble. "How GE is disrupting itself." *Harvard Business Review* 87 (10) (2009): 56–65.

Ito, Banri, and Ryuhei Wakasugi. "What factors determine the mode of overseas R&D by multinationals? Empirical evidence." *Research Policy* 36 (8) (2007): 1275–1287.

Jolly, Dominique, Bruce McKern, and George S. Yip. "The next innovation opportunity in China," *Strategy+Business*, September 2015.

Keupp, M. M., A. Beckenbauer, and O. Gassmann. "How managers protect intellectual property rights in China using de facto strategies." *R & D Management* 39 (2) (2009): 211–223.

Khanna, Tarun, Krishna Paelpu, and Philip Andrews. Haier: Taking a Chinese Company Global in 2011. Case study 9-712-408, Harvard Business School.

Koopman, Robert, Zhi Wang, and Shang-jin Wei. "Estimating domestic content in exports when processing trade is pervasive." *Journal of Development Economics* 99 (2012): 178–189.

Leibowitz, Glenn, and Erik Roth. "Innovating in China's automotive market: An interview with GM China's president." *McKinsey Quarterly*, February 2012.

Lewis, Joanna. *Green Innovation in China: China's Wind Power Industry and the Global Transition to a Low-Carbon Economy*. New York: Columbia University Press, 2013.

Liu, Xiaohui, and Trevor Buck. "Innovation performance and channels for international technology spillovers: Evidence from Chinese high-tech industries." *Research Policy* 36 (3) (2007): 355–366.

Llewelyn, David, and Peter J. Williamson. "China's IP protection minefield: separating fact from fiction." *Intellectual Asset Management* 69 (January 2015): 34–44.

Luo, Y., and R. L. Tung. "International expansion of emerging market enterprises: A springboard perspective." *Journal of International Business Studies* 38 (4) (2007): 481–498.

Ma, Hong, Zhi Wang, and Kunfu Zhu. Domestic Value-Added in China's Exports and Its Distribution by Firm Ownership. Working paper 2013-05A, US International Trade Commission, 2013.

Manolopoulos, Dimitris, Klas Eric Söderquist, and Robert Pearce. "Coordinating decentralized research and development laboratories: A survey analysis." *Journal of International Management* 17 (2) (2011): 114–129.

Martin, J. A., and K. M. Eisenhardt. "Rewiring: cross-business-unit collaborations in multibusiness organizations." *Academy of Management Journal* 53 (2) (2010): 265–301.

Mazzucato, Marina. *The Entrepreneurial State: Debunking Public vs. Private Sector Myths*. London: Anthem, 2013.

McGregor, Richard. *The Party: The Secret World of China's Communist Rulers*. New York: Harper Collins, 2011.

McKern, Bruce, and George Yip. "Innovation: The key to China's structural transition." *Harvard Business Review China* (October 2012): 96–98.

Mertha, Andrew. *The Politics of Piracy: Intellectual Property in Contemporary China*. Ithaca: Cornell University Press, 2007.

Mokyr, Joel. *The Lever of Riches: Technological Creativity and Economic Progress*. Oxford University Press, 1990.

Needham, J. *The Grand Titration: Science and Society in East and West*. London: Allen and Unwin, 1969.

OECD Factbook 2010: Economics, Environment and Social Statistics. Paris: Organization for Economic Cooperation and Development, 2010.

OECD *Review of Innovation Policy: China*. Paris: Organization for Economic Cooperation and Development, 2008.

Ostry, S., and R. Nelson. *Techno-Nationalism and Techno-Globalism*. Washington: Brookings Institution, 1995.

Peng, M. W. *Business Strategies in Transition Economies*. Thousand Oaks: SAGE, 2000.

Peng, M. W., and D. Y. Wang. "Innovation capability and foreign direct investment: Toward a learning option perspective." *Management International Review* 40 (1) (2000): 79–93.

Peng, M. W., S. L. Sun, B. Pinkham, and H. Chen. "The institution-based view as a third leg for a strategy tripod." *Academy of Management Perspectives* 23 (3) (2009): 63–81.

Porter, Michael E. *The Competitive Advantage of Nations*. New York: Free Press, 1990.

Qi, M., Y. Wang, H. Zhu, and M. Y. Zhang. "The evolution of R&D capability in multinational corporations (MNCs) in emerging markets: Evidence from China." *International Journal of Technology Management*. Forthcoming.

Quan, X., and H. W. Chesbrough. "Hierarchical segmentation of R&D process and intellectual property protection: Evidence from multinational R&D laboratories in China." *IEEE Transactions on Engineering Management* 57 (1) (February 2010): 9–21.

Ramamurti, Ravi. "The obsolescing 'bargaining model'? MNC-host developing country relations revisited." *Journal of International Business Studies* 32 (1) (2001): 23–39.

Redding, G. "Overseas Chinese networks: Understanding the enigma." *Long Range Planning* 28 (1995): 61–69.

Reger, Guido. "Coordinating globally dispersed research centres of excellence—the case of Philips Electronics." *Journal of International Management* 10 (1) (2004): 51–76.

Rein, Shaun. *The End of Copycat China: The Rise of Creativity, Innovation, and Individualism in Asia*. New York: Wiley, 2014.

Roy, Subroto, K. Sivakumar, and Ian F. Wilkinson. "Innovation generation in supply chain relationships: A conceptual model and research propositions." *Journal of the Academy of Marketing Science* 32 (1) (2004): 61–79.

Sanna-Randaccio, Francesca, and Reinhilde Veugelers. "Multinational knowledge spillovers with decentralised R&D: A game-theoretic approach." *Journal of International Business Studies* 38 (1) (2007): 47–63.

Santos, José F.P., and Peter J. Williamson. "The New Mission for Multinationals." *MIT Sloan Management Review* 56 (4) (2015): 45–54.

Santos, José, Yves Doz, and Peter Williamson. "Is Your Innovation Process Global?" *MIT Sloan Management Review* 45 (4) (2004): 31–37.

Schmitt, Maja. "Intellectual property protection in China from a multinational company perspective." In *China Strategies*. Hong Kong: Apex Asia Media, 2015.

Simon, Denis Fred. "Whither foreign R&D in China: Some concluding thoughts on Chinese innovation." *Asia Pacific Business Review* 13 (3) (2007): 471–480.

Simon, Denis, and Cong Cao. *China's Emerging Technological Edge: Assessing the Role of High-End Talent*. Cambridge University Press, 2009.

Skarczynski, Peter, and Rowan Gibson. *Innovation to the Core: A Blueprint for Transforming How Your Company Innovates*. Harvard Business School Press, 2008.

Song, Jaeyong, and Jongtae Shin. "The paradox of technological capabilities: A study of knowledge sourcing from host countries of overseas R&D operations." *Journal of International Business Studies* 39 (2) (2008): 291–303.

State Council, PRC. *The National Medium- and Long-Term Program for Science and Technology Development (2006–2020)*. Beijing, 2006.

Stening, B. W., and M. Y. Zhang. "Challenges confronting higher education in China." In *Higher Education in Hungary and the World: Tendencies and Potentialities*, ed. Z. Szalai. Budapest: Mathias Corvinus Collegium, 2011.

Strategic Research Group of China's NIS Construction. *The Developmental Report on China's National Innovation System*. Beijing: Strategic Research Group of China's NIS Construction, 2008 (in Chinese).

Sun, Y., M. von Zedtwitz, and D. F. Simon, eds. *Global R&D in China*. New York: Routledge, 2008.

Sun, Yifei, Maximilian von Zedtwitz, and Denis Fred Simon. "Globalization of R&D and China: An introduction." *Social Science Electronic Publishing* 13 (3) (2007): 311–319.

Tan, Yinglan. *Chinnovation: How Chinese Innovators Are Changing the World*. Singapore: Wiley, 2011.

Teece, David J. "Profiting from technological innovation." *Research Policy* 15 (6) (1986): 285–305.

Teece, David J., and Gary P. Pisano. "How to capture value from innovation: Shaping intellectual property and industry architecture." *California Management Review* 50 (1) (2007): 278–296.

Vernon, Raymond, and L. T. Wells. "International trade and international investment in the product life cycle." *Quarterly Journal of Economics* 81 (2) (1966): 190–207.

Von Zedtwitz, Maximilian. "Initial directors of international R&D laboratories." *Research Policy* 33 (4) (September 2003): 377–393.

Von Zedtwitz, Maximilian. "Managing foreign R&D laboratories in China." *R & D Management* 34 (4) (2004): 439–452.

Von Zedtwitz, Maximilian, and Oliver Gassmann. "Market versus technology drivers in R&D internationalization: Four different patterns of managing research and development." *Research Policy* 31 (2002): 569–588.

Von Zedtwitz, Maximilian, Sascha Friesike, and Oliver Gassmann. "Managing R&D and new product development." In *The Oxford Handbook of Innovation Management*, ed. Mark Dodgson, David M. Gann, and Nelson Phillips. Oxford University Press, 2014.

Von Zedtwitz, M., O. Gassmann, and R. Boutellier. "Organizing global R&D: Challenges and dilemmas." *Journal of International Management* 10 (2004): 21–49.

Von Zedtwitz, M., T. Ikeda, L. Gong, and S. Hamalainen. "Managing foreign R&D in China." *Research Technology Management* 50 (2007): 19–27.

Williamson, Peter J. BROAD Group: Chinese Innovation in the Air. Case study 311-115-1, Cambridge Judge Business School, 2011.

Williamson, P. J., and A. Raman. "The competitive advantage of emerging market multinationals." In *The Competitive Advantages of Emerging Market Multinationals*, ed. P. J. Williamson, R. Ramamurti, A. Fleury and M. T. Leme Fleury. Cambridge University Press, 2013.

Williamson, Peter J., and Eden Yin. "Accelerated innovation: The new challenge from China." *MIT Sloan Management Review* 55 (4) (2014): 27–34.

Williamson, P. J., and M. Zeng. "Chinese multinationals: Emerging through new global gateways." In *Emerging Multinationals in Emerging Markets*, ed. R. Ramamurti and J. V. Singh. Cambridge University Press, 2009.

Winchester, Simon. *The Man Who Loved China: The Fantastic Story of the Eccentric Scientist Who Unlocked the Mysteries of the Middle Kingdom*. New York: HarperLuxe, 2008.

World Intellectual Property Organization. *World Intellectual Property Indicators 2014*. Geneva, 2014.

Wu, Xiaobo, Rufei Ma, Yongjiang Shi, and Ke Rong. "Secondary innovation: the path of catch-up with 'Made in China'." *China Economic Journal* 2 (1) (2009): 93–104.

Vernon, Raymond. *Sovereignty at Bay: The Multinational Spread of US Enterprises*. New York: Basic Books, 1971.

Yin, Eden, and Peter Williamson. "Rethinking innovation for a recovery." *Ivey Business Journal* 75 (3) (2011): 28.

Yip, George. *Total Global Strategy: Managing for Worldwide Competitive Advantage*. Englewood Cliffs: Prentice-Hall, 1992.

Yip, George, and Bruce McKern. "Innovation in emerging markets—the case of China." *International Journal of Emerging Markets* 9 (1) (2014): 2–10.

Zeng, Ming, and Peter J. Williamson. *Dragons at Your Door: How Chinese Cost Innovation Is Disrupting Global Competition*. Boston: Harvard Business School Press, 2007.

Zhang, Chunlin, Douglas Zhihua Zeng, William Peter Mako, and James Seward. *Promoting Enterprise-Led Innovation in China*. Washington: World Bank, 2009.

Zhang, M. Y. "The intersection of institutional entrepreneurship and industry convergence: The evolution of mobile payments in Korea." Presented at Academy of Management Conference, San Antonio, 2011.

Zhang, M. Y. "Innovation management in China." In *The Oxford Handbook of Innovation Management*, ed. Mark Dodgson, David M. Gann, and Nelson Phillips. Oxford University Press, 2014.

Zhang, M. Y., and B. W. Stening. *China 2.0: The Transformation of an Emerging Superpower … and the New Opportunities*. Singapore: Wiley, 2010.

Zhou, P., and L. Leydesdorff. "The emergence of China as a leading nation in science." *Research Policy* 35 (2006): 83–104.

Zhu, S., and D. You. "An empirical research on the influence of intellectual capital on innovation performance at the background of open innovation." *Journal of Xiangtan University* 37 (4) (2013): 72–76.

ABOUT THE AUTHORS

Yi Ta Chng is a consultant specializing in strategic innovation practices in Asia and in emerging markets. He founded and served as CEO of Whatif! Asia, a leading innovation consultancy with major clients across multiple categories specializing in strategic innovation, in creating new business processes, products, and services, and in building organizational innovative capabilities. He was previously Vice President for Emerging Markets at Johnson & Johnson, spearheading that corporation's growth in developing markets. He was also a general manager at Procter & Gamble, leading P&G's growth in Asia (particularly China, Japan, Korea, and Southeast Asia) and managing its global hair-care strategy from London. (yitachng@chng.org)

Dominique Jolly is now Professor of Business Strategy and Chair of the Walker School of Business and Technology at Webster University in Geneva. He is also a visiting professor at the China Europe International Business School in Shanghai. Formerly he was Faculty Dean of the SKEMA Sophia-Antipolis campus and head of the Strategy, Entrepreneurship, and Economics Department. He has been running missions in China since 1998 and has actively contributed to the development of the SKEMA Business School's campus in Suzhou since its creation in 2008. He works as a consultant for several large companies. He also advises international organizations and foreign governments on innovation and technology. (Jolly@Webster.ch)

Bruce McKern is an educator and corporate advisor on business innovation and strategy. He is a visiting professor of

International Business and a former co-director of the Centre on China Innovation at the China Europe International Business School. Currently a visiting research fellow at Oxford University's Technology and Management Centre for Development, he was recently a visiting fellow at Stanford University's Hoover Institution and at INSEAD. He has been president of the Carnegie Bosch Institute at Carnegie Mellon University, director of the Stanford Sloan Master's Program in the Stanford Graduate School of Business, and dean of two Australian business schools, and has held private and public executive and board appointments. Author or editor of eight books, including *Transnational Corporations in the Exploitation of Natural Resources* and *Managing the Global Network Corporation*, he is on the editorial board of *Management International Review*. (bmckern@ceibs.edu; bruce.mckern@gmail.com; robert.mckern@qeh.ox.ac.uk)

Maja Schmitt was, at the time of writing, the Intellectual Property Director for DSM China. She has a PhD in polymer chemistry and is a UK and European patent attorney who has led IP departments in the Netherlands and in China. (maja.schmitt@dsm.com)

Lin Xu is an independent strategy and innovation consultant in Shanghai. She has been doing executive training and consulting for multinational and Chinese companies for more than ten years. Her recent clients include Alibaba, Samsung, Sharp, Zegna (Japan), Toyota Tsushuo, and Marubeni. She is also a columnist for some of China's top management journals. She holds a master's degree from Hitotsubashi University. After receiving a PhD from the Massachusetts Institute of Technology, she taught at Babson College. She was also the founding CEO of China-Lab, a well-known Beijing-based Internet consulting company. (2008linxu@gmail.com)

George S. Yip is Professor of Strategy and Co-Director of the Centre on China Innovation at China Europe International Business School in Shanghai (until mid 2016) and Professor of Marketing and Strategy at Imperial College Business School in London. He serves on the editorial advisory board of the *MIT Sloan Management Review* and was the founding co-executive editor of *Chinese Management Insights*. Previously he was vice president and Director of Research and Innovation at Capgemini Consulting and dean of the Rotterdam School of Management at Erasmus University. He has held faculty positions at Harvard Business School, the University of California at Los Angeles, the Cambridge Judge Business School, and the London Business School. He has held management positions at Unilever and Price Waterhouse, and has served on various boards. His books include *Strategic Transformation*, *Managing Global Customers*, *Asian Advantage*, and *Total Global Strategy*. (gyip@ceibs.edu, g.yip@imperial.ac.uk, and www.georgeyip.com)

Yongqin Zeng is a senior director of the Healthcare Research Department of Philips Research China and is the head of the Philips China R&D Open Innovation team. She joined Philips Research in 2000. Having worked on education and innovation on electronics for more than fifteen years, she has been working on innovation management since 2005. She has led various Philips Research departments across industries, including wireless communication, LED lighting systems and services, and healthcare equipment and medical informatics. She holds BSc and MSc degrees from Chongqing University and a PhD from Imperial College, all in electronic engineering. (yongqin.zeng@philips.com)

INDEX